To my darling wife, Terri, and three incredible children, Amber, Aaron, and Jack. I love you all and hope you are not getting tired of the fact I keep writing books.
Joe (Dad)

With thanks to my family and friends who are always there for me through thick and thin.
To Joseph: who would have thought it?!
To my son, Robert: whatever you do, don't take a job in marketing (unless you really want to, of course).
And to my wife, Valerie, the real writer in the family, with love.
Maarten

CONTENTS

FOREWORD

ZERO n.: 0 (with n = infinity)

In the dramatic year 2000, Science magazine journalist Charles Seife published Zero: The Biography of a Dangerous Idea. He took his readers on a fascinating and accessible historical ride, explaining the role of this iconic number in humankind's eternal quest to understand why it is that we, and the universe, exist.

Zero was, is, and to date remains a highly controversial notion in science thinking. As Seife shows, "Zero is behind all of the big puzzles in physics . . . dividing by zero gets you infinity . . . it destroys the fabric of mathematics and the framework of logic." Within the pure logic framework of Pythagoras and his ancient Greeks, zero and infinity were numbers that ruined everything, so they were simply banned. During the Renaissance and Age of Enlightenment, people started to test their way around in science, rather than rely on pure ratio or unconditional belief in God. They experimented, they played, and they observed. They used their own brains. For scientists ranging from Isaac Newton to Steven Hawking, zero and infinity were back, and some illogic was accepted. It appears that in the recent past decades of more logic-oriented string theory and cosmology, zero and infinity have had to take a backseat again. Seife concluded that the eternal fight to demystify existentialism continues, and zero continues to star in a provocative role.

In 2013, Joseph Jaffe and Maarten Albarda propose their own existential version: Z.E.R.O. Without Newtonian comparison aspirations, they are indeed more like sir Isaac and his Enlightenment peers. They observed where the apple fell (and still falls) in the connection world, thought about why, experimented themselves, and finally observed and learned from numerous other people who dared to experiment and from those who did not. They built a case for a new connection theory, called Z.E.R.O. As with any theory, one can be for or against, love it or hate it. But if you care about consumer connections in the next decades, it will not leave you indifferent. It is a theory that empowers any marketer, anybody involved in media, and anybody in business to think as the resourceful business marketer any modern marketers ought to be.

Joseph and Maarten aim to reawaken in us the starving artist–type creativity that comes only from hunger, not from a full belly. They rekindle the notion to not act just on last year's big budget, increased marginally after a long fight with the boss during the yearly budget routine, to do pretty much more of the same versus last year—just with a twist: "Now we have apps!" or "Now with social media," or more recently, "Now we are using big data!" They try to bring out in every marketer the intrapreneur that hides inside, the businessperson who acts as if every dollar or euro invested is his or her own. They challenge the marketers and their support ecosystem to make any major connection investment decision a zero-based one, in content as well as in investment. This attitude of ownership is the deeper value that will drive any business-minded professional to read this book, to reflect on it, to debate its merits, and most important, to act and to experiment on the basis of new insights created.

The Z.E.R.O. theory combines art, science, and discipline to create connection models that are much more effective and much more sustainably cost-effective than the still-prevailing TV-first models most senior leaders in companies have grown up with (including myself a while ago). But as yet, despite the enormous amount of ink that flowed on the subject of new media and despite the growing empirical evidence on the impact of digital, the TV model is proving indeed to be very hard to evolve from. It is in itself empirical evidence of Newton's own First Law. According to his law of inertia: "An object at rest tends to stay at rest. An object in uniform motion tends to stay in uniform motion . . . unless acted upon by a net external force." We have for more than 60 years wired generations for TV, and what a powerful wiring it is proving to be indeed. There is nothing wrong with TV itself, by the way. People love *watching* TV (video) on multiple screens more than ever. This is not about the power of classic 30-second advertising on TV the medium. This is about the fast-waning effectiveness and efficiency of TV advertising–based connection models. We can do better.

The "net external forces" for change are there. At least two key ones you will find explored in this book in more depth are (1) the enabling power of digital in the hands of the consumer, creating a more even playing field between companies regardless of their marketing budget size, and (2) the unsustainability of a ballooning marketing line item on the profit and loss (P&L) statements for any company that remains wedded to a core TV 30-second+ model, instead of the zero-based, fans first/go direct model. The opportunity cost of the good old TV Gross Rating Point (GRP) in most countries is simply going up too much. GRPs become an unaffordable connection commodity. According to a March 2013 forecast by Aegis Media, TV will still account on average for 80 percent of the connection investments around the globe in 2014. According to data from Accenture/Ebiquity, cost per GRP increased between 2012 and 2013 by 5 percent in the United States, 14 percent in China, and 28 percent in Argentina. Few marketers were able to raise prices to the people for their brands that much or more, so there has to be incredible pressure on the brand margins just to *maintain* the TV 30-second+-based model, let alone increase its impact (as we know people mostly zap through the commercials).

By no means do the authors suggest Z.E.R.O. is the holy grail, nor do they propose a one-size-fits-all approach. They know every company is different. There may be *n* versions of the Z.E.R.O. truth, with *n* equaling infinity. But applying the principles and insights in this book, within your own context, will increase your probability of getting infinitely better at connecting with the people you serve today and tomorrow. Your stakeholders will thank you for it. And some may do so by writing you checks that include multiple zeros.

But as Seife forewarned us all before: Z.E.R.O. remains a dangerous idea. Read at your own peril.

—Chris Burggraeve
www.vicomte.com
Founder, Vicomte LLC and Adjunct Faculty
Global Programs @NYU Stern
Former CMO, Anheuser-Busch InBev (2007–2012)
Former President, World Federation of Advertisers (2010–2013)

PREFACE
THE OBESITY EPIDEMIC

More than one-third of U.S. adults (35.7 percent) are obese. By 2030, this number will have risen to 51 percent of the adult population.[1] Childhood obesity is even more alarming; the incidence has doubled in children and tripled in adolescents in the past 30 years, increasing to 18 percent for both groups.[2]

Many studies attempt to shed light on what causes obesity—or certainly what exacerbates or accelerates the propensity to put on enough weight over enough time to qualify as being obese. One of these causes is most certainly one's gene pool. As an overweight person my whole life, I can testify to my lifelong battle with the bulge from my childhood years through adulthood. In 2012, I shed 40 pounds in an attempt to (for the final time . . . yeah, that's what I said the previous ten times) take back my life. Weight gain is like a ninja. It quietly stalks you, studies up on you, waits patiently for the right time to strike, and then sneaks up on you until—pop—that pants' button is liberated from its safe house at the expense of your dignity.

Weight gain is almost certainly a cultural phenomenon as well.

In a country and culture where *more is more*—where supersizing and Big Gulps are as American as apple pie and chants of U-S-A, U-S-A—it is hip (literally) to go big or go home. Entire television shows, such as *Man v. Food*, were created to embrace gluttony.

And today it is an epidemic. It is estimated that the cost of treating those additional obese people for diabetes, heart disease, and other medical conditions will add up to nearly $550 billion over the next two decades.

Not to make light of the seriousness of this disease, but it is apropos to highlight another epidemic and battle of the bulge, this time one that focuses on our media market: the sloppy legacy world of advertising and its cohort of "paid media" forms of attention-sucking parasites. Like weight gain, it is similarly suffering from collapsing underneath its own obtuse girth. Like weight gain, it is threatened by harmful additives, preservatives, and artificial stimulants that maintain a false sense of security. Like weight gain, it is similarly conned by the deadly cocktail of inertia, tenure, and incumbency.

But things are changing. Supersizing is history, relegated to the annals of Wikipedia, thanks to one "*Steak* in the ground" movie by filmmaker Morgan Spurlock by the name of *Super Size Me*. Big Gulps are an endangered species, thanks to the efforts of New York and Chicago mayors Michael Bloomberg and Rahm Emanuel, respectively.

The same cannot be said in the media world, with yet another year of prematurely sold out (there are medical remedies for this condition) Super Bowl inventory at a paltry $4 million for a 30-second pop and a 2013 upfront TV sales season with predicted price increases of 7 percent and more.

Cultural acceptance and corporate lethargy are equally culpable as they relate to a media world that continues to operate blissfully unaware of a tidal wave of change that threatens to destabilize the very foundations of the model as we knew it.

As former agency and brand marketers, we've lived through a series of media tremors, each one getting exponentially larger and more disruptive than its predecessor: the Internet, social media, the rise of mobile, and a bevvy of other platforms, unified by an unholy trinity of technology, consumer, and market forces that are both irreversible and devastatingly permanent.

We believe that a storm is coming—a perfect storm that may very well result in the bottom falling out of an entire industry that not only supports and perpetuates an inconvenient truth but underpins pretty much the entire economic engine of growth that comes from people buying stuff from other people.

The impact could be cataclysmic. Ultimately that depends on whether you work in the magazine business, sell artery-blocking products called Twinkies, peddle Kodachrome, or fly the friendly skies with union-loving tenured flight attendants who are more likely to belong to AARP than AAPL (Apple's Stock Ticker).

You may feel this doomsday scenario is a tad overly dramatic, but as you'll read in this book, it isn't as far-fetched as you might think. Hopefully, you won't be a casualty of the media apocalypse, and to ensure your survival, we've provided an extensive road map for the post-marketing journey ahead. Call it your zombie survival kit, but more important, think about this as a way to survive and thrive regardless of the outcome.

Welcome to the world of Z.E.R.O., where the only constant is change.

A NOTE FROM THE AUTHORS

Z.E.R.O. is coauthored by two halves of a whole perspective: Maarten Albarda, a first-time author and seasoned marketing executive at global blue-chip companies like the Coca-Cola Company and AB InBev, who is now running his first business, and Joseph Jaffe, a four-time author, ex-agency executive, and entrepreneur, who is currently running his second startup. Maarten and Joseph see the world the same way, albeit from different perspectives. It is this diversity of thought, expertise, and experience that is represented in Z.E.R.O. in three distinct ways:

1. *A unique spin on authentic voice:* Maarten writes his chapters as Maarten and Joseph as Joseph. It's pretty easy to tell them apart, as the style varies quite dramatically. Joseph's approach is fairly informal and conversational. He writes like he talks, and if you listen closely, you can even hear his South African accent. Maarten writes like Albus Dumbledore. (Can you tell who is writing this now?)

2. *Debate and disagreement:* Maarten and Joseph share the same vision on Z.E.R.O., but at times they'll disagree with each other. These lovers' quarrels are called out from time to time.

3. In the action plan (Section III) in particular, Joseph will weigh in at the end of Maarten's chapters with his agency-biased take and Maarten will do so likewise with a brand-centric opine in Joseph's chapters.

This approach may not work for you, and if this is the case, we hope you'll give us the benefit of the doubt for trying something pretty novel and, in our opinions, creative. If you do like it, don't encourage Maarten because he'll want to do it all over again!

Most important, we hope the book is valuable—even invaluable—to you. We're not sure when last (if at all) a book was written (1) this openly and honestly and (2) with a balanced perspective, representing both the brand and agency sides of the table.

At any time, if you're unsure of who's doing the talking and want a name and face behind the rant, you can contact us on Twitter via #zeropaidmedia (we're listening), @malbarda, or @jaffejuice.

Of course, you can also contact us the classic way via carrier pigeon, or use e-mail if the pigeons have migrated south or are pining for the fjords.

From Joseph: I want to thank my coauthor and friend Maarten for undertaking this journey with me. In reality, we've been on a journey together since we met in 2005 or thereabouts. Maarten, I'm incredibly proud of you for becoming an author and a better social media participant at times than even me! I also want to thank my mother because I do so in all my books. She will be 70 the same year this book comes out, and I hope her eyesight does not permit her to read that I just disclosed her age. In the world of zero to hero, she is the latter.

I also want to thank my Evol8tion work colleagues and in particular my cofounder, Gina Waldhorn, for putting up with me!

Finally, a shout out to Richard Narramore at John Wiley & Sons, Inc. You began this journey with me back in 2004 and today, I am your first four-book author. Why stop there?

From Maarten: Pretty quickly into our first meeting, Joseph and I hit it off both professionally and personally. I don't think we could have written this book together if both things had not happened at the same time. When Joseph came up with the Flipped Funnel Bowtie idea (as further explored in this book), I told him that it was a truly BIG marketing idea, which was exactly right for the emerging always-on marketing economy.

I also must credit my two grandfathers, both smart businessmen in their time. Especially Opa Goedhart, because without his intervention I would have never gotten into marketing.

To our industry at large, I would like to say: Trust me when I tell you Joseph does not hate you. He loves you so much that he just can't help himself, so when he speaks, he dispenses tough love. I think more people should listen to Joseph, as I don't know anybody who is as passionate and original in their thinking about marketing, advertising, and communications as he is.

The Problem

Madison Avenue
We Have a Problem

The world has changed. There's something you haven't heard today . . . 100 times or more. It seems as if everyone and everything keep reminding us about the never-ending and accelerating forces of technology disruption, consumer changes, and innovation evolution in the marketing world.

Sounds exciting except for the fact that we're doing absolutely nothing about it. Zero. Well, that's not entirely true. Our budget setting is done using a *zero-sum* approach. We look at what we did *last* year and then use that as a proxy to determine—incrementally—what we should do *next* year. When it comes to spending our budget, we *use it or lose it*, preferring to add to the clutter in order not to detract from our media bank account. Optimization is all about robbing Peter to pay Paul, and the more adventurous of us are akin to Robin Hood, whereas the more conservative of us (the overwhelming majority) fall back on the adage "No one ever got fired for putting TV on the plan" (or these days, perhaps it should extend to Facebook as well).

That approach—and the 1990s crutch of marketing mix modeling—may determine how many incremental cents we get back from our marketing dollars but it doesn't factor in a whole host of variables such as wastage and the aforementioned forces of change. The legacy models simply cannot predict the value of an additional 100,000 Facebook likes, a Foursquare promotion, the production of original content for your brand's YouTube channel, the lift of a real-time tweet, or the first-mover advantage of collaborating with an early-stage startup.

Commitment to change is window dressing at best, with a superficial mark on a checklist of tactical to-dos. Proof of this lack of depth is evident in anemic innovation budgets that are the first to go when the budget comes under pressure.

Think that's an overly skeptical picture? Think again. Just look to Super Bowl XLVI (2012) or XLVII (2013), which have the bragging rights of being the most watched television events in U.S. history. You would think that this stage would promote a cacophony of originality, a plethora of innovation, an invariable explosion of creativity. You would be wrong.

More from less is not a nice-to-have anymore in the corporate world. It's pretty much the price of entry nowadays. With an increased commitment and scrutiny on prudent spending and an ever-watchful eye from the Street and government on fiscal responsibility and ethical integrity, the Don Draper days of advertising are surely limited to a scripted drama series on AMC.

In addition, with the increasing digitization of (all) media comes the inevitable transparency of performance, against a backdrop of measurability and therefore accountability. Put differently, more from less applies doubly so when efficiency and effectiveness are based on actual performance.

More haste. Less waste.

And then there's good old John Wanamaker who uttered those immortal, clichéd words: "Half my advertising is wasted; the only problem is I don't know which half."

Only that statement isn't really accurate anymore, because we *can* measure what works and what doesn't, and increasingly, the disturbing truth (or ugly truth) is that what isn't working is *way* more than 50 percent.

In May 2013, Sir Martin Sorrell, the chief executive officer (CEO) of the advertising and communications holding company WPP, conceded[1] that his clients were wasting 15 to 25 percent of their advertising budgets, only *he* didn't know which 15 to 25 percent. This could be interpreted in three ways:

1. Sorrell was shrewdly downplaying Wanamaker's 50 percent (or Jaffe and Albarda's way more than 50 percent) guestimate.
2. He was conceding that his holding company was responsible for "wasting" 15 to 25 percent of the dollars.
3. He was opening up the door for some new budgets, shifts, and optimizations.

Let's give him the benefit of the doubt that it was number 3, especially when according to Nielsen,[2] only 3 of the top 10 U.S. television programs in 2011 reached more than 20 million viewers, and in the United Kingdom, not one program reached 14 million viewers or more. Just 20 years ago, this number was 10 out of 10 in the United States,[3] and in the United Kingdom, all 10 programs reached more than 17 million viewers, with 4 reaching more than 20 million.

So where are the viewers?

- YouTube serves more streams per day than "nearly double the prime-time audience of all three major US TV Networks COMBINED,"[4] and 72 hours of video is uploaded every minute (Figure 1.1).

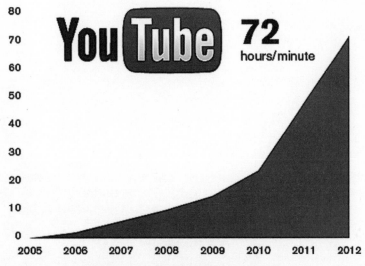

Figure 1.1   Uploads per minute[5]

- According to a new report from Nielsen, the number of U.S. homes that have broadband Internet but only free broadcast TV is on the rise. Although representing less than 5 percent of TV households, the number has grown 22.8 percent over the past year.[6] *Cutting the chord* is a phenomenon on the rise in a world where a set-top box is becoming taboo.

That's significant because it opens up a series of important insights about the changing media landscape:

- Fragmentation—20 years ago, there were 28 channels[7]; today there are more than 250 channels.[8]

  Figure 1.2 shows the number of media channels beginning in 1704, with the first newspaper advertising (a lot changes in 309 years) and progressing at a reasonable pace until 1941, when the first commercial television broadcast aired. And then pretty much nothing happens (and why would it given that the goose had laid its golden egg?) for roughly 40 years until television (in an ironic twist) fragments itself. Then in 1990 a massive disruption in the form of the Web rockets the number of channels to new levels, followed by the early signs of social media in 2000 and all leading up to the introduction of the DVR.

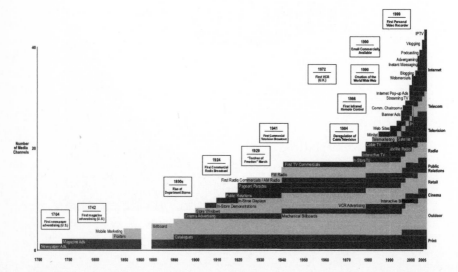

Figure 1.2   Historical growth and fragmentation of media touchpoints

Three significant insights should catch your trained eye:

1. What was once a walk in the park (the flat line of ZERO innovation thanks to television) has since become a vertical ascent up Mount Everest.

2. The increments of the chart begin at 50 years (based on level of activity) and end at 5-year increments.

3. The chart itself stops in 2005 (when it was tabled).

4. Can you only imagine what it would look like today, considering in 2005, the likes of YouTube, Facebook, Twitter, and the iPhone did not even exist?

- Differentiation—One size no longer fits all; consumers want choice, but they also want relevance.

- Proliferation—of alternatives. Where have all the young viewers gone?

- Devastation—expressions and perceptions of value and business models have turned on their heads.

In August 2013, *Washington Post* (Yes, THE *Washington Post*) was aquired for $250 million by Jeff Bezos. Licensed to acquire. Not Amazon.com, but Jeff. That's one-quarter of what Yahoo! paid for Tumblr.

The World Has Changed. The Consumer Has Changed. Marketing Has Not.

A scorpion approaches a frog swimming in a river. "Take me across the river on your back," says the scorpion to the frog.

"Are you crazy?" says the frog. "If you get on my back you will sting me and I will die."

"If I sting you, then I will die, too," explains the scorpion. "For I cannot swim and rely on you for my sole survival."

Thinking this makes sense, the frog concedes and allows the scorpion to mount his back. Midway across the river, the scorpion stings the frog. As the life drains from the helpless amphibian, he turns to the scorpion and says, "Why?"

"It's just my nature," explains the scorpion. "It's just my nature."

Is it really? Is it your nature to cut off your nose to spite your face? Are you the scorpion who would rather die than change? Or are you the victim—the helpless frog who either dies by the hand of the sword (scorpion) or perishes in water a different way (the boiling frog syndrome)?

When I left the corporate agency world in 2002 and founded my consulting practice around "new marketing for a new consumer," I wrote the minimanifesto that introduces these immediate paragraphs on my website. Today, some 10-plus years later, I am saddened, appalled, and utterly shocked by the lack of progress, innovation, and creativity in our space. Some people choose to remind me that the 30-second spot is not dead and in fact is enjoying "record rates" as defined by the Super Bowl.

Chapter 2 and onward will suggest otherwise.

Chapters 2 and onward will outline how the silver linings are so exceptional (as in the exception) that the only norm is the slow and steady demise of the traditional media model as we know it.

Chapters 2 and onward will suggest that the end is near. Dramatic perhaps, but a fairly conservative estimate of an apocalyptic postadvertising era and quite possibly a postmarketing era, depending on whether *you* are prepared to draw a line in the sand and make some fairly dramatic, irreversible, and critical changes to the way you plan, buy, sell, connect, engage, optimize, analyze, measure, and retool.

If we're wrong, then it will have cost you the marginal price of a book or the rounding error of a few percentage points of your already underthreat budget, should you choose to anemically allocate toward the window-dressing line item of innovation or experimentation.

However, if we're *right*, then maybe, just maybe, you'll have made the successful journey and transition from zero to Z.E.R.O., and ultimately to hero, and, in doing so, saved your (professional) life, your job, your brand, and even your industry. Admittedly, that's a fairly dramatic continuum, so we'll let you pick your poison (back to the frog) or adjust your risk accordingly, depending on whether you choose to be wholeheartedly selfish (the *me* in *media*) or take a much more long-term position on the future health and wellness of the marketing profession.

No empire rules forever—not the Roman Empire, the Ottoman Empire, the Ming Dynasty, the British Empire, the Nazis, or even the Murdochs. Some would assert Brand America could learn a lot from the hubris of fallen predecessors. Some would contend that marketing and marketers might want to take the same position, especially given a "craft" that is barely 65 years young (on the bright side, it is AARP eligible!).

What is to come will both light a massive (we hope) fire underneath your lard bottoms and provide a clear and viable path to marketing salvation.

A Perfect Storm Is Coming

S o here's the multibillion-dollar question: If there is a semblance of validity in the "world is changing, but we're not" argument, what's preventing change? Why are organizations slow to move—if at all? Why are we not seeing more innovation in the game? Who is standing in the way of navigating companies through the turbulent waters of change?

The reasons are numerous, and they begin with the *basic psychological barriers* to change. Human beings are predictable and habitual animals organized around norms, routines, best practices, and the comfort of the past (versus the uncertainty of the future).

We're also forgetful animals with extremely short-term memories. Once upon a time we had to literally sweat blood to justify having digital itself on the plan, but today it would be accurate to state, "No one ever got fired for putting Facebook on the plan." How quickly we fall back into our bad habits of boosting the incumbent—Facebook as the new TV—at the expense of backing the challenger.

That's because rocking the boat doesn't necessarily offer up enough incentive to do so—the perceived return associated with success is completely overshadowed by the perceived risk of failing.

This—juxtaposed against an extremely short-term-focused industry and extremely *impatient corporate climate*—makes for a tough value proposition toward boldly going where no marketer has gone before.

"Change is good, but not on my watch" is another (in)famous quotation that highlights the eternal hope that "this too shall pass," as Rupert Murdoch once famously said about the Internet.

This brings up a generational debate that the old guard will need to retire, die, or be *killed off* (as in encouraged to take that retirement package) in order to be replaced by the next wave of—younger—leaders, more likely than not to be digital immigrants (versus digital outsiders).[1]

That may be true, but it could also be a blatant red herring. Age is less a factor in determining expected moves in the media market versus, for example, seniority as in title, role, or corporate mandate. I've seen way too many digital people fail to produce when given integrated or leadership roles within large organizations; likewise, I've seen plenty of grizzled veterans sounding like digital mavens once released (read: retired) from the shackles of the pressure, expectations, and idiosyncrasies of the monolithic corporation.

In other words, *it is both attitude and aptitude within an environment that encourage, support, and adjust for change.* And they are not easy, or abundant.

Furthermore, the current *incentivization methodologies* and *compensation schemes* do not support the move toward a more diversified media-discerning approach versus the incumbent status quo of being media dependent. Bold moves such as bypassing the upfront, launching a product using digital only, or implementing a formalized ambassador program to flip the funnel become scapegoats for external failure, as opposed to catalysts for change or explanations for success. So why bother?

At the end of the day, the system infrastructure is both antiquated and misaligned with today's consumer reality or quite frankly *anybody's* reality, including marketers themselves, Wall Street, and so on.

Although recent research suggests an increased tenure (an almost doubling from two to four years) for the typical chief marketing officer (CMO) against the climate of ever-shrinking tenure and job security or even a healthier culture of job rotation within a global company, there is no net present value of investing forward. In other words, there are no incentives for incoming CMOs to continue the efforts of the previous regime, nor are there residuals or royalties that reward the impact or results from legacy efforts.

The *zero-sum budget setting approach* (which is different from zero-based budgeting) looks at what was done in the prior year to predict or extrapolate what will happen in the upcoming year. And let's be honest: We can't even predict what will happen tomorrow in today's hurly-burly world. Just a year or two ago, the word *Pinterest* might have been thought to be a punny typo. Today, it is one of the fastest-growing social networks, having—seemingly overnight—cornered the market on hobbies, arts, crafts, and the like.

Any change is incremental at best and negligible (window dressing) at worst. In 2005, the CMO of one of the world's largest consumer packaged goods companies challenged his entire marketing staff to rethink digital, citing the fact that if they *tripled* their digital spend, they'd only be at 3 percent (you do the math!). And still this move took several more years to happen based on an increased urgency or need to play catch-up.

Twenty years prior to that, in 1985, Intel's then chief executive officer (CEO) Andy Grove famously fired himself, leaving the building with his box in hand before reentering as a new employee with a clean slate and no baggage per se. The symbolic act of starting over created a blank canvas on which to present a fresh set of ideas, vision, and approach that was not necessarily tied to any fiefdoms, political capital, and/or ingrained biases.

Companies often create similar role-play exercises in training programs or senior executive education courses, whereby they challenge their executives to create plans without television, paid media, and/or advertising; construct programs that pivot around organic word of mouth, advocacy, and/or content creation; devise innovative ways to harness the power of new media; and so on—and yet very few of these theoretical exercises find their way from the classroom to the boardroom.

Perhaps the problem comes down to measurement, or the lack thereof. In one corner is the safety net of marketing mix modeling and volumetrics, which become the default justification for the old way of doing business. It is not uncommon to hear executives confidently and defiantly state that they *know . . . with certainty . . . and no room for error . . .* that for every dollar they spend on paid media, they can predict the resulting sales.

Let's assume for a moment that this statement is true. Why then do we see advertising agencies constantly passing through the revolving door of reviews and clients? Why is the world's most scientific marketer, Procter & Gamble (P&G), chasing single-digit sales growth with double- or triple-digit advertising? Why are companies like Research in Motion (now called BlackBerry), Kodak, JC Penney, or Hewlett-Packard (HP) not able to advertise their way out of sticky situations?

The answer, of course, is that it is impossible to accurately and confidently pin success or failure alone on paid media. Way too many variables exist, and they positively and negatively affect a campaign's ability to resonate, change behavior, and turn passives into promoters, window shoppers to buyers, and even lapsed customers or dissidents to converts. It isn't a stretch to infer that when things go well, we tend to take the credit ourselves; but when things underperform, we immediately look for the closest scapegoat. Case in point: When sales flatline, replace the CEO (P&G's Bob McDonald, JC Penney's Ron Johnson), fire the CMO, blame the creative team, and/or hire a new media agency.

Speaking of which, the continued rise of digital is, in part, influenced by its promise of acute measurability, which is equally subjected to the same scrutiny when it comes to accuracy, representativeness, and insight. Many companies have fallen head over heels in love with search, for example, because of its one-two punch of measurability and optimization, coupled with its pay per performance.

In many emerging fields, such as social media, measurement is either evolving (work in progress), is incomplete, or lacks standardization. In many cases, investment level shifts are negligible or incremental at best, and because of this, they deliver such marginal results that it is difficult to truly learn from them or discern their contribution to the business.

Analysis paralysis versus paralyzed with fear? Which wins? Probably neither, which is why the true response always lies somewhere in the middle.

Finally, consider the very real problem of *scarce resources*—time and money, but not necessarily solely as they relate to media budgets. Scarcity can also relate to *talent*.

On the most senior end of the pecking order is the very real challenge of not rocking the boat. Today's CMO got there not by managing risk but by mitigating it. Which CMO is going to be the first to call the sell side's bluff by walking away from fixed, scarce impressions? What if that CMO is wrong? What if the result is that the company's fiercest competitors jump into the fray like rabid underfed hounds to, in essence, push the company out of the consideration set?

On the lower end of the totem pole is the bright-eyed and bushy-tailed newbie brand manager or media planner, filled to the brim with technology-laden ideas and tactics but hopelessly left out of the decision-making process because of layers of often unnecessary politics, dysfunction, and professional courtesy or just plain old lack of credibility stemming from inexperience.

But the real issue here is not about seniority; it's about having enough able-bodied employees who are well versed in alternative and progressive approaches that represent contingency scenarios to the status quo. There simply are not enough people out there who meet these requirements. They either don't have enough career experience and seniority, or they don't have enough subject matter expertise, technical knowledge, and/or practical, hands-on involvement. Without enough of these traits, it isn't possible to collaborate on a way forward that embraces and marries the best of the old (best practices, universal truths, proven techniques, and fundamental beliefs) with the best of the new (social media, consumer-generated content, microcreationism, mobile, digital everything).

This is true for both marketers *and* the agencies that serve them.

The End Is Near

Simply put, under current operating conditions, the paid media model and market will not be able to sustain itself and, without taking action, is likely to result in severe to catastrophic outcomes— from financial underperformance to job loss to even a collapse of the current media ecosystem.

Sound like the ranting of some subway-dwelling loon or perhaps that Noah guy warning that the drizzle is going to get worse? Either way, it behooves an industry fundamentally built on a limited and scarce supply side and a generally fluid but ultimately stable demand side to think about hedging bets, diversifying portfolios, and considering contingency plans— just in case.

Cultural Armageddon

Digital's continued rise might please the new media boosters and evange-lists out there, but it comes at a price and presents a catch-22 to the "real" world:

- What happens to scripted drama and comedy on television when ad dollars are no longer abundant enough to support actors' salaries?

  In 2011 in the United States, sci-fi/epic *Terra Nova* (*Jurassic Park* meets *Star Trek*) lasted only 11 episodes, spurring debate as to whether this was the last expensive production we'd see in new television shows.

  Interestingly enough, Netflix was rumored to pick up this series, demonstrating the shifts in power (e.g., from producer to distribu-tor), which began with the commercial-free premium channels such as HBO. Today, Netflix has proved this new clout with its successful launch of original programming in the form of *House of Cards* and a resurrection of *Arrested Development* and in an industry first, was even nominated for an Emmy Award.

  In a few cases,[2] brands such as General Electric (GE) (Focus Forward films) and Subway (with their online comedy *The 4 to 9ers*) have found audiences online, but these are extreme exceptions to the norm.

- What happens to our culture when reality shows dominate any other kind of content because of their low production costs? How many more singing or talent shows can we endure?

- As much as we'd like to celebrate the rise of citizen journalism, consumer-generated content, and blogging or even microblogging (Twitter), what happens to researched, fact-based, audited, verified, and validated objective and professional reporting and journalism, when—well—there are no journalists left?

  o Newspapers[3] lost revenue in 25 consecutive quarters between 2006 and 2013, and consequently 13,500 journalists received pink slips between 2007 and 2010.

  o U.S. newsrooms have lost 25 percent of their staff.

- In the desperate "need for speed" in today's 24-hour news cycle, Fox News reported during the 2013 Boston Marathon bombing that one of the suspects was Zooey Deschanel (the actress) instead of

Dzhokhar Tsarnaev—not an easy spelling mistake. And CNN's John King infamously gaffed[4] when reporting a "dark-skinned male" had been taken into custody, when in fact the second suspect was still at large and wasn't—as we now know—dark skinned.

- With the rise of Kindles, iPads, Nooks, and e-readers in general, what will happen to bookstores like Barnes & Noble or Waterstones and, more alarmingly, libraries? That's somewhat rhetorical, as we kind of already know: Borders RIP.

  o Amazon.com now sells more e-books than printed books.

  o 25 percent of young adult book sales at HarperCollins were e-books in January 2012.

- With everything going digital, how will rights management and protection of copyright balance out in the wake of huge public (successful) backlash at the proposed SOPA and PIPA bills tabled by the U.S. Congress or the new Digital Economy Act[5] tabled in the European Union.

  o Both bills were builds to the existing Digital Millennium Copyright Act (1998). On the flip side, should legislation—which admittedly and unsurprisingly is backed by the music and film industries—succeed, what happens to free speech, expression, mods, mashes, hacks and artistic interpretation, citizen reporting, and so on?

Put all of this together, and you could be scratching your head to the point of drawing blood. If this is all true (and it is), why do we continue to support an advertising funnel that serves one purpose—and one purpose only: perpetuating a status quo that preserves and protects inefficiency, false job security, and incumbent assumptions that are not even remotely shared by its target audience!

As is often referred to, the old command-and-control approach presupposes a consumer as a target, a captive audience, a sitting duck, helplessly waiting to be fed propaganda and indoctrinated with brand babble.

But what happens when the targeters become the targeted? After a now infamous episode where rogue employees uploaded rather disgusting videos of kitchen shenanigans, Domino's bravely instituted "Pizza Turnaround" as a public mea culpa for their legacy of lies about great-tasting cardboard.

That's not being snarky at all—Domino's actually showed video footage from real focus groups of consumers talking about how Domino's pizza tasted like cardboard.

The Game of Numbers

Three old Jewish friends are sitting around the park, feeding the pigeons and lamenting over how tough things are (see Chapter 3 on economic change). "Oy vey," says the one. "Things are so tough in the garment business these days. We have to discount everything by 50 percent. Can you imagine that? Two for the price of one? It's ridiculous!"

"You think that's bad," says the second one. "The watch business is so crazy right now, we literally give away our watches at cost in order to break even."

In a rant fitting with a Monty Python scene, the third one interjects: "You lucky, lucky bastards. The jewelry business is so bad right now; we give away diamonds for free and throw in $1,000 per transaction in the process!"

The other two look puzzled and say, "How on Earth do you make any money?"

"Don't worry," says the third, "we make it up on volume."

How's that working out for you? Is our business any different, when we continue to spray and pray as a means of supporting our command-and-control philosophy? We've built in unacceptable levels of wastage on the, at best, sketchy assumption that we'll make it up on volume, that we'll still reach enough people to convert the needed volume. Sadly, this is partially true, but where we go off the rails is on the deferred tax or price we'll pay down the road for taking the easy way out, essentially polluting the drinking waters of attention with the endless supply of clutter.

We often refer to an execution as off strategy when it is at odds with a brief that clearly states a sacrosanct précis of brand value, attributes, equity, and guidelines. Does this same strategic disconnect apply when we fish where the fish are but also piss into the waters because we've had too much beer to drink?

One hand feeds us, while the other sprinkles rat poison on the meal! It *has* to stop.

We're living in a perverted version of *Groundhog Day*, where what is old is new again in the form of content strategy, content factory, content library, content is king—you get the idea. It's fantastic that content is king. When *wasn't* it? When did it abdicate the throne in favor of the court jester with his bright and shiny objects (tweet, tweet)? Some smartasses have even suggested context is king. Or queen. Or crown prince.

They're not necessarily wrong, but I'm not sure even these prognosticators have grasped how important context is in the context of sealing paid media's fate and the impending perfect storm. To illustrate the point, let's go back to the one-two sucker punch of (1) build it and they will come and (2) make it up on numbers.

Lee Clow, legendary TBWA\Chiat\Day creative force behind Apple's classic commercials, is often quoted as saying, "The problem isn't advertising; it's bad advertising." Not untrue, but what happens when the solitary vestal virgin is swallowed in a sea of two-bit whores? Isn't that *off strategy*? Didn't your mother warn you not to mess with the wrong crowd? We're losing the numbers game on all fronts, but it is the qualitative strategic front that is probably the most troubling insofar that it is the silent assassin. You can create the perfect commercial for the perfect brief and the perfect brand, but when it is inserted it into an imperfect ecosystem, there is only one outcome: imperfection (and although that might work for erring humans and divine forgivers, it's not going to help you keep your job).

Off Strategy, Off Funnel

The world has changed. We simply do not live in a market that reflects, supports, or fulfills against an Industrial Revolution–led mass merchandising ecosystem characterized by the traditional sales and marketing funnel and its conventional AIDA (awareness → interest → desire → action) methodology, which has been largely unchallenged until now. Challenged until *Flip the Funnel*, that is, my third book and in which I outlined the traditional funnel as being flawed, oversimplified, out of date, linear, and open. This book will espouse the virtues of the flipped funnel in much more detail, but for now think about this simple premise: The traditional marketing funnel has four components: awareness, interest, desire, and action. How much of your marketing budget is allocated to paid media, and how much of your paid media is spent against awareness versus the other three combined? I believe (anecdotally, of course) that it's around 85 percent.

More important, how much of this expenditure—or expense—is efficient (works) versus inefficient (doesn't work or is wasted)? Can you even work it out?

And although it might be true that we don't always know what we don't know (the argument in favor of awareness, whereas search implies a baseline of awareness and interest), it stands to reason that great advertising might be more the product of luck, spontaneity, serendipity, and impulse. Truly being in the right place at the right time but for all the wrong reasons (meaning it had nothing to do with you).

If Awareness Is Universal Currency, It's Devaluing Quickly

Awareness is the $10,000 entry fee into the no-limit Texas Hold 'Em World Series of Poker, with a grand prize of a whopping $8.6 million. The only problem is that there are another 8,000 players competing for the winner-takes-all grand prize. It's a pretty apt metaphor because anyone who knows poker will tell you that in a heads-up all-in battle, the professionals have about as much chance (50 percent, at best) of flopping the winning card on the river as does the amateur schmuck wearing an unwashed hoodie and Oakley sunglasses sitting opposite them.

Sounds exactly like the Super Bowl, doesn't it? Shuffle up and deal, loser!

Paid Media's Last Stand

Put all of this together, and you're heading toward a point of no return. The fact remains: Advertising has not evolved beyond its attention and awareness as the heavy blunt instrument of choice for marketers and the brands they steward. Paid media is still the weapon of choice for an industry that is woefully out of sync with an economy and consumer who has made progress in leaps and bounds from an Industrial Revolution to an information revolution to today's digital, connected, mobile, and social evolution and revolution!

Perhaps it's time to acknowledge the elephant in the room: If you tell a lie long enough and enough times, eventually everyone will believe it—and so will you. Paid media does not deliver on three out of the four core elements of the traditional funnel, and it's failing fast on the final bastion it has clung to for decades: awareness. Not only is its efficacy and efficiency fading, but—as noted before—the mix of clutter, crap, and waste at ever-increasing prices is taking its toll in terms of lowering a bar to the point where even a contortionist will struggle to limbo his way underneath it.

Over the course of the next several chapters, we will review the intersection of the following key ingredients in the recipe for disaster:

- Business
- Economic
- Consumer
- Media
- Creative

In isolation, any one variable might not be enough to cause anything beyond an uncomfortable tremor, but combined, they could very well usher in the "big one."

Normally, the following mantra would present a pretty comfortable three-phased approach to hedge bets in the race against time:

Defend the past.
Seize the present.
Chase the future.

But when a perfect storm is approaching (*mediageddon*, if you like), it might read instead:

Forget the past.
Act in the present.
. . . or there won't be a future!

CHAPTER

3

The Economic Case

T he world economy has not only become borderless but also relentless, restless, and impatient. Add to this the volatile state of economies around the world, and you will understand that these factors are greatly contributing to the perfect storm that allows our Z.E.R.O. concept to become so relevant today.

Bob Johansen, distinguished fellow of the Institute for the Future, calls the world today a VUCA world. VUCA stands for volatility, uncertainty, complexity, and ambiguity.[1]

I find this an amazingly simple and at the same time appropriate acronym. The four VUCA ingredients perfectly describe the world we live in, and whether you look at economic, business, media, or geopolitical world affairs, they all seem to be driven by VUCA.

In business, the combination of VUCA and access to global, real-time data means that Wall Street or any other investor hotbed—London, Hong Kong, Frankfurt, and so on—has completely lost sight of Warren Buffett's investment rule #9: "Buy and hold . . . for a long time." Instead, the prices of gold, oil, and coffee seem to go up and down on the whim of world events and quarterly business performance of companies and brands.

On December 6, 2012, research firm IDC announced that Android seemed to be winning the operating system battle in the mobile world, and Apple lost 6 percent of its value in a day, losing an accumulated shareholder value of $35 billion. Did anything materially change in the way Apple was making money between December 6 and 7 (or December 8, for that matter)? Did iTunes, all the Apple hardware, and other moneymaking business pillars lose their relevance, power, and ingenuity overnight? Did the Apple ecosystem collapse? Was Apple the next Kodak? Of course not. It was the Street and its nervous inhabitants feeding data into huge algorithms, sparking a sell, sell, sell frenzy.

For a brand marketer, this short-term thinking means that there is a constant and enormous pressure to deliver results—now. Despite efforts to develop three-year or even five-year marketing plans, companies typically live by the demands of the Street for the next month, next quarter, and the next 12 months.

This leads, on one hand, to very shortsighted brand business building (instead of always-on, brands are more likely to follow an always-on-promotion strategy; more about this later). On the other hand, it also leads to a continuous and relentless cost and efficiency drive. The ascent of procurement from raw materials purchasing into every aspect of business is a clear indication of this.

Don't get me wrong: Some of my best friends work in procurement. And as a shareholder in many businesses, I want those businesses to be cost-conscious. However, I do get annoyed when the price at the pump keeps going up, seemingly hand in hand with the profits at big oil, despite the oil barons stating it is the government and not themselves reaping the rewards.

Equally, as a consumer I find it inexcusable that banks and airlines nickel and dime passengers with fees and cost charges while at the same time reporting big profits. In 2012,[2] the nation's 15 largest airlines collected baggage fees totaling $3.5 billion and ticket change fees of $2.6 billion, representing increases of 3.8 percent and 7.3 percent, respectively, compared with 2011. Delta Air Lines received the most change/cancellation fees, collecting $1.6 billion in 2012. Delta's baggage fees added up to $865.9 million and they made $778.4 million on change/cancellation fees, according to an article in USA Today.

HSBC was fined $1.92 billion for money laundering charges in 2012. This, apparently, roughly equates to its profits for one quarter. Meanwhile, the company happily charges you each time your account is overdrafted.

Again, I am no Ralph Nader. I understand business and value creation for shareholders. But the drive to create shareholder value seems to get more and more in the way of building brands for the long term.

The trouble is not in your face; you have to look deep in the bowels of big brand business-building machines such as Procter & Gamble (P&G), the Coca-Cola Company, and AB InBev to understand the reasons for the disconnect between the profit jockeys (aka the finance department on behalf of Wall Street) and the brand builders (aka the marketing department on behalf of, at least in theory, the brand's consumers).

How Budgets Are Set

In most companies, budget setting is determined by one of two approaches: really bad practice or just bad practice! In the worst-case scenario, the finance department and/or CMO looks at the previous year's budget for a given brand, asks the media department for a proxy media inflation number, and applies that to determine the coming year's budget. If media inflation is really high (for example, in BRIC markets—Brazil, Russia, India, and China), the finance guys set a target to keep the inflation at zero for the marketing department, putting enormous pressure on the brand plans and media buying agency to deliver something that is potentially unrealistic and unhealthy for a brand. Actually, they *always* set zero inflation as an objective. And if they don't, the procurement guys will.

Both at Coca-Cola and AB InBev I led efforts to understand the true state of our budgets globally by reviewing the budget growth over a five-year period. (I recommend selecting a random base year and going back a good few years.) For those past five years plus the upcoming year, I looked at the actual budgets and then adjusted them with the published media inflation for that market; for good measure, I did the same with our negotiated media cost.

What this showed was that in most markets (the exception was typically China), our real budgets had actually fallen, and even though our media agencies had done a great job in negotiating the cost of media, even that was typically not enough to keep the budgets flat. And again, that was true over a period of five years. In other words, even though costs had increased for everything from the price of media to the products'

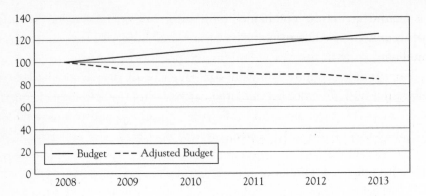

Figure 3.1   **Budget versus inflation-adjusted budget example**

ingredients and packaging itself, we were spending the same or less behind each brand in real-time dollars.

The second worst (or lesser of two evils) scenario is when the finance or strategy department uses modeling to determine what the budget should be for each brand in a portfolio. The problem with this approach is that in most businesses, the econometric model was developed in the 1990s and has been steadfastly fed a diet of TV plans. As a result, it can (rather accurately) predict how much market share can be gained or lost by using more or less TV ads. It uses Gross Rating Points (GRPs) and often also a measure of share of voice (SOV) or share of market (SOM) for this.

And therein lays the problem. It looks at TV in isolation of today's fragmented media world. Or, at best, it looks at it in relation only to other traditional media, because there are some data available for it. It is completely incapable of telling you if it might be more beneficial to shift some TV dollars to creating always-on content to be shared through social media, or driving an increase in Facebook fans, or expanding your digital search footprint into mobile. (Spoiler alert: You should do all these things, and all at the expense of TV.)

To make matters worse, many advertisers still rely on the SOV/SOM analysis to determine how competitive their budgets are or will be. The index of the two data points is usually seriously flawed because SOV typically reflects TV in isolation, without taking any other media, especially digital, into consideration. Imagine you are competing against Red Bull or Starbucks. These companies have huge marketing budgets but are rarely seen on TV as a regular advertiser. Good luck with your SOV/SOM analysis!

So, in summary, most companies' budgets are set to satisfy the drive for efficiency and are based on outdated models and principles.

How Marketers Are Incentivized

The drive for cost-efficiency and profits has led to an increased demand for marketing return on investment (ROI). And this is a good thing when in the hands of enlightened leadership that is willing to look beyond the short-term financial demands of the Street.

We are living in an era where more and more data are available as a result of the use of digital media. This increase in data should technically lead to far more measurable, trackable, and accountable plans than ever before.

The reality, however, is that marketers seem increasingly overwhelmed and confused in the new data maelstrom. There almost seems to be too much data, so they resort to either the tried-and-tested GRPs and ignore everything else (see previous point on the second-worst scenario), or they try to oversimplify the complexities of today's media world. (For example, they may target the total number of fans and fan growth, which leads to social media promotions that ask you to like a page to enter or worse, idiotic calls-to-action like in Figure 3.2. Seen those? Liked them?)

And to add a second layer of accountability, CMOs will promise their chief executive officer (CEO) to put out only advertising that is *tried and tested*. In reality, this means that the advertiser typically brings in either Millward Brown or Ipsos and has either of these wonderful institutions pretest the TV copy and adorn it with their standardized "one-number score." The one-number score is a score for the tested commercial on a number of communication criteria relative to the average score of all tested commercials. This magical number determines the future of not only the spot in question but pretty much the career prospects of any of the marketers involved with the spot, as well as the agency. Too many misses, and you're out!

The consequences are three-fold:

Consequence 1: It prevents bad copy from reaching consumers (where *bad* means it doesn't communicate the key brand message and/or brand extrinsics/intrinsics). This is, in principle, a good thing. If you are going

Figure 3.2   If you LOVE us, love us (don't LIKE us)

to run TV ads, they might as well be ads that have a chance of conveying the intended message.

Consequence 2: The downside is that the quest for acceptable one-number scores as the sole metric of a marketer's capabilities promotes the creation of TV ads in the marketing department. There is incentive to deliver a spot that passes the one-number score test, because it is what the marketers and their agencies are measured against. Marketers can also add this accolade to their résumé and career trophy cabinet, which in turn helps them get promoted.

Consequence 3: For the agency it incentivizes them to propose the creation of TV spots because every "passed" spot will be part of the bonus the client pays over and above the razor-thin margins at the end of the year (more about agency remuneration in point 3 later).

The System Is Rigged

So the quest for the one-number score drives media investment toward TV, because it is the only measurable medium in pretest.

Why do marketers use these types of poor targets? It is because CEOs are asking their CMOs to be accountable for the considerable amount of money they are responsible for, similar to the people who build factories or procure packaging.

The good news is that the average tenure of a CMO has increased from 23.2 months in 2006 to 45 months in 2012. The bad news? According to research published in November 2012, most senior leadership still views "CMOs as being outside of their internal circle of key business decision-makers (such as CFO, COO and CIO)."[3]

This is from a study published by UK firm Fournaise Marketing Group in 2012. According to this study, among more than 1,200 CEOs of large corporations and small and medium-sized businesses based in North America, Europe, Asia, and Australia, 80 percent are "not very impressed" with their marketing teams.

CEOs do not believe that marketers add value to the bottom line, and they have stopped giving them measurable targets to deliver ROI for the significant marketing investments they make. A large majority of these CEOs admit to having moved once basic marketing functions such as innovation and pricing to other, apparently more accountable and trust-worthy, executives.

> *Whether we like it or not, what CEOs are telling us is clear-cut: They don't trust traditional marketers, and don't expect much from them,*
> —Jerome Fontaine, Fournaise's global CEO

Nice!

The real rub here is the admission that apparently many CEOs have given up giving marketers clear, business-linked performance targets. Shame on those CEOs. We live in an age where there are now more and more sophisticated tools available that help you calculate a form of actual marketing ROI (volume, share, and brand key performance indicators versus marketing investment).

And so we all bloody well should. There are some really, really clever algorithm jockeys who can create magic with all these data. All that is needed is an enlightened senior leadership that demands a better (or "any") level of marketing ROI measurement. This should not be expressed in outputs such as "CPM/GRP/CPT" for traditional media, nor should they or can they be "Page Views/CTR/Fan Count/Number-of-Likes" in digital.

In my experience, it is totally possible to develop marketing models that will eat all your data and create very insightful "what-if" tools. These smart models are able to suggest a mix of touch points (across a range of all touch points, not just traditional media) that have a high probability of delivering "awareness" if that is what your brand is after. And they will offer a different mix if you are, for instance, after "reconsideration" or "response/participation."

About 20 percent of CEO-CMO relationships were based on a CMO who was not afraid to be measured and evaluated by ROI/value creation and a CEO who perceived marketers as key players/partners in the success of the business.

CEOs should not be allowed to label the CMO as a second-class business executive. And CMOs should not accept being treated as such by demonstrating to the C-suite what marketing, *their* marketing, adds to the bottom line. Love is, after all, a two-way street.

How Agencies and Other Partners (Suppliers) Are Paid and Incentivized

The final consequence of the economic pressures on today's businesses operating in a VUCA world are that, in an effort to downsize the cost of marketing as low as possible, payment terms and conditions for agency time and media space have been driven to dangerously thin levels. And still there seems to be room for improvement (read: reduction) if you ask most advertisers.

A long time ago, in a universe far, far away, agencies created TV ads, bought the media space for these ads, and pocketed 15 percent commission on each placement. It was a peaceful and gentle world, where the focus was typically on the creative execution (ads) and not on the agency's bottom line. Okay, perhaps it was not that tranquil, if we can believe the exploits of the *Mad Men*.

Over time, the process evolved. Initially, agencies evolved their approach to a payment system whereby clients paid for the number of hours that people worked on a briefing. This worked well for a while and was probably a more fair reflection of an agency's actual cost of business on a given piece of a client assignment. After all, it meant that a complete rethink of the brand's strategy and campaign earned the agency more than the development of a simple shelf wobbler. It certainly saved clients money.

But as time moved on, budgets went flat (see earlier discussion) and the world became more fragmented. Clients started to shave these cost, leading to some clients today paying less than 2 percent (sometimes less than 1 percent) of their total spend toward the complete bundle of strategy development, planning, buying, execution, optimization, and postbuy reporting of each plan. Media agencies were born to deliver these specialized media products to advertisers and to benefit from the economies of scale to develop high-end back-office systems and resources.

What? You don't actually see all of these services from your agency today? Well, that's probably because the agencies, in response to the negative growth of their advertiser and media owner–generated revenues, started to shave and silo their offerings. (Sidenote: Oh, how I hate this *negative growth* expression commonly used in our vocabulary. If it is negative, it is not growth!)

Media agencies were forced to become more and more creative (and less and less transparent toward their clients) as to how they could deliver on the clients' expectation of paying less than 1 percent while at the same time delivering a more and more sophisticated product tailored to the ever-expanding fragmented media world and delivering anywhere between 10 and 15 percent profit margin to hungry agency group CEOs (for example, Sir Martin Sorrell, Maurice Levy, or any of the other advertising barons) who themselves were pressured to deliver to the Street.

One obvious way is to seek scale and more scale. Enter the media groups such as Magna Global and Group M Media. And now even that is no longer enough, so Messrs. Levy and Wren combined Publicis Group and Omnicom Group in the summer of 2013 into PublicisOmnicomGroup. It is obviously in the media agencies' interest to keep the media world manageable and simple so that they can automate their low-margin media buying and optimization product as much as possible and sell high-margin consulting and strategic planning on top of that. Plus, they want to sell you, the advertiser, all sorts of specialized functions separately, such as sports marketing, search optimization, social media listening, and so on.

But back-office savings through scale will only get you so far. The real money for media agencies is in making money from your budgets. And in that game scale certainly counts. More on this in Chapter 12.

In summary, as we have demonstrated, the economics are not working toward a changed approach to connection planning, which is perhaps why TV is still 65-plus percent of most marketing budgets. Only the brave are moving on, even though they recognize the complexities and uncertainties of today's media world. The lethargic are staying behind—and are setting themselves up to potentially go under in the perfect storm that is rapidly approaching.

CHAPTER

4

The Business Case

To say that we live in a highly competitive world is an open door the size of the opening door of NASA's now-closed vehicle assembly building at the Kennedy Space Center (there are four doors there, each large enough to let a space shuttle pass through). For the purposes of this book, we will limit ourselves in this chapter to the competitive complexities of managing large marketing/brand portfolios. But to be honest, whether you manage a complex or simple brand portfolio or even just one brand, the challenges are essentially the same.

Some numbers first: In 2012, AB InBev managed well over 200 beer brands worldwide. Unilever, according to their website, manages 34 brands, some of which contain many different product lines (such as Dove and Knorr). The Coca-Cola Company manages about 90 trademarks worldwide. All of those brands typically consist of various line extensions, flavor ranges, packaging sizes, and so on.

Each brand and sometimes each subbrand is supported by an ecosystem consisting of brand marketers, agencies, and support personnel, such as legal, finance, and procurement. This ecosystem is designed, trained, and incentivized for growth and survival. Shrink and you'll die; the name of the game is market share growth and value creation in brand revenues and ultimately company share price.

The authors have nothing against this system. We love the world of capitalism, free choice, and consumerism. But, the ecosystem and how it is executed leads in many cases to behaviors that in the long run turn against the simple (and therefore elegant) goals of growth.

As mentioned earlier, almost all executives will tell you that "change is good" yet they typically think to themselves, "but not on my watch." Those who deny this are lying to you as well as to themselves. The problem is that what typically grows a business and what marketers are evaluated against are often diametrical opposites. Chief marketing officers (CMOs) and chief executive officers (CEOs) have historically struggled with misaligned agendas. And more recently, the agendas of CMOs and chief information officers (CIO) have started to overlap, adding more complexity and ambiguity to the evolving landscape.

Growing a business typically requires vision, a strategy, innovation, and a measure of risk taking. Practically, this means that executives need to have time to spend away from the short-term goals and focus on the long term. Now let's examine the career of a typical, very senior executive at one of the world's largest fast-moving consumer goods (FMCG) companies. Let's call him Dave (and that is not his real name).

Dave started his career in 1988 as a brand assistant on brand A. It was a lowly job, but Dave was recognized as a talent. And although the average U.S. worker stays in his or her job for 4.4 years today (according to a Millennial study in 2012), Dave managed to get promoted one year after starting and became assistant brand manager on brand B. And yet another year later, in 1990, Dave lost the "assistant" in his title and became brand manager of brand B.

He then got a horizontal promotion a year later and became brand manager of brand C. Thinking that the grass must be greener somewhere else, Dave left the FMCG company in 1991 to join the music industry, where he immediately became a vice president of marketing. This lasted until 1994, after which he rejoined the FMCG company as marketing director for product category D. Three years later, in 1997, he made a horizontal move and became marketing director for product category E. To round out his experience, a year later he became marketing director for product category F.

We are now in 1999, and Dave becomes general manager for product category G. This is the FMCG company's biggest and historically most important category, so Dave is clearly destined for great things. And thus, in 2001, he becomes general manager of North America for a wider definition of product category G, so let's call it G+ (no, not that one!).

A year later, our Dave does us all proud and becomes vice president for all of North America. Finally he stays in place for a bit, and we don't hear from Dave until 2007 (five years!), when he is promoted to president of North America operations. And a year later, he is president of North America all out.

Now needing to brush up his résumé, in 2009 he becomes global president of product category H, and to stay true to his career trajectory, in 2010 he becomes global group president of product category H.

And that's where Dave is today. It is, as we write this book, the middle of 2013. No doubt Dave and the Dave watchers are wondering what will be next. Retirement? Or one more move? It is time Dave; it has been two years already!

If you think we made this up, we have to disappoint you. This information was pulled from the corporate website for a real FMCG company and is a true description of Dave's career.

Dave is clearly one of the key leaders of "FMCG" (the company we are not naming). He makes decisions about big budgets and approves, hires, and fires marketing executives and agencies. The longest he has stayed in one role was (1) when he was vice president for the whole of North America, a position in which he already makes the types of decision referenced in the previous sentence, and (2) when he left FMCG for the music industry. But when he was learning his trade of how to market, build, nurture, and evolve brands, he moved virtually every year to a new brand and/or category, each as wildly different as condoms one year and contact lens saline solution the next. (To avoid any guesses, Dave did not work in either of these categories. In fact, we're not even sure this FMCG company manufactures these products.)

What does this mean? Any innovation project Dave started was finished by someone else. Any project he finished (and most likely reaped the rewards of) was started by someone else. Each time Dave took on a new assignment, he—unwittingly, unknowingly, and/or unintentionally—created discontinuity.

Dave is a best-case scenario. After all, he has been relatively *successful*. The last thing inexperienced managers and/or those trying to impress superiors in a war on promotion are likely to do is to admit someone else's work was smart, but rest assured, they'll know exactly where to lob the blame if things work out less than optimally.

Credit Where Credit Is Due

Marketer incentives in compensation are still grounded in antiquated, out-of-touch-with-reality TV copy pretest as referenced in Chapter 3 and TV reach, frequency, gross rating points, and cost (did you reach the target enough times, and preferably more so than your competitor, and/or at a lower price versus the competition, compared to last year?).

Higher-level brand marketers' metrics typically also have volume, share, and—if it is an enlightened company—brand health objectives (although most companies like to track purchase intent for this in an attempt to bring it back to sales).

David Ogilvy famously said, "We sell or else," but he also said, "Encourage innovation. Change is our life blood, stagnation is our death knell."

So the danger is that many FMCG companies squander the long-term health and opportunity of a brand for short-term successes. This is why you are still bombarded today with promotions like "two for one," "x% extra," trial sizes, blister packs, and so on. This is the collective wisdom the industry has come up with during our great era of marketing. Procter & Gamble (P&G) famously implemented an "everyday low prices strategy" in the mid-1990s in an attempt to wean the company of these promotions. It failed because the competition did not follow P&G's lead and in fact turned up the promotional noise. P&G lost market share, and we all know what happened next: The everyday low prices strategy was nixed, and P&G is running promotions with gusto. More recently, department store chain JC Penney tried to do the same and failed as well (this was cited as one of the reasons CMO Ron Johnson lost his job in early 2013).

There are a ton of research studies that show that none of these short-term strategies lead to a long-term market share or value gain. A good starting point is the work done is the work done by Carl Mela, Sunil Gupta, and Donald Lehmann as published in the journal of marketing in 1997.[1] Can you spot the two promotional periods in the hypothetical graph shown in Figure 4.1?

Yet, in the career rat race, marketing executives keep doing what they have been doing for decades—and still hope for growth.

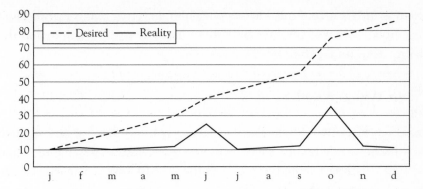

Figure 4.1   Promotions: Desired versus actual results

You could argue that this model leads to an enormous amount of waste and destruction of shareholder value. What if the brand had launched a true innovation (beyond the product, new packaging, or a promotion) and managed to pull away from the competition?

So back to what this means in the context of this book. Short tenure leads to short-term thinking and removes risk taking from the equation. Why risk something new, when I can do what I have always done and what has served my career and those before me, above me, and around me very well?

Why try new connections when nobody has ever been fired for propos-ing a TV schedule? Why explore two-way conversations with consumers when the bullhorn, spray-and-pray method has served us so well? "Do you have any proof this new digital approach is going to work?" was the question posed by a client to Joseph a few years ago. Joseph answered with the only correct answer: "How certain are you that your current media strategy is working?"

What about some of the new touch points? True, brands today spend more in digital than 10 years ago. But this is driven mostly by competitive pressures and inevitable consumer migration. And in social media, it is typically driven by the question "How big is yours versus mine?" No, not that, but measured in fans, likes, and followers. Not exactly blazing an innovation trail, now is it?

When Maarten started his job at AB InBev in mid-2009, he went around the world on a fact-finding and discovery mission to learn the beer business and its marketing. He met with his marketing teams globally, and they proudly showed off their activation plans, many of which included a Twitter account for their brand.

When asked why they had this account, what purpose it served, and what they hoped to accomplish through Twitter, the best answer that came back was that the Twitter account existed because Twitter existed and the agency/brand manager had seen other brands on it and decided their brand needed to be there, too. Or so their agency had told them. And all this had resulted in a whopping 230 followers and 27 lifetime tweets by summer of 2009.

The same argument is often used to defend or justify the creation of apps. Most apps are developed for Apple's operating system, even though consumers around the world en masse use Google's Android to the tune of two to one. But that platform is not what the art director, app director, or creative digital director use. They are loyal Apple disciples.

And never mind that your app will be competing with 1.4 million apps in the combined Apple/Android app universes. Good luck getting noticed (our best advice is to think before you app).

But hey, in the 12- to 18-month tenure as a brand manager you can always claim credit for launching a kick-ass promotion every quarter, and perhaps launching the brand onto Twitter, Facebook, Pinterest, Instagram, Tumblr, Vine, Snapchat, or whatever the latest shiny digital toy is. Done so because there was a sound, visionary strategy behind this? Hardly, but it was done nonetheless and it must be a reflection of my awesomeness, right? Now go ahead and promote me!

CHAPTER 5

The Media Case

The author of *Life after the 30-Second Spot* (John Wiley & Sons, 2005) has a particular affection for the 30-second spot (a sadistic one), but it is important to note that the assertion always was a metaphor for a particular way of doing business: command-and-control, spray-and-pray, hit-and-hope, carpet bomb, shock-and-awe—pick your poison in terms of describing a paid media model built on scarcity and building in an unknown, acceptable level of wastage.

I have planned, bought, and negotiated media all my life. I helped Leo Burnett Amsterdam enter the commercial TV era in the Netherlands in 1989. I managed significant media budgets for clients at JWT, Leo Burnett, and McCann-Erickson, and then for the Coca-Cola Company and AB InBev. Over the years, my belief was that it was certainly worth it to pay attention to new, innovative ways of dissecting TV schedules (using any and all of the new ways that agencies, researchers, and occasionally media owners came up with).

With all this historic perspective and understanding of today, we'll explain in this chapter why we believe Armageddon is upon TV land. We will not tell you anything new with the following data points.

Data Point 1: More TVs and More Channels, But Not More Viewing

TV viewing has not significantly increased, despite an enormous increase in channels and the fact that TV sets have become hugely

Average Time Spent per Day with Major Media by U.S. Adults, 2009–2012 (in minutes)

	2009	2010	2011	2012
TV	267	264	274	278
Online	146	155	167	173
Radio	98	96	94	92
Mobile (nonvoice)	22	34	54	82
Print*	55	50	44	38
–Newspapers	33	30	26	22
–Magazines	22	20	18	16
Other	44	47	45	36
Total	632	646	678	699

Source: eMarketer, October 2012
Note: time spent with each medium includes all time spent with that medium, regardless of multitasking; for example, 1 hour of multitasking on a PC while watching TV is counted as 1 hour for TV and 1 hour for online;
*offline reading only

Figure 5.1   Average time spent per day with major media

more affordable, which resulted in a set being added to almost every room in homes from New York to New Delhi. In Figure 5.1 you can see that between 2009 and 2012, TV viewing among adults has moved up only a little, despite the continued increase of sets, channels, and digital.

The average number of TV channels receivable for U.S. homes rose from 63 in the year 2000 to 135 in 2010. Note that this is the average and that since 2010 the availability of digital/high-definition (HD) distribution has increased significantly. In addition, viewers in the United States (and other markets) now have more and more access to online videos on TV. In other words, the number of channels has only continued to increase since 2010.

Finally, for those who think that the trend of increasing TV ownership is happening only in advanced TV markets, have a look at the data in Figure 5.2. In emerging markets, more than 75 percent of households have two TV sets or more.

Number of TV Sets per Household

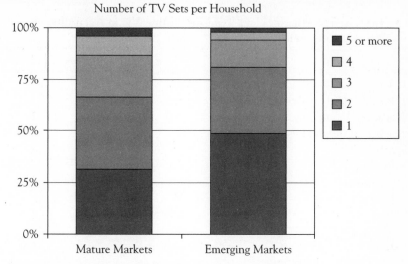

Source: XFD Display Search Global TV Replacement Study, July 2012

Figure 5.2   Number of TV sets per household[1]

Data Point 2: Cutting the Cord—New Ways to Watch "TV"

An increasing number of consumers are cutting the cord, nixing the satellite feed, and bypassing the real-time broadcast in large and growing numbers. Dish Network chairman Charlie Ergen said on an earnings call in November of 2011:

> *Young people who move to an apartment or get a house for the first time don't subscribe to any MVPD [multichannel video programming distributor] and they just . . . get their network programming from Hulu and they get Netflix. . . . As an industry where people pay between $70 and $92 a month, that's a lot of money to a young person today who is getting their first job when they can go out and watch Hulu for free and Netflix for $7.99. So it's a threat.*

In Figure 5.3, we can see that the average viewer across Brazil, France, Italy, Spain, the UK, and the United States is still spending quite a significant amount of time with traditional TV. But all other devices are quickly becoming viable alternatives to watching any type

Devices Used to Watch Select Types of Online Video According to Internet Users in Select Countries,* March 2013					
% of respondents					
1. On TV set without set-top box					
2. On TV set connected through set-top box					
3. On PC/laptop					
4. On mobile phone/smartphone					
5. On tablet					
	1	2	3	4	5
Full-length and TV series	51%	63%	47%	14%	33%
Live content (i.e., sports, news, TV programs)	48%	53%	38%	21%	29%
User-generated content (i.e., videos on YouTube)	17%	16%	61%	50%	51%
Short videos/clips	16%	14%	49%	49%	44%

Source: Accenture, "Video-Over-Internet Consumer Survey 2013," April 8, 2013
Note: *Brazil, France, Italy, Spain, UK and US

Figure 5.3   Devices used to watch select types of online video.

of content. And technology firm Alcatel Lucent predicts that by 2020, the share of traditional TVs will have fallen to less than 50 percent of all viewing.

Data Point 3: I Am Watching . . . and Texting . . . and Tweeting . . . and . . .

And even when consumers watch TV, they are choosing to be distracted by using other devices at the same time.[2] The culture of multitasking is actually giving birth to a nascent industry of TV companion apps and sites. Zeebox, NASCAR, the Olympics, Glee, and many other TV shows and events offer fans a platform to immediately discuss, criticize, share, vote, or ridicule what they are watching. The water cooler moment used to happen tomorrow. No longer; it is immediate and occurring in real time. Nielsen reports that a whopping 85 percent of viewers have their tablet or phone within easy reach while watching TV.

So let's summarize: TV is everywhere and omnipresent. But viewing is stagnant, splintered across more and more channels by an increasingly distracted consumer. And for many, the content is watched on demand, and sometimes ad-free, away from the stations where advertisers buy the bulk of their ads.

You can't ignore these trends, unless, of course, they're completely made up, in which case you should ignore them. But they aren't and so you shouldn't. And although that last statement makes no sense at all, what makes even less sense is that marketing and media departments around the globe are demonstrating about the same lack of common sense by hoping this will all blow over, exhibiting the ostrich approach of sticking their heads in the sand and defaulting to the same old, same old of incrementalism when developing connection strategies.

Arguably, the final nail in the coffin comes in the form of the coveted and hallowed 24- to 39-year-old demographic group that has largely been held to represent the aggregate buying power of the consumer. In the United States in February 2012, only two programs—reality show *Dancing with the Stars* (21) and *Monday Night Football* (20)—broke the 20 million mark on average in terms of audience delivery. The highest scripted program was drama *NCIS*, with 18 million viewers. As a comparison, online social games FrontierVille and FarmVille boast numbers of 18 million and 33 million weekly users, respectively.

In the week ending February 26, 2012, only one television program broke through the 20 million mark: the Academy Awards (aka the Oscars, one leg of the holy Trinity, along with the Super Bowl and Grammys, that itself needed the tragic death of Whitney Houston for a viewership boost) with 39.3 million viewers.

Digging barely one layer deeper reveals that just 15 million viewers were adults aged 18 to 49. Forget 24- to 39-year-olds; try 18- to 49-year-olds, which made up only 38 percent of the viewers who potentially viewed any given commercial at any given time, assuming of course they weren't TiVo-ing, texting, multitasking, relieving themselves, spacing out, talking, tweeting, or Facebook messaging.

And this doesn't even begin to factor in the grudging realization that consumers are simple human beings with very forgetful physiological traits that work strongly against advertisers or that only 47 percent of people around the world trust TV advertising, according to Nielsen research from

November 2011. TV was bested by my best friends ("Recommendations from people I know"), complete strangers ("Consumer opinions posted online"), newspapers, websites, and e-mails. How do you rate your chances of convincing your audience about the awesomeness of your product or service through TV ads, even with the best one-number score possible?

We're talking critical relevance and resonance disconnects in a hardening world that is littered with noise, distraction, and competing platforms for our increasingly starved and threatened attention.

As a case in point, the story around the water cooler the day after the Oscars in 2012 was not about commercials; it was about a tired, geriatric-heavy billing (a 63-year-old host, a 78-year-old winner of the category best supporting actor, best picture going to the silent movie *The Artist*, and a leading lady who said, "Enough already!"), together with nipplegate courtesy of Jennifer Lopez and the personification of Angelina Jolie's leg (the latter two courtesy of Twitter—@JLosNipple and @AngiesRightLeg).

To participate in the world's greatest reach vehicle (although arguably Facebook's 1 billion-plus users puts this to shame) should come at a premium, but putting it in context:

A 30-second commercial in the first Super Bowl in 1967 cost just $40,000. By 1980, the year of Mean Joe Green's Coke commercial, the price was up to $723,000 per spot.

In 1984, it cost Apple nearly $1 million to air the iconic "1984" spot that set a new standard for blockbuster ads.

In 2012, the price hit $4 million, which advertisers willingly paid.

At what point did (exponentially) increasing prices become proof positive of efficacy?

More important, is it worth it?

It could be if the creative team was able to deliver a "clutch" performance (big match temperament if you like). Why has the industry not been able to create a 1984-like equivalent, as was the case for Apple? One might argue that 2011's VW Darth Vader came close—at least from a number of views standpoint—but let's be honest: Will we be talking about this spot in a few years' time, let alone in 25 years? Probably not. If you live in the United States, can you name three commercials from the most recent Super Bowl? Good, bad, or indifferent? Bueller? Bueller? Bueller?

As a sidebar: Apple went into 10 years of decline after 1984, ultimately leading to Steve Jobs's ousting from the company, according to Regis McKenna, who led Apple's first ad/public relations shop at the time. To be sure, the 1984 ad did put a stake in the ground that has served as a rallying cry, cultural call to action, and differentiating attitude that has, in recent times, kept Apple separate from the pack and made it the pack leader.

In 1984, 36 percent of the 42 spots contained humor; 14 percent, animals; and 17 percent, celebrities. In 2008, a whopping 83 percent of the 53 spots focused on humor (and arguably, most were decidedly unfunny); 43 percent, animals; and 32 percent, celebrities. In the past, the use of puppies or babies in commercials guaranteed success. Today, that might be amended to include those that feature Betty White, but even with these ingredients, success is no longer a sure thing.

Per the graph below, in 2012 there were 55 spots in total (up from 32 in 1984 as a benchmark). Of these, a whopping 31 percent were for automotive brands, essentially zeroing themselves out of contention by adding to the noise (quantity) instead of fine-tuning the signal (quality). Forty-six percent of all Super Bowl ads did include a URL or any digital/social continuity. And of those that did, it was for a paltry few seconds and not used for anything more than hawking us to friend the company. But good news! Hashtag inclusions were up to 38 percent of all commercials, coming from 7 percent in 2012 which represents an increase of 31 percent. Did you use any of the suggested advertiser hashtags during the Super Bowl? I didn't either.

Ad Technology Integrated into Super Bowl Ads, 2012–2013

% of total and % change

	2012	2013	% change
Corporate URL/microsite	58%	46%	−12%
Hashtag	7%	38%	31%
Facebook	11%	7%	−4%
Shazam	6%	2%	−4%
Total	68%	75%	7%

Source: Altimeter Group as cited by Jeremiah Owyang in his blog, February 4, 2013
Note: ads aired from kickoff until the end of the game; excludes CBS promotion ads

Figure 5.4   Ad technology integrated into Super Bowl ads

How is this even possible? Why are we continuing to regress? Why is no one saying anything, waving their hands in the air out of sheer exasperation and utmost protest?

Well some are—or at least they're beginning to.

Maarten addressed this very issue in a Festival of Media keynote speech in Asia in November 2011. At the time, he was employed as vice president of global connections at AB InBev.

A player receiving a red card—issued by the referee to players who commit a serious foul—in football (soccer for our American readers) is immediately sent off the field for the remainder of the game. A yellow card is a referee's warning to the player to modify his or her on-pitch behavior. If you get a second yellow card in the same match, it is upgraded to a red card. A red card also leads to a follow-up punishment of a match ban for anywhere from two or many more matches, depending on the severity of the offense as judged by the football association, and a financial penalty, which is usually laughable given athletes' huge salaries.

I began my speech by giving an emphatic red card to television, but at the end of the address softened (or weakened) this to a yellow card. A lesser verdict perhaps, but notice had been served.

TV represented about two thirds of the global spend on average for AB InBev in 2010. And the tube had yielded historic successes for the AB InBev beer brands. Of late, however, it was becoming more of a crutch than a guiding light (to quote David Ogilvy on lampposts and drunks).

I pinned down the problem at hand to three specific points:

1. *The cost/benefit ratio was out of whack.* In terms of cost, the only way is up; in terms of delivery (eyeballs), it's only creeping down. Furthermore, relevance and engagement scores, especially for young adults, were following a downward trajectory.

   The United States showed a 10.5 percent cost increase compared with 2009, but the issue was in no way limited to the U.S. market. According to a study by Accenture, between 2009 and 2012, prices in Indonesia rose by 22.5 percent; Thailand, 12.5 percent; Vietnam, 22.5 percent; Russia, 19 percent; and so the list goes on.

   I then drew the simple analogy of TV advertising as a raw material for marketing. For any other raw material, if the cost keeps going up, you are going to look for an alternative ingredient. Think fossil fuel being replaced by biofuel, or oil-based plastic being replaced by recycled PET. It has always been very difficult to argue that any of the other traditional media are a viable alternative to TV, but in today's digital world, online video is now a true alternative at usually a lower cost—and with the added benefit of being able to buy it with a guaranteed audience delivery, paying only for those people within the target who actually watched the entire 30 seconds. Try to negotiate that with any of your TV networks of choice!

2. *Budget allocation was based on flawed allocation models and methodology* (see Chapter 4).

3. *The planning ecosystem and methodology were similarly out of date.* The old model of planning from a brand-centric starting point (linear) starkly contrasts with a consumer-centric methodology or perhaps a social networking hub approach that does not put anything in the center but focuses on connections, influence, and the spread of ideas.

   Instead, the focus was on reach and frequency, and although large brands do need a certain amount of reach and frequency to ensure viable impact, the model focused on reaching and not on engaging or rewarding or even recognizing the consumer. Nor was the approach built around an always-on consumer world but rather on campaign periods with a defined start and end date.

So are these points the exceptions or the norm? Are they shared by all of the leading global advertisers or just the pipe dream of an anomaly dissident? To be clear, the issue at hand is not about targeting the 30-second spot as a stand-alone culprit, but at the same time, it still does make up the lion's share of paid media investment. This also is not about whether paid media works. This is not a binary and thus oversimplified litmus test. It's about degrees of efficacy, waste, and ultimately optimization. It's about a rebalancing or a return to normalcy that aims to correct the spiraling disconnect or chasm between cost and benefit of paid media. And yes, it's about alternatives that may very well be more efficient but equally more effective to boot.

So what's the consensus in the market as it relates to the amount, distribution, efficacy, and balance of paid media?

The short answer is there isn't one.

Some of the world's largest brands have tried to take bold steps to shock the system, but at the end of the day, they succumbed to pressure or did not have the staying power to see through their vision, which may have proved to be on the money. Experience has taught us that living on the edges (at the extremes) almost never works, especially when treated as a public relations gimmick or negotiation tactic.

Procter & Gamble (P&G) announced early in 2012 that it would be laying off 1,600 staffers—including marketing—in an effort to cut costs. Then chief executive officer (CEO) Robert McDonalds told the Street that he would have to "moderate" his ad budget based on the reality that Facebook and Google were more efficient compared with traditional media. That may be true, but it's not the whole story: The reality was that continuous increases on a $10 billion annual ad budget were in fact hurting the company's margins (see our point about raw materials earlier). A year later, the actual layoffs totaled 6,250, most of which were in brand management. P&G's marketing budget did not decrease as it learned the hard way from Facebook that free comes with a price as Facebook and Twitter started charging for promoted content.

General Motors pulled back from the TV upfront in the second quarter of 2012 and pulled out of Facebook entirely, but later it backpedaled, announcing a return to Facebook and its greased wheels of like revenue.

Coca-Cola's chief marketing officer, Joe Tripodi, stated, "We estimate on YouTube there are about 146 million views of content related to Coca-Cola. However, only 26 million views were of content that we created. The other 120 million views were of content created by others." Coke has done a little better in terms of creating a diversified approach to their free versus fee content. When last we checked, Coke deploys a healthy mix of both paid media and nonpaid media (more on this classification later when we go into the Z.E.R.O. vision), but things are changing fast.

Whichever way you look at it, the media world has been—and continues to be—rocked with shockwave after shockwave of new approaches, platforms, definitions, channels, outlets, pricing mechanisms, and measurement. How well are you structured to plan, buy, measure, and optimize accordingly?

How quickly are you changing and adapting to these new paradigms and frameworks? What is your hubris-humility media scorecard right now?

CHAPTER

6

The Consumer Case

I t's all well and good to fish where the fish are, but what happens when they're not biting anymore? What happens when they've figured out a way to outsmart us or beat us at our own game?

Stranger things have happened, including—but not limited to—Sharknado!

In essence, there has been a reversal of roles so to speak, where the targeted have become the targeters. Going back to the strategic argument again, shouldn't we have smelled something fishy when we didn't have a problem calling our customers "targets?" And certainly, terms such as *shotgun approach* or *spray-and-pray* should have gently prodded us in the direction of gun control. Even in the digital realm, we felt at home with phrases such as *hits* (ouch) or references to diseases (*viral marketing*) to affirm our self-worth and proxies of success. Even the tech world refers to its customers as "users," to which I say, the only profession that refers to its customers as users is the drug profession and trust me, you're not that addictive! The times are a-changin', and the tides are turning and the prognosis is not all too good for the ivory tower–dwelling advertising community.

The numbers game itself is cranking toward a deafening crescendo. The economics don't support it. The media math doesn't prove it. The strategic blueprint doesn't accommodate it. The business priorities don't allow for it. The market cannot justify it. However, the tipping point may manifest itself in the only variable that matters in this messy mix: the

47

consumer—your prospect, your customer, your ex-customer, your competitor's future customer.

Consumers have too many sources these days to be informed, persuaded,
and reminded about things that matter and even things that don't.

I purchased a Kindle Paperwhite from Amazon.com recently for $119
(it's actually a birthday present for myself, but don't tell the kids that
because they think it's from them). It's my third Kindle. Apparently I
need three, plus iPhone and iPad apps for all the books I don't get a
chance to read. I most certainly need an eight-week battery, a nonglare
screen that functions perfectly in the baking sun, a paperlike consump-
tion experience (the background looks like paper instead of a computer
screen), and of course the backlight for all those lonely plane trips and in-
bed reading times. I never got any of that from an ad, although Amazon
did *allegedly* run TV advertising for the Kindle (no one's perfect!). I got
it from Amazon.com directly through this evolutionary new medium and
platform called electronic mail (or e-mail for short if you're looking to
abbreviate it). And now you got it from me. Maybe you'll buy it based
on reading this. I can tell you that I absolutely love it and would give it
five stars. And even if you don't believe me, you can go to Amazon and
read the 14,340 reviews (at time of printing), which are predominantly
great. Throughout this process, paid media was inconspicuously absent,
as it should have been.

Speaking of reviews, during the final weeks before the 2012 general election in the United States, candidate Mitt Romney had his now infamous
"binders filled with women" gaff during the second presidential candidates'
debate. Immediately following this moment, 1-inch binders started selling
like hotcakes on Amazon.com. After all, people wanted to commemorate
and immortalize this moment in time (and store it next to their lockboxes).
Perhaps it stemmed from "reviews" on Amazon like these:

*** out of 5
*As an intern on the Romney 2012 election campaign, I was tasked with
procuring binders for Governor Romney. While these binders are well
made, attractive and reasonably priced, and while I'm sure they would
make an excellent choice for those wishing to store written or printed docu-
mentation in a secure and easily accessible manner, they are unfortunately
too small to put women in.*

**** out of 5

This is a nice binder, but not quite up to five star standards. As a petite lady, I did not anticipate any problems fitting inside this binder. In fact, I expected to be able to share it with at least one or two of my friends. The binder is much too small to contain women, and in fact does not even fit one woman very adequately.

* out of 5

A few words about this product: it is a horrid product, now before I get accused of elite bias I do understand that this binder by Avery is an economy peasant product, but that is no excuse. The space is incredibly limited, in fact 47 percent of it is useless and doesn't even do what it is supposed to do; and on top of that I was under the false impression that this model came pre-loaded with women (in fact when I discovered this fact, I threw the binder so hard it hit the glass ceiling in my home). Hell, this binder won't even work as a flip flop (and I know about flip flops). So to say again, I was highly disappointed that it lacked the appropriate storage space for women and that it did not come with women.

There's so much life going on around us, every moment of every day. Why are we so oblivious to the real conversations with real people, as opposed to the fake ones we regurgitate on a frequent basis in the form of paid media? Is it any wonder that our relevance is fading so fast?

Consumers Have Moved On

Consumers have left us behind. We're no longer relevant or resonant to them in the form of sales plugs and commercial pitches. They have way too many tricks up their sleeves and methods of mass (media) destruction.

We're clinging to the last strands of hope in the form of live TV events such as sporting events or preroll commercials that can't be skipped. Hope may spring eternal, but you don't have that much time left to wait it out.

Fundamentally, the essence of marketing hasn't changed: Make a great product and let it market itself via satisfied customers. Unfortunately, that statement, as simple and *commonsensical* as it appears, is fraught with artificial impediments and unnecessary layers of ambiguity, interference, and mitigated efficacy.

To start, most products are not great. They're mediocre at best. Parity is the first prize at this hog show. Commoditization is the low barrier to entry, and obsolescence is the low barrier to exit. Standing out from the crowd is virtually impossible, and what makes this even more pathetic is that we waste billions of dollars on the faulty premise that great advertising will help us break through the clutter and into the hearts and minds of our *targets*. Come on, people!

Most products are okay. Meh. Whatever, dude. This is one reason why there needs to be an intangible value-add in the form of service and experience—to separate the chaff from the chaff. And yet, we continue to paint dollops of lipstick on a pig and our consumers are not amused.

Probably the best example of this tremendous point of no return is the movie business. No longer can a studio dupe a savvy audience into seeing a movie not worth the paper the overpriced ticket is printed on. Sites such as Rotten Tomatoes create an arguably near-frictionless and transparent connection between the integrity of the content and the intelligence of the moviegoers. With a one-two punch of "critic" (old white guys) and "user" (not just old white guys) reviews regarding whether to see or skip the movie, potential customers are ultimately emboldened and empowered to make an informed decision based on the wisdom of crowds. Or they can choose to ignore it all, throw caution to the wind, and see the movie regardless.

It's this final point that is often overlooked by lazy marketers who want the viral without having to work for it. I'm a Trekkie. I love sci-fi. I love fantasy. I saw *The Hobbit* despite its length and the grumbles about one book having to be split into three movies to maximize the box-office bucks. (Give Mr. Jackson credit; the 3D scenery and special effects were breathtaking.) I also love musicals (go figure) and saw *Les Misérables* even though some reviews lambasted Russel Crowe's lack of ability to hold a tune. (I thought he did *okay*, with a lowercase o.) In the case of *The Hobbit*, I didn't know the movie was split into three parts, so this heads-up was helpful. On the flipside, I would have preferred to have judged Mr. Crowe's flatness on his own merits, as opposed to the bias of a review in *People* magazine.

The point here is that the crowd has, quite literally, mixed reviews, and using the crowd is similarly a function of choosing when to take heed and when to turn away. But even at its worst, it's almost 99.9 percent better than the advertising approach, which spends a lot more money than it should to say, "I'm coming." The model has its own built-in marketing mechanism in the form of movie trailers *at the movie*. When done well, it taps into similar genres or themes, much like the way Amazon.com says, "People like you who bought book A also purchased book B." Where it breaks down (and where the paid media model is breaking down) is the disingenuous and compromised cronyism, combined with narcissistic indulgence that takes the form of putting an ego on a billboard, Super Bowl ad break, or "for your consideration" spread designed to win one of those gold statuettes.

Perhaps if there was a significant shift in favor of meaningful conversations with influential experts, opinion leaders, and fans, there would be a much more profitable split between the cost of goods sold and the revenue at the box office.

In May 2013, I was invited to attend the media premiere of *Star Trek Into Darkness* in IMAX 3D. As a Trekkie, I was bound to love the movie regardless (unless, of course, it was an unmitigated dagger to the purist spine), but even if you *aren't* a Trekkie, you'd love J. J. Abrams's follow-up to his fantastic origins *Star Trek* movie starring Chris Pine and Zachary Quinto. And then there's the IMAX 3D part, which—let's put it this way—I'll never be able to see another movie conventionally after witnessing this masterpiece. All scenes outside the *Enterprise* in *Star Trek Into Darkness* were filmed with IMAX cameras. You could tell.

Question: How much did it cost Paramount to invite a predisposed raving fan (and alleged influencer with Klout) to a free showing of the movie and provide him with a warm soda and stale popcorn? Answer: Not much. Perhaps if Paramount had done more of this influencer outreach, the opening weekend likely would have done slightly better than $84 million and pushed it over the $100 million mark. Perhaps if it *hadn't* done any influencer outreach, the movie would have done much worse.

And speaking of which, what about the other part of the equation: the "raving fan" myth?

Let's start with proving the negative: If a product sucks, people *will* talk about it. Bad news travels fast. In fact, I often include a slide in my presentations that features a beautiful image of Jack's beanstalk with a caption that reads, "The seeds of conversation are not magic beans." There is no "instant viral success . . . just add paid media" quick fix. Paid media is an amplifier, but one that is as harmful as it can be helpful when a product has a defect, no matter how small. And let's face it, most have a defect. Just ask retiring Steve Ballmer.

The only time instant impact occurs in marketing today is when it's a tidal wave of negativity and a public relations bedwetting crisis.

Word-of-Mouth Is a Red Herring

Human beings talk. That's a fact. I have proof. I have met several of these humans on my time on this Earth and true to form, their mouths move and words come out. Slapping our grubby paws on top of it and calling it word-of-mouth doesn't mean we have a clue in terms of how to influence, maximize, activate, optimize, or measure it.

The bad news is that consumers have one another—and Twitter and Facebook—to mobilize, literally and figuratively, their collective wisdom on any topic at any time and figure out a binary *buy* or *don't buy* decision. Sure, there's serendipity and impulse and the occasional billboard or signpost that someone manages to make a sale, but for the most part, entire industries (public relations, social media) have built a pretty solid revenue base on convincing enough boards that their money is better invested in "earned" versus "paid." The really bad news is that these snake oil salespeople are just a slightly evolved version of their paid predecessors. The fact that peer-to-peer has become the new vehicle or delivery mechanism of choice for marketing messages and communication does not mean we have a clue in terms of how to control it, monetize it, or profit from it. Case in point is Twitter, which continues to stumble its way into a paid media model, when it's best case scenario is just to sit back and enjoy the halo effect of doing what people do best: talk—or tweet, or twalk if you're from Brooklyn.

So Where's the Rub?

Building a great product and letting it market itself with the help of raving fans is still the *prime directive*. It's the one thing and the only thing that we should be preoccupied with on a regular basis, yet we continue to lose our way, distracted by everything but the very things we should be focused on.

Our reliance on paid media as a cure-all, a default or reliable go-to pathway, is about to come to a rude halt and it's being driven by consumer culture.

Paid Media Is a Temporary *Cultural* Phenomenon

Increasingly and continuously, new generations of consumers (digital natives) are coming of age and mainstreaming; born into a world where the Internet (rules of engagement) dominates. This is a world that begins with two-year-olds not understanding why they can't pinch, swipe, click, and swoosh a magazine page or television screen like they do on a tablet.

We are assuming, of course, that magazines will even be around when these two-year-olds eventually get the keys to the car.

If you fundamentally believe the preceding statements, then surely you realize that unless you're in the business of selling denture cream, your days are numbered. The consumer contribution to the perfect storm is centered on an acute shift in terms of autonomy, reliance, independence, and efficiency (the pull), as well as integrity, influence, credibility, believability, and persuasiveness (push), that, together, combined for a lights-out KO.

What is your contingency plan for the scenario where consumers predominantly find out about new products, recommended services, or even make serendipitous impulse purchases from alternative sources—third parties and other emerging channels? How do you break through your self-created clutter when the noise is so deafening to begin with? What is your role within these developing ecosystems? Will you survive by forcing your customers to like you or force fitting your marketing messages into their streams?

Native advertising is the new industry term, and it refers to advertising disguised as content. It is a huge part of both Facebook's and Twitter's advertising approach, predicated on an assumption that the more naturally advertising is embedded into a standard user experience, the more likely it is to be perceived as organic. Personally, I see this as no different from a commercial on TV or a print advertisement. It is still interrupting the natural flow of content and a consumer's interaction with that content in a typically commercial-free mind-set.

Native advertising has many more challenges, including disclosure and transparency ones that will ultimately require much cleaner and clearer demarcations between vacation photos and shills from Expedia or Travelocity.

Google's approach was always better from a visual management of expectations—paid ads were either on top or on the right-hand side; they were never hidden within the organic feed itself.

It should never be the obligation or onus of the consumer or user to have to differentiate or distinguish between a marketing message and content itself. Never.

I'm not sure we (the industry) have a game plan or winning formula when it comes to giving our consumers a truly compelling reason to have to sit through another marketing message, public relations pitch, proposition to like, or dull activation of a brand looking to establish relevance, resonance, or relationship with a prospect again. And no, "If advertising goes away, so does your content" is not a winning argument. If I worked for a brand right now, I would set up a covert operation called Project Bolivian,* an initiative designed to explore life *after* the 30-second spot or success and health in a post-advertising world. More on this to come under "What's Your Heresy?"

Consumers Love Ads—No They Don't

I don't want this argument to be about bashing the Super Bowl. I'd love to be invited by one of the large networks or publishers to attend a Super Bowl one day; hell, I'd love to work on an innovation-filled Super Bowl project if given the opportunity—although I won't hold my breath.

Let me just say that I think the Super Bowl is a great institution (but I'm not ready for an institution yet†). One might argue it's paid media's last stand—after all, name one other mass reach vehicle or platform that can even touch one fifth of the potential. (From a quality standpoint, does 100-plus million drunken fans really count?) The folks over at Facebook could argue by a multiple of 10 that their billion users overshadow viewers of the Super Bowl; however, I'm not sure a billion individuals, each

---

*This is an ode to Mike Tyson, who when knocked out against Evander Holyfield said he would probably fade into Bolivian, when clearly he meant *oblivion*.
†To quote Mae West.

with 130 friends, is the same thing as one mega melting pot of advertising mediocrity.

Playing devil's advocate (or angel's nemisis, in this case), let's argue in favor of the premise and widely held belief that the Super Bowl is a cultural flash mob, an advertising mecca that people look forward to once a year when they can watch the next iteration of the farting donkey, talking baby, dancing monkey, or strutting Go Daddy spokesperson.

Is it really? When someone says, "I watch it for the ads," isn't that person in fact saying, "There's nothing else to watch," "I don't want to feel left out," or "I hate football." Is this really a cultural part of Americana or a scene right out of *The Usual Suspects*—a lie told for so long that it has become the de facto truth.

It is a strategic minefield built on paper-thin ice to build an entire media strategy on this popular contention that advertising has a place in our lives, and that even if it doesn't, we'll dedicate one day a year to welcome the intruder into our living rooms.

Of course, whether you live in the United States and follow football or live in the United Kingdom and support football (the other kind), you're still exposed to the same archaic and faulty houses of cards that justify the spending of hundreds of millions of reals, pesos, euros, yen, pounds, and dollars on the unwavering conviction that you will be able to tell the difference between Coke and Pepsi, Heineken and Budweiser, MasterCard and Visa, Sony and Samsung, Burger King and McDonald's, or Nike and Adidas.

Case in point: In 2012, Ad Age reported that of 1,034 U.S. consumers who completed its online survey, 37 percent incorrectly identified Nike as an Olympic sponsor. Only 24 percent correctly named Adidas, the brand that actually paid $155,000,000 for the sponsorship.

So what about the other part of the consumer equation, the believability part . . .

CHAPTER

7

The Creative Case

In a previous chapter, I outlined a more ephemeral argument against paid media from a strategic perspective. You can break it down to two core components, namely, tactics over strategy and the disproportionate delivery against the traditional funnel in favor of awareness above all else.

What about the creative argument? Forget the medium; what about the message? Surely, it stands to reason that great advertising will always prevail and shine through, right? After all, the networks air *The Year's Best Commercials* and *Best Commercials of All Time* specials, don't they (no conflict of interest here)? The Super Bowl is all about the advertising, so says NBC's *The Professionals*, led by ex–ad man Donny Deutsch, who eagerly comments on the best and worst commercials like Joan Rivers does about Oscar fashion on the red carpet. We all talk about the VW commercial from Super Bowl 2012 where a small boy dressed as Darth Vader uses the force to start his dad's VW (actually, he used the remote starter, which apparently is an important selling point for fathers who have sons who want to be Darth Vader when they grow up). So how many VWs sold that year? And assuming you even recall the ad was for VW, do you remember which model? (*Crickets . . .*)

"Advertising is a tax paid for being unremarkable.*" If that is true, then this tax is rising fast, which is good news for the government—not to mention production companies, media sellers, and agencies—but bad news for you.

_____

*Google tells me that quote is attributed to Seth Godin.

What If . . .

What if all advertising was unremarkable? Even the best advertising. What if advertising's day in the sun was waning? What if buying attention was no longer effective through our intrusion-based or interruptive paths to the hearts and minds of our consumers?

If advertising is a tax for being unremarkable, then *frequency* (one of two cornerstones of the paid media model; the other is "reach") *is a tax for being unmemorable*; instantly forgettable. It is, if you think about it, an almost perfect proxy for how ineffective your advertising actually is—and extrapolating this one step further, how ineffective *all* advertising is.

Apple's 1984 commercial aired only once. All things being equal, a commercial should only have to air once. Its sheer creative brilliance should be enough to prompt one of three actions:

1. A DVR rewind or review
2. A recommendation/referral to a friend
3. A purchase

Every single time an ad is repeated or rebroadcast, it is a blatant "tell" that the message did not achieve any of these goals and thus its purpose. It was not seen, it was not understood, it was not liked, it was not relevant, it was not clear, or it was not successful in moving a viewer to take some kind of action.

That's a lot of permutations of disaster.

Maarten's Response: Joseph and I don't always agree on everything. Here's my take on this argument, which isn't meant to be taken completely literally but nevertheless warrants a hearty discussion. I buy his argument to a degree. Studies in the 1990s talked about effective frequency of 2 point-something (Erwin Ephron). I do believe that in certain fast-moving consumer goods/low-interest categories, frequency can help a product stay at the "top of shopping list," although in-store advertising has proven to be even better for that.

There are exceptions, of course, such as the Turkish Airlines commercial featuring Lionel Messi and Kobe Bryant. Within a short period of time, it had amassed more than 100,000,000 views on YouTube, which at the time was a record for a brand. This spot did not have to air on TV at all because it became a viral sensation. It had global reach, and the airline didn't have to spend a penny on paid media. Doesn't one of the most successful pieces of television creative prove the very point that paid media is completely and utterly irrelevant and wasteful?

This *airline's commercial could have (and arguably should have) aired— once—during the Super Bowl. But here comes the rub in the form of the second part of the argument:* Who cares?

If the brand in question (it's Turkish Airlines, but if I hadn't told you, would you have remembered?[1]) had been replaced with its direct competitor or even one from a completely different and non-competitive industry, would the message have been any different? Would the "integrity" of the *narrative* have been compromised or changed? Would consumers have loved it any more or less? Would they have told more or fewer people about it?

You know the answer, don't you? The message would have been completely unchanged. The reaction from the consumer would have been completely unchanged. The number of people booking tickets on Turkish Airlines or purchasing ice cream would have been unchanged. On the flip side, Messi's brand equality just increased.

Beeeeeeeeeeeeeeeeeep. Time of death: 7:33 AM (as I ride the train into Grand Central this brisk winter's morning).

Let's dissect this commercial to prove the point: It features a little boy in first class (lucky bugger) who sees the four-time Ballon d'Or winner and world's best football (soccer) player Lionel Messi onboard. He takes a soccer ball to get autographed, but just then, he notices Kobe Bryant sitting a couple of rows behind. Bryant and Messi enter a frenzied battle to win the boy's attention and give him an autograph. We're talking one touch and spinning balls on fingers, intricate houses of cards with self-spinning windmills, and even balloon animals. But just then, a flight attendant offers the boy ice cream, and he loses complete interest in both superstars, drops the ball, and takes the ice cream as one of the balloon animals deflates (Figure 7.1).

Figure 7.1   Kobe vs. Messi: Legends on Board commercial

Huh? The ice cream is *that* good? Unless it's Turkish Delight, I'm not sure it's possible for the Turks to rival the Italians in the gelato department. And what about Kobe versus Leo? Christiano or Gareth weren't available? It's a little bit of a disconnect for me to see a basketball great from yesterday (sorry Kobe, but LeBron is the man now) going head-to-head with the Argentinian maestro who plays football across the pond.

Of course, taking this too literally is missing the point, so here's the point: *borrowed interest.* How much did it cost Turkish Airlines to make a commercial that ultimately British Airlines—or Disney—could have made just as easily?

Was it really necessary to have to lean on Leo like a crutch in order to boost an airline that wants to stand out from the crowd? Is the ice cream *that* good? For what it's worth, the Turkish Airlines business menu is phenomenal, with a cacophony of meze-type dishes that make it look more like a Michelin-rated restaurant than the prototypical "meat, chicken, or fish" airline. So why wouldn't that be the message as opposed to the artificial hype of magic ice cream and meeting Lionel or Kobe? Boggles the mind.

The Apple That Broke the Camel's Back

Even Apple figured out that when you have a great product, the best thing to do is to show the product (as the hero) versus esoteric, ambiguous, or abstract imagery (remember its silhouetted treatment for the iPod?). One of Apple's more recent commercials shows a hand swiping and swooshing on an iPhone to showcase the device's sublime form and functionality, together with its app advantage. The commercial in question ends with the line "If you don't have an iPhone, you don't have an iPhone." It's perhaps the *worst* and simultaneously the *best* tagline in history. It might as well have said, "nya nah na na na" or from the great skit from Eddie Murphy:

> *You don't have no ice cream!*
> *You didn't get none! You didn't get none! . . . 'cos you are under welfare;*
> *you can't afford it.*

Way back in the day, I looked up the word *creativity* in the dictionary and a particular phrase struck me: "productive originality." In other words, doing things differently (originality) to get a result (productivity). I remember thinking that creativity was our salvation—the antidote to Einstein's definition of *insanity*, namely, doing the same thing over and over again and expecting a different result.

Sadly, this is not what we see today in the marketing arena. We don't witness originality but rather a tired and endlessly futile attempt of fire-the-agency (aka agency-roundabout), intertwined with incremental messaging tweaks.

Our paid media mind-set is so embedded into our operating psyche that we are quite conceivably doomed from the outset. In January 2013, Verizon, a phone, Internet, and cable company (among other things), launched a series of commercials in the United States for its high-speed fiber optic offering, citing "real-life" FiOS customers who were so giddily in love with the service, they were tweeting about it like preachers with verbal diarrhea (Figure 7.2). Verizon even gave them unique Twitter handles to prove they were humanoid (Figure 7.3).

Take Liana Rowe, for example (@LianaRowe). Lo and behold, Liana's Twitter profile photo was the same person I saw in the commercial. Her bio informed me that she lives in New York and "everyday is a new adventure!" It also states "Verizon Disclaimer" and includes a nondescript URL. When you click on the URL, you are tantalized with the following

Figure 7.2   Verizon FiOS TV commercial featuring a real Verizon customer

Figure 7.3   @lianarowe's Twitter account

syrupy goodness: "This Twitter user is a real FiOS customer incentivized by Verizon to share his/her own opinions and thoughts on FiOS service. The thoughts and opinions expressed by participants in this program are completely independent of Verizon."

Give this brand a Grand Prix right now!

Figure 7.4 Defending Verizon

Liana had 365 tweets, had 178 followers, and was following 109 people as of May 22, 2013. Clearly the mass exposure on national network television during the NFL playoffs was working! Interestingly enough, on August 5, 2013, her tweet count was still 365, and she was following the same amount of people and had lost a whopping 9 followers. This pretty much conclusively shows the incredible devastating effect of what happens when mass media support is withdrawn!

Her tweet stream is a sublime mix of defending the fact that she is not a robot, not disclosing how much she was paid, proclaiming that Verizon is not racist (Figure 7.4), and stating that she can talk about anything she wants (but she just chooses to gush about #TalkFios).

Oh, and Liana first tweeted (Figure 7.5) on January 26, 2010, that she "is not quite sure how to use this" (meaning Twitter). Thankfully, almost three years later, she discovered her authentic voice in the form of shilling for Verizon.

I'm sorry, ladies and gentlemen, this is not creative nor is it persuasive. It's not solving the dearth of creativity. It's making it worse.

It is fitting to end the perfect storm warning for paid media with a critique on the creative crisis. Of all the variables mentioned, the one that is capable—by itself—of saving our souls (or damning them to eternal purgatory) is the creative one. The problem is that our industry is so ill that no amount of medication will seemingly help anymore. We have an identity crisis, bordering on schizophrenia: Are we trying to sell or not? Why are we so obsessed with measurement when we can't seem to measure anything properly? We choose to obey metrics that make no sense (what is *reach* anyway?) and ignore ones that offer tremendous promise (like voluntary and quality time spent as a proxy for *real* likeability).

Liana Rowe @LianaRowe   19h
@MichaelHarrispx Thank you! Glad you're enjoying the commercial!
#TalkFios
💬 View conversation

Liana Rowe @LianaRowe   19h
@DavidjcCote I'm sorry to hear that, try reaching out to
@verizonsupport and see if they can help! Good luck!
💬 View conversation

Liana Rowe @LianaRowe   19h
@LloydLaFlare Not annoying at all! I'm happy to share my experience
with Fios and make new friends! #TalkFios
💬 View conversation

Liana Rowe @LianaRowe   9 Jan
@leozuniga So glad you're happy with Verizon Fios! Thanks for
sharing! #TalkFios
💬 View conversation

Liana Rowe @LianaRowe   27 Dec
Hey Guys! I've had a great experience with Verizon FiOS! If you have
any questions, feel free to hit me up! #TalkFiOS
Expand

Liana Rowe @LianaRowe   26 Jan 10
is not quite sure how to use this...
Expand

Figure 7.5   @lianarowe's first tweets

Firing Blanks

Perhaps the problem is that creativity has long been the sole domain of—
and maniacally hoarded by—the creative teams in the advertising agencies. And to add insult to injury, it seems to be confined to an extremely
narrow advertising context (messaging). Here's how I *know* we are beyond
the pale: We can't even fix *that!*

The amount of time that it takes to truly build a defensible set of brand
icons and assets is just too long, unrealistic, and out of sync with the natural biorhythms of time, change, and consumer decision-making ability
and loyalty.

Take the color green, for example. Are we talking about BP or
Starbucks? Or take blue. Does it refer to IBM or KLM? Or how about red?
Vodafone or Virgin?

My feeling has been that if the audience can't name the brand within
the first 3 seconds of a commercial, you're wasting your time, hoping that
the other 27 seconds will somehow be able to hook and hold a consumer's
understanding, attention, consideration, and preference. The litmus test
of advertising should be as binary as a pH indicator or pregnancy test:
it should be impossible for another brand to insert itself into the same

banner, billboard, spread, or spot via simple substitution and maintain the integrity of it.

You simply do not have the time, and your consumers simply do not have the patience to establish this rapport. The clock is ticking.

To a hammer, everything is a nail. And until we secure a new set of tools, we will be relegated to whacking every elusive nail with our ineffective blunt instruments until we run out of thumbs (ouch).

Sure there are ways to fix the creative conundrum, but they are decidedly unsexy. If given the choice between works of art that can't sell squat but that win awards and infomercials that made the late Billy Mays a multimillionaire, shareholders would choose the latter every time, but would creatives do likewise?

In a world of extreme multitasking, two-, three- and even four-screen viewing, shortened attention spans, and consumer attention deficit disorder, advertisers need to get it into their thick skulls that paid media, led by television, is no longer the dominant medium; it is often relegated to what I'd call subservient or submissive state versus active or dominant. It is background music or noise; it is Muzak. And therefore, audio and visual cues need to be adjusted to reflect this pragmatic truth.

Maarten's Response: Again, I am not sure I agree. I think there is significant evidence that second-, third-, and fourth-screen use actually enhance the viewing experience, rather than diminish or destroy it. I say so in Chapter 5 about media. I think the point is that the amount of "conscious viewing" or "appointment viewing" has changed significantly, not so much in the amount consumed (see Figure 5.1 in Chapter 5, which shows that between 2009 and 2011 we added a "whopping" 11 minutes of additional viewing time for all U.S. adults. I am going to guess that for young adults the number is even lower). What changed is how, where, and when the content is being viewed. Many of the "other screens" deliver viewing with a very different ad environment (from one ad to zero). This in itself does not bankrupt TV commercial creativity. What changes the demands for creative is that the traditional network TV–captive audience is changing (and dying out—generationally). The not-so-captive audience cannot and won't be wooed by simple spray-and-pray. Isn't that the point?

The Z.E.R.O. Vision

CHAPTER
8

Is It Time to Blow Up the Entire Model?

We can debate all we want until the proverbial (cash) cow comes home, but as long as we bring a scalpel to a task befitting a hatchet, incremental change will be marginal and short-lived at best.

The multibillion-dollar (or insert your local currency here) question is this: Can brands *survive* at all in this ubiquitously digital, increasingly social, exponentially mobile, always-on, always-public free-for-all chaos?

To help us answer the question, here are a few reframes of the same question:

- *How* can brands survive in this chaos?
- Will brands evolve to a better state of being/operating in this stormy environment?
- How can brands differentiate themselves and achieve elements of sustainable competitive advantage amidst this climate of constant flux?
- Can brands in fact *thrive* in this volatility?

Help Me Help You

The quick answer is a cautiously optimistic yes. The glass is at a very minimum surprisingly half full, as opposed to leaking vociferously, hemorrhag-
ing, or being altogether shattered. That is of course, entirely dependent
on your frame of mind, sensibility, and, most important, course of action
from here on out; and it requires and begins with the same advice given to
an airline passenger being instructed on emergency or evacuation procedures: First put on your mask or life jacket before helping others. In other
words, you can't help others if you're dead.

The first step to solving a problem is to admit there is a problem to
begin with. Accountability is paramount, and ownership is key: The
change starts with you.

Something's Got to Give

> The fact remains: Under current economic conditions and against
> current, adjusted inflationary conditions and run rates, brands are
> not going to be able to maintain or sustain their marketing communi-
> cations objectives and goals using paid media. Put differently, media
> inflation is outpacing marketing budgets to such an extent (and
> it's increasing), that we are heading to that point of no return.
> And it's a tipping point to boot.

Let's summarize:

Exhibit A: Eyeballs are fleeting and migrating to alternative platforms
and outlets . . .

Exhibit B: . . . but we're paying more for them . . .

Exhibit C: . . . except that it's not a fair fight because our budgets are
not growing proportionately to fuel the increases (relative) . . .

Exhibit D: . . . which means, in a world where we're expected to *produce*
more from less, we're actually *paying* more for less, and that translates into
inefficient delivery and deficient results, and essentially the only predictable outcome is an inevitable one.

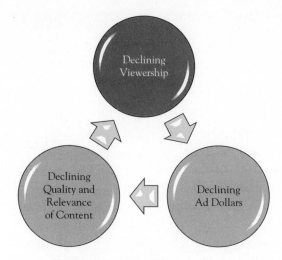

Figure 8.1   The Vicious Cycle

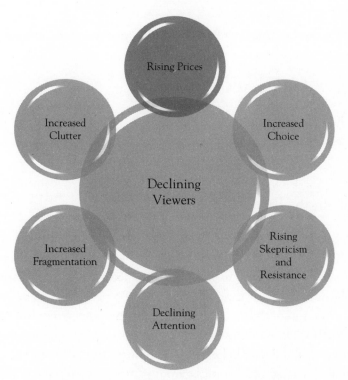

Figure 8.2   Understanding viewer decline

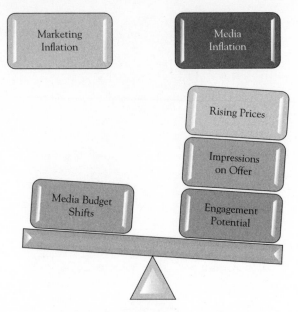

Figure 8.3   Media inflation usurping marketing innovation

Figure 8.4   The end of the line

Are You on the Bus?

At this point, you're either on the bus or you aren't. You either agree with the situation analysis that things are getting worse and the only way they will get better is by doing something about it, or you don't. You either are concerned to a fault that something's got to give, or you're in denial. You're either intensely focused on diversifying your portfolio, or you're sticking with what you know.

At its core, you either believe you're smarter than us—and not just us, but endless reams of infographics, punditry, research, and most important, results (yours as well as those of your partners-in-crime that grace the dailies, trades, and bankruptcy courts with increasing frequency), or you don't. But this isn't really *us* versus *them*, is it? Perhaps that's the problem with the antagonistic (guilty as charged), confrontational, and combative way *new* has sized up *old*, nontraditional to traditional, digital to analog. You've been called dinosaurs enough times by young, impertinent, snotty, arrogant, and self-appointed social media experts or digital saviors who count their credentials using the currency of Klout scores, retweets, and likes to convince yourselves you really are going the way of the dodo.

Make no mistake; the end is nigh (or nigh-ish), and it's as much a threat to the consumer nation as it is to big business. It is as much a cancer to culture as it is a death sentence to mainstream media.

And in this scenario the enemy is our friend (frenemy—just ask Sir Martin Sorrell and his love-hate relationship with Google) *and* the enemy is us.

The solution is not more advertising—or iAds or convincing (begging) consumers to watch more ads or pay for the newspaper or click more or be comfortable with their privacy being hawked in order to sell more stuff to "friends." It's a complete overhaul of the incumbent operating system in favor of a clean-slate approach, a reprioritization of our goals relative to the market reality. It is a restructuring and reconciliation of our dollars against the true drivers of growth.

What's Your Heresy?

In 2012, Andrew Winston gave a keynote at WOBI's World Innovation Forum in New York City. He introduced the notion of embracing the very thing that you fear most, that which threatens your very existence or presents the biggest threat to your health, wellness, or financial future. The idea was not just to identify this heresy but to incorporate and integrate it into the inner sanctum of your strategy, to make it your point of origin. All planning, decision making, and contingency planning would subsequently be based on this heresy.

The entire concept of hacking an API is a prime example of embracing your inner and outer heresy. Today, hack-a-thons are a dime a dozen, being held by some of the most surprising sources you'd expect, such as the Mayor's Office of New York City, with their Reinvent NYC initiative.

Closer to home, the Coca-Cola Company turned over its digital assets to its consumer base through its Content Factory initiative (Figure 8.5).

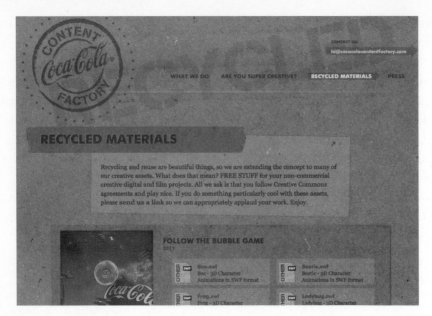

Figure 8.5   Coca-Cola's Content Factory initiative

The ultimate (and as it turns out false) security blanket for major corporations is the illusion of control. It is the very thing that they struggle the most to let go or give up, and it is this stubbornness that is ironically the single biggest contributor to their lack of innovation, evolution, and ability to inject fresh, creative, and progressive thinking into a sluggish beast. What better way to turn this on its head than to open source the entire "secret sauce," or proprietary methodology of a brand proposition? Twitter's entire ecosystem was arguably created and supported by the developer community with a cacophony of apps from TweetDeck to Twittelator. Instagram is not much different.

What would happen if the record labels gave away their music for free? What would happen if book publishers embraced self-publishing or threw out their physical printing and distribution model in favor of an exclusive e-book approach? What would happen if automakers eliminated dealerships in favor of digital showrooms? Would you be surprised to learn that all three scenarios (in varying degrees) are already in motion in the form of singles and ringtones (versus album sales), traditional publishers like Simon and Schuster entering into self-publishing in 2012, or Tesla and

Audi launching experiential showrooms with few or no salespeople and physical cars?

To put some flesh on the bones of this organizing idea, here is a heretical scenario to serve as the ideal backdrop and illustrative foundation against which to introduce the Z.E.R.O. hypothesis: Consider a world where advertising does not exist. Government has completely regulated all forms of corporate communication; consumer advocacy groups have fought back and won significant and game-changing lawsuits against media companies; and technological innovations have, one-by-one, obliterated once-traditional communications channels.

Think this is a scene right out of *1984*, *Total Recall*, or *Fringe?* Think again. Consider this:

- In 2006, the Sao Paulo government outlawed[1] all forms of outdoor advertising in Brazil's industrial and corporate mecca.

- In 2003, the Do Not Call registry was enforced[2] by the U.S. government.

- In May 2006, the soft drink industry voluntarily banned soda dispensing/vending machines[3] from schools in the United States.

- In early 2008, in New York State, all fast-food or restaurant items were required by law[4] to reflect accurate calorie counts.

- In 1998, a startup out of Silicon Valley called TiVo introduced a personal video recorder that allowed consumers to skip or fast-forward through commercials.

- In 2012, the Russian government banned[5] all advertising for all alcohol-containing products and severely limited their distribution.

Still think this is an unrealistic futuristic scenario? Legendary Yankees catcher and captain Yogi Berra once said, "If you come to a fork in the road, take it!" He was famous for these nonsensical sayings, which upon further reflection made complete sense. With deference to Yogi, I like to say, "When there's writing on the wall, read it."

In May 2013, Tom Phillips, senior director of communications for Microsoft Advertising, wrote an opinion piece citing a world without advertising. He listed lost jobs, the void of cultural memes like "Got Milk?," reporters having nothing to talk about in the agency and advertising world (!), the Super Bowl, an empty Times Square and Yankee

Stadium, and finally iconic campaigns such as Wendy's "Where's the Beef?" These are all valid examples, but they are virtually insignificant in context of the bigger, global picture, especially when we have to go back to decades-old campaigns to make a point about the next several decades to come. Even putting aside Phillips's, obvious conflict of interest, the fact remains: Consumers have moved on. Brands are still relevant in some places, even their advertising presence is welcome, but this is a numbers game now and the odds are horrendously stacked against us.

Protesting "I'm not dead" didn't work for Dr. Malcom Crowe,* and it won't work for us either. Instead of desperately protesting to preserve the status quo, why not embrace our inner heresy and make the assumption that advertising is dying or plan against the worst (or best depending on your perspective) case scenario that we may very well be operating in an environment where advertising is a luxury tax?

Is it really so outlandish to expect the cash-strapped government to impose the same kinds of onerous tax penalties on advertising as it does on tobacco, alcohol, and other harmful drugs? After all, when facing the prospect of falling of fiscal cliffs at a regular occurrence, desperate times surely call for desperate measures.

Developing a go-to-market plan without an iota of advertising or paid media seems like a useful and productive exercise in any event. At the very minimum, it's a healthy and arguably cathartic process designed to uncover a host of viable alternatives that either would have been buried until the very end of the planning process (when neither time nor money remained for any meaningful investment) or not uncovered at all. On the opposite end of the continuum, it's a life-and-death insulation against the doomsday scenario.

I always like to start with two underlying assumptions:

1. If given the choice, consumers would without exception choose to ignore, avoid, or obliterate advertising
2. See assumption 1.

---

*Spoiler alert: This lead character in *The Sixth Sense*, played by Bruce Willis, did not realize he was dead until the end of the movie.

If your agency were challenged with the simple premise that advertising was a luxury tax at best and an unnecessary evil at worst, would they do things differently? If you held the belief that advertising effectiveness was the exception, versus the norm, wouldn't you approach your planning with a severely prudent fiscal lens?

Your heresy is not limited to paid media. Consider these uncomfortable scenarios:

- What if fast-food restaurants refused to serve obese customers?
- What if cable companies embraced à la carte pricing and earned the bundle, versus commanding it?
- What if consumer package goods manufacturers cut out the supermarket in favor of selling directly to customers?
- What if automakers collaborated to create a nationwide grid of recharge stations, much like the Israeli initiative Better Place that folded on May 26, 2013, the same day this paragraph was written (see Figure 8.6)? But don't you dare think this is the end for smart, electric, and/or sustainable cars. To the contrary. Up and coming Tesla recently announced their plans to deploy a similar battery exchange solution to that of Better Place. Timing. Luck. Execution (but not necessarily in that order!).

Quit talkin' like a crazy person . . .

What's Your Legacy?

Determining your heresy is a spiritual journey of self-discovery and enlightenment designed to promote brand health and wellness and ensure job fulfillment, growth, and continuity.

This section is just about done, but it's worth revisiting the reasons why we resist change, avoid change, and even downright sabotage change in order to sustain our fiefdoms, preserve the status quo, and maintain our corner office position.

As the old saying goes, "The more things change, the more they stay the same." Rishad Tobaccowala, a friend, luminary, and thought leader in the media space, has a much smarter take on it: "The more you want things to stay the same, the more you *have* to change."

Figure 8.6   Better Place battery exchange station in Israel

I interpret this many ways, but right at the top of the list is a Darwinian evolution of modern marketing man or woman—a survival of the fittest predicated on keeping your job by constantly iterating, adapting, and progressing.

Staying the same in this case is a status quo of sorts, yet it's based on anything but. Put differently, by staying the same, you'll fast-track your departure and demise.

Surely, there has to be more to our miserable existence than eking through our daily grind on the dingy and underwhelming path to tenure. I simply cannot accept that any chief marketing officer or agency leader is a cockroach of sorts (something Tobaccowala has adopted as a mantra[6]), looking to evade the stomping boot of shareholder EBITDA* and survive solely based on a physiological constitution of scraping through.

Isn't it a much more admirable and worthy aspiration to think about your legacy? What will be written about you when you retire? (No, I don't mean the forced retirement or the public relations–spun misdirection of a pink slip.) What will your Wikipedia entry read? Will you even have a Wikipedia entry? What is Wikipedia? (Hopefully you know the answer to that last one.)

What will you tell your grandchildren when you explain that you made ads for a living and they recoil in disgust? Will you show them a binder filled with media plans (created by women)? Will you dust off the cobwebs of your CLIOs, Addys, Lions, and Pencils to reflect on that amazing billboard, radio jingle, or banner ad?

How did you change society for the better? How did you influence your industry? Which professional lives did you mentor, elevate, and nurture? Are these questions you've even been asking? Or are prepared to answer?

What's your legacy? Surely it is one that reflects life after the 30-second spot!

Whether you take the What's Your Heresy or What's Your Legacy positions—or both—there are specific pathways to follow and exercises to undertake to extrapolate, project, and reverse engineer a working plan designed to get you from here (chaotic) to there (less chaotic). Rome wasn't built in a day.

The Z.E.R.O. framework is your Sherpa on this path.

---

*EBITDA stands for earnings before interest, taxes, depreciation, and amortization.

CHAPTER

9

Introducing Z.E.R.O.

Occam's razor: The simplest explanation is often the correct one.

Charity Begins at Home

The solution begins inside the corporation. It's an internal solve that flips the funnel by recognizing that waste is never acceptable and that the true engine of business is not fueled via acquisition but in fact by retention. It's an innate belief and the activation of that belief that *in a perfect world the optimal marketing and media budget would be zero.*

Zero spend

Zero paid media

Zero advertising

Zero "bought" attention

Zero waste

We believe that in a perfect world the optimal paid media spend would be zero: that all businesses (large and small) and all brands (existing, newly formed, and newly launched) would not need paid media to launch, build, or sustain their presence, relevance, or resonance with their target market, prospects, customers, advocates, community, or constituencies (internal or external).

I MAY NOT ALWAYS DRINK BEER, BUT WHEN I DO, I PREFER DOS EQUIS.

Admittedly, this isn't a perfect world and this is perhaps why paid media will continue to be a part of many companies' marketing plans. This doesn't justify it though. In fact, it could be argued that the very reason the status quo is perpetuated is itself evidence of an imperfect model.

It is our belief that paid media should not be the *first* part of a plan. It should not be the default or go-to play in the marketer's handbook. And it should most certainly not dominate the plan both in terms of mindshare and share of budget. It may have been proved once upon a time, but it is no longer proved to be an efficient or effective *investment*.

Paid media is a cost, an expense item—an expenditure that fails any reasonable austerity measure. Buying media is buying attention, like buying friends. It's reserved for the fat kid who is refused a Happy Meal at McDonald's (see "What's Your Heresy?" in Chapter 8).

Paid Media Is Reserved for PEONs

The word *peon* is defined[1] as a low-ranking or unskilled employee. It is not a stretch to describe the incumbent marketer or media or agency "professional" as a peon—at least when it comes to persisting with a status quo–driven agenda that insists on advertising its way out of any problem; misguides, misleads, and/or misdirects an otherwise informed consumer; and does not adapt, evolve, or innovate quickly enough, especially in an increasingly digital, social, and connected world.

As we will shortly reveal about Z.E.R.O., the word P.E.O.N. is also an acronym. It is the lesser of the two acronyms that will be introduced in this chapter.

P.E.O.N. stands for paid, earned, owned, and "non." The first three you will no doubt have heard ad nauseam. The final one almost certainly not.

Paid, earned, and owned is often spoken of as a compound phrase— paidearnedowned—inextricably linked. But of course we know this is not the case. It is a cliché of sorts, a throwaway term—both superficial and empty.

Paid media at face value represents all forms of paid advertising and communication (both above and below the line), in other words, all the rented space you buy to promote, showcase, and shill your brand. Earned media encompasses the public relations and publicity realms. For categorization purposes, we define owned media as predominantly digital, incorporating third-party hubs such as Facebook pages and/or YouTube channels. You'll notice that we did not include your website, your trucks, your packaging, your people, or your stores. That's because these are assets—owned assets. These are very different from owned media. (More to come on that shortly.)

This leaves us with nonmedia, defined as human-to-human or peer-to-peer connections, interactions, or transactions. Nonmedia is better than media. It is richer, more authentic, more influential. Nonmedia might include "mouths" and the "words coming out of those mouths" as opposed to word-of-mouth, which probably gets bucketed in the earned category.

In *Life after the 30-Second Spot*, I introduced one of my bold new approaches to traditional advertising: *consumer-generated content.* This may not sound particularly innovative to you, except that it was written in 2004, before YouTube existed. I was very deliberate to use the word *content*, as opposed to *media* (consumer-generated media), and I was equally meditative to refer to *consumers* versus *users* (the drug reference once again.) Unfortunately for me (or you), the phrase did not stick. In fact, it regressed to a sucker one-two punch of *user-generated media.* That doesn't mean I stopped using my original term, and it certainly doesn't mean I've given up! Likewise, I am hopeful that the idea of nonmedia will catch on and, at the very least, we will pay equal homage to this fourth leg of the attention table. You play a major role in helping me continue to chase this particular windmill.

Media, a So-Called Term . . .

Ernie Kovacs, a television personality from the 1950s, once described television as "a so-called medium, because it is neither rare, nor well done." This could very well cover any form of paid media or, for that matter, all media (earned and owned to boot).

The media model is built around scarcity, with the laws of supply (finite and decreasing) and demand (finite and stagnant) creating an artificial ecosystem of inflationary pressure on pricing, when in reality, there is instead an abundance of impressions available relative to the truly scarce resource: attention.

Media was a term we (the biz) created to force our way into the homes of our unsuspecting "targets"; it is the generalized phrase to describe the blunt instrument of communication as we talk to our audience—that is, talk down to and at our audience, as opposed to, for example, listening and responding to them or joining their conversation.

Media is both commoditized (neither rare) and dull (nor well done) when it comes to communicating with any class, consistency, or inspirational originality.

Most important, it is decidedly *not* consumer- nor customer-centric. It is one-way traffic, so to speak, and therefore must die. Okay, perhaps that was a little over the top, but it stands to reason that any lip service paid to even the most remote desire to be somewhat customer-centric would demand a different approach.

Nonmedia does just that. It's not a sexy term (and therefore will almost certainly not stick), but then again if the notion of being compared to contagious germs and bacteria worked (viral marketing), why wouldn't this?

A nonmedia budget is essentially a human budget. It is a major portion of the *flipped funnel,* and if we are to seriously attempt to adapt and evolve the way we do business, then we need to elevate this as a strategic imperative with immediate effect.

Employees connecting with fellow employees, employees connecting with customers, and customers connecting with customers all qualify as nonmedia. Word-of-mouth is the lubricant that greases the wheels of the nonmedia machine. It truly does not belong in the earned media camp—at least if we're talking about authentic, organic, credible value exchanges. The other kind of word-of-mouth in the form of likes, shares, retweets, and forwards can gleefully stomp in the increasingly noisy sandbox of earned media.

Setting the Attention Table

Getting back to a consumer-centric approach in modern-day marketing or postmarketing requires a true apples-to-apples benchmarking to help categorize and segment the primary forms of engagement.

The most elegant and succinct way to do this is as follows:

Paid media is all about *buying* attention.

Earned media is all about *creating* attention.

Owned media is all about *building* attention.

Nonmedia is all about *paying* attention.

Nonmedia may be human-centric, but it is increasingly powered by technology—in this case, even an old-school passenger manifesto printed on a dot matrix printer.

Referring to the incident mentioned in the tweet from Figure 9.1, I declined an upgrade because I was sitting with my family (in fact, they asked, "Are you traveling alone or with your family?"), but I did get to upgrade my mother compliments of the new U.S. American Airways.

The *earned media* of my tweet stream and this mention in this book are my way of saying thank you for paving the way to Z.E.R.O.

On its simplest level, P.E.O.N. implies that paid media is but one of four forms of media. And all things being equal, it should command 25 percent of all media budgets accordingly. This is obviously not even remotely the case.

P.E.O.N. sets the stage by putting four supporting pillars in place that help build the foundation for current and future engagement. It covers predominently the traditional funnel but, increasingly so, offers a bridge to connect with and incorporate the flipped funnel (as introduced in my book *Flip the Funnel*, John Wiley & Sons, 2010). P.E.O.N. runs on a lesser of evils higher ground, offering an added dimension to the existing palate of tools used to break through the clutter and create signal from noise.

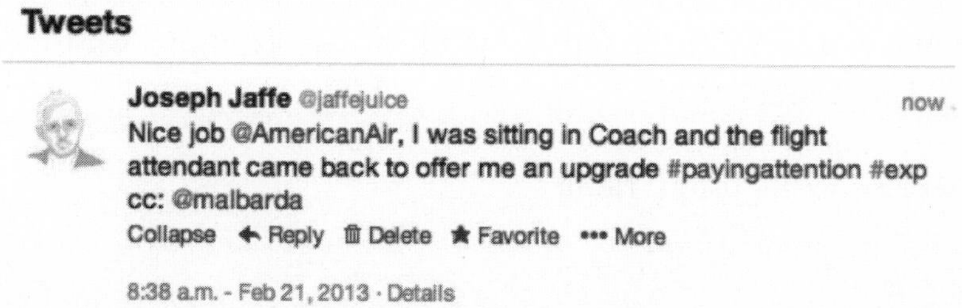

Tweets

Joseph Jaffe @jaffejuice   now
Nice job @AmericanAir, I was sitting in Coach and the flight
attendant came back to offer me an upgrade #payingattention #exp
cc: @malbarda
Collapse ← Reply 🗑 Delete ★ Favorite ••• More

8:38 a.m. - Feb 21, 2013 · Details

Figure 9.1   Paying attention

Interactions

Figure 9.2   Paying (it forward) attention

P.E.O.N. assumes that paid media is necessary—after all, the P of *paid* comes first in the acronym. But what if it didn't? What if there was no need to acquire new customers from the ether of the outside world because *there were enough customers to sustain and grow the base from the inside?*

We believe that P.E.O.N. gives rise to a revolutionary contention that brands don't need to spend another cent on media because, all things being equal, they have enough to grow their business from the inside out.

Enter Z.E.R.O., a model that may very well top up with a responsible portion of paid media, but it begins with the heresy that the optimal paid media budget is zero.

Z.E.R.O. itself is an acronym that outlines why and how we believe that in a perfect world, brands would be media discerning, versus media dependent. It stands for:

Z = Zealots

E = Entrepreneurship

R = Retention

O = Owned assets

The Z.E.R.O. framework is built on these four pillars, which not only support our primary hypothesis but also outline a strategic and balanced way forward, namely, the effective prioritization and combination of advocacy, innovation, customer centricity, and direct to consumer engagement:

- *Zealots:* Zealots have an intense focus on tapping into and harnessing the power of advocates, enthusiasts, evangelists, and ambassadors, much like then Senator Barack Obama did during the historical U.S. general election in 2008: a flip the funnel idea like the Ambassador Program or simply a referral-based ecosystem is designed to grow the business from the inside out, starting with the most passionate power users.

  When it comes to the power of passion-initiated conversation, earned media impressions trump paid, especially in a YouTube world. So-called free media is not just about efficiency, it's also about authenticity, credibility, permission, and trust. *KONY 2012*, a short film designed to make African cult and militia leader and indicted war criminal Joseph Kony (in)famous in order to help with his capture, has more than 98 million impressions on YouTube, and by the time you read this, that number will be even higher. Of course, you can also go all Gangnam Style on your way to becoming YouTube's most watched video of all time. All you need to do is dance around on your invisible horse.

- *Entrepreneurship:* Entrepreneurial spirit and corporate marketing go together like caviar and dog poop—or at least that's how it used to work. Movements such as Lean Startup are teaching mighty companies like General Electric and Intuit to "Think Different" as they attempt to inject innovation and risk taking into these companies' lethargic DNA.

- *Retention:* Retention as an acquisition driver becomes the consummate way to grow a business from the inside out by focusing—or even obsessing—on *real* customers above potential ones. Customer centricity (as opposed to consumer centricity) is really a combination of a renewed focus on service and experience, with an equal prioritization and shift (mind and body) toward a retention-based approach. This particular facet really embodies the spirit of Z.E.R.O. It costs nothing to remember your customer's real name or Twitter account name.

- *Owned assets:* To truly make the shift from being media dependent to media discerning, brands need to free themselves from the shackles of being renters and move to where they have the potential to be landlords. And why not? Brands have long sat on a mountain of disparate assets, but they have never fully connected the dots to bring them together under one unified front.

Putting It All Together

In 2012, Tottenham Hotspur Football Club toured the United States and played a match against the New York Red Bulls in Harrison, New Jersey. Being a lifelong Spurs fan (and having passed this on to my poor son, who now has to experience the same pain I have had to endure), I found out that Red Bull's season ticket holders would have an opportunity to attend an open practice between the two teams and meet the players. So, crazy zealot that I am, I purchased two season tickets, even though I would never actually attend a single Red Bulls game. How crazy is the Red Bulls organization? "Totes cray" as my other son would say. Crazy smart, that is! Whether intentional or not, they gave themselves a chance to convert a prospect into a client by leveraging their owned assets and tapping into the advocacy of a true "fan" (not the Facebook kind). As an aside, the real reason I didn't return was that I live too far away—but if I didn't, I'd probably be renewing my season ticket right about now!

Or switching gears, consider Sit or Squat, a mobile app that locates the nearest public restroom and gives a host of context, including cleanliness, whether the restroom is open or not, a rating system, and even photographs (yuk!). As it turns out, Procter & Gamble's Charmin brand acquired Sit or Squat and now owns 100 percent of the share of voice in this direct-to-consumer service-based utility. Although there was an initial cost to the company and no doubt continued maintenance and optimization, what Charmin now has is a pretty sublime opportunity to connect with its customer base and bundle in consideration, engagement, emotion, and value. It also has an organic opportunity to build this or if required—with paid media support—a platform to exponentially ramp

**Figure 9.3   Posing at the open practice with Spurs' manager,
André Villas-Boas**

this up. Imagine the possibilities if Pampers and Always were to join forces (and budget) with Charmin.

Microsoft recently wrote off $900 million of excess surface inventory. What if they had deployed a Z.E.R.O. approch to put these tablets in the hands of their portfolio customers' hands—and in particular, their most fervent fans?

Primary Hypothesis and Z.E.R.O. Manifesto

To reframe the setup and (re)state our vision statement: In a perfect world, media budgets would be zero, because existing customers would be driving sales—directly via upselling, cross-selling, increased frequency, recency, and basket size, and indirectly via referrals, recommendations, feedback, word-of-mouth, and content creation (testimonials, reviews, endorsement). Marketing budgets would be predominantly focused on an inside-out approach designed to maximize reach via organic nonmedia first versus paid media first. Brands would be content curators capable of seeding ideas and starting memes, movements, and idea viruses—each of which would have the *potential* to become transformational branding, positioning, or strategic platforms that differentiate, sustain, and power brands and businesses.

Beat the drum. Crow at the top of your lungs. Sing with us:

In a perfect world, brands would be media discerning, not media dependent.

In a perfect world, brands would no longer be tenants but landlords.

In a perfect world, paid media would be a nice-to-have and not a have-to-have.

In a perfect world, brands would control their relationships with their customers and not cede them.

In a perfect world, brands would build direct bridges between themselves and consumers and not need facilitators or intermediaries.

But, alas, this world is not perfect. This doesn't mean we have to accept it, be resigned to it, or comply with it. We can change. We can change it. We can be the change agents our stakeholders deserve, the ones our shareholders demand and our customers expect.

Truly, nothing is perfect, and imperfections are what make us human. *To err is human; to forgive divine.*

Why then do we not hold this true for our marketing efforts? Media today is a giant imperfection with small, siloed, unscalable, and somewhat serendipitous lightning-in-a-bottle perfections. It's not enough to save the day. It's not enough to save your job.

We are on a journey to perfection, knowing full well that we will never get there but emboldened with the confidence and knowledge that literally every step taken to a world without paid media is a step in the right direction.

That's the elevator pitch, now let's take a more in depth look at each of these four pillars, beginning with the almost uncomfortable association of customers as religious die-hards.

Awaken, Zealots, Awaken

In a perfect world, we wouldn't need paid media because we would have a rising army of passionate advocates.

Rogers's diffusion of innovations curve talks about innovators (2.5 percent), early adopters (13.5 percent), early and late majority (34 percent), and laggards (16 percent). This bell curve can be just as easily applied to a customer-centric segmentation model or, in this case, an advocacy-driven one. Satmetrix's Net Promoter Score (the percentage of promoters less the percentage of detractors) does something similar, statistically representing that only a 9 or 10 response to the question "On a scale of 0 to 10, how likely would you be to recommend to a friend" qualifies as a promoter. Pretty incredible to think of 7 or 8 as being passive or indifferent and 5 or 6 (putting the *satisfactory* in *satisfaction*) as being classified as a detractor!

Along similar lines, shouldn't it be possible to identify the top 2.5 percent of consumers (or better yet, your customers) as advocates, loyalists, and even zealots in almost every sense of the word (except the literal falling on swords)? Of course it is. It isn't even difficult to find them; most of the time they find you—whether you like it or not. In some cases, they've tattooed your brand onto their skin (a strong case why rebranding and spending millions of dollars on dumb logo tweaks is a sore point with your zealots). In less extreme cases, it could be a season ticket holder or a tenured "made" customer based on consecutive years of elite status. (For example, American gives lifetime Platinum status for its AAdvantage members who have flown 2 million miles.)

Zealot, a word with a connotation that made even the uber provocateur Seth Godin a little uncomfortable. And that can't be a bad thing, right?

Merriam-Webster defines a zealot as follows:

1. *capitalized: a member of a fanatical sect arising in Judea during the first century* AD *and militantly opposing the Roman domination of Palestine*

2. *a zealous[2] person; especially: a fanatical partisan <a religious zealot>*

I'm pretty sure that a Harley-Davidson fan does not get up every morning and curse out the Romans, although I'm equally certain he is fanatical about his hog. It would appear that the definition itself offers very little in terms of meaningful insight into understanding advocacy at its purest, except for one very important word: *fanatical*. As in *fan*. As in *raving fan*. As in *raving lunatic*.

Personally, I don't care which phrase you use as long as you truly are in sync with the act of submitting wholly to the very people who keep you in business: your base, your core, your power users, your customers for life.

When I talk to companies, they generally fixate on the following two objectives because they relate to advocacy: "How do we get more promoters?" and "What do we do with the ones we already have? (How do we activate them?)" I give them a simple strategic plan with distinct roles for marketing to play:

Convert the detractors.

Engage the passives.

Activate the advocates.

I'm always struck by how few companies have specific programs in place to address any, if not all, of these three mission-critical roles.

Zealots by definition are not quiet. Passives are. Passives are the silent enemy—the rotten core that will destroy a brand from the inside out. The real enemy ultimately is apathy—indifference or agnosticism if you will. Getting someone to care and give a damn is 80 percent of the battle, and this is why I'd prefer a detractor over a passive any day.

My views are a little more extreme (okay, a lot) than yours need to be. When I've keynoted at Satmetrix conferences in the past, I often joked with the audience that my ideal net promoter score should be, you guessed it, zero. My goal is to challenge, to be a true provocateur. I don't expect everyone to agree with me. In fact, if that happened, I would have failed my mandate of challenging the status quo—the average, which by definition, should be shared by 50 percent (no more) of the room.

You could say I'm a bit of a zealot when it comes to presenting, especially about subjects I'm passionate about. I'm not sure it's possible to have an introverted zealot, a reserved or timid super-promoter. If anything, I would consider any silent minority of promoters to be either neglected or underutilized by a brand: They are a sleeping giant and, if disturbed in a bad way, could make for a very unpleasant headache for companies.

This is why I've suggested to companies to consider subsegmenting their promoters into zealots (promoter-promoters), dormants (passive-promoters), and defectors (detractor-promoters.)

Zealots without a voice are both a myth and a potentially fatal mistake. Awaken the beast at your peril! It generally is just a very clear indicator that a company is not paying attention—whether in the form of doing a better job listening to the various online and social channels, doing one's time on the various customer care phone lines or chat sessions, or just plain walking the floor and having genuine conversations with employees and customers.

In today's marketplace, there is a strong convergence taking place between "those who buy (a lot)" and "those who talk (a lot) to (a lot of) people." For this reason, tapping into zealots is a double-edge sword. If not properly utilized, we could very well fall on our own swords in the process (and we're back to vengeful zealots of lethal biblical proportions).

As Figure 9.4 highlights (taken from *Flip the Funnel*), we have an opportunity to expand the middle ground by turning the funnel into a megaphone, as Seth Godin would say, or creating formal ambassador programs that recognize and reward zealots based on their business (referrals) and brand (content creation and conversation) contributions.

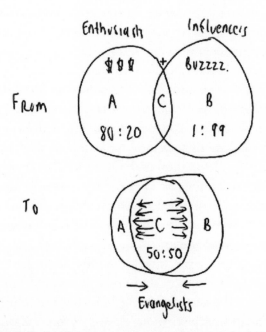

Figure 9.4   The fall of influencer marketing, the rise of advocacy marketing

According to the Z.E.R.O. manifesto, with an army of fanatical fans (or zealots) advocating on your behalf, why on Earth would you need to buy another person's attention again?

Loyalty and Advocacy Are Not One and the Same

Loyalty is to advocacy what satisfaction is to being truly remarkable. Most companies (Red Bull, you can sit down) have not remotely figured out how to harness true passion—unadulterated, unrefined, and often raw, unconditional devotion to a cause, purpose, idea, and, yes, even brand. For some reason, loyalty exists in a sort of purgatory, somewhere in the domain of customer relationship management. Ordinarily, this would be fine, except for the fact that it is not being given the investment, commitment, mindshare, and strategic clout commensurate with its potential, impact, and value to the business.

I recently visited with one of the largest consumer packaged goods marketers on the planet, and management point blank refuted the value that loyalty programs bring to the bottom line. They even tossed a bunch of spreadsheets into my face to support their point of view. I returned the spreadsheets with an offer to work for free to prove them wrong. Perhaps the starting point of our divergent perspectives lies in the chasm between weak loyalty and impenetrable advocacy.

A customer who sticks around is not necessarily a loyal one and should not be confused with one. My Coke Rewards relaunched its rewards catalog to be more aligned with advocates versus loyalists. For the longest time, I thought AT&T sucked—big time. And I didn't hesitate to tell anyone who would care to hear it, as well as those who didn't. And here I was—a customer, a loyal customer since 1997. Even when legislation was passed giving customers the opportunity to switch providers without losing their numbers, I remained a customer because of my resigned belief that pretty much all cellular providers sucked (the same can be said for airlines and cable TV providers).

As the saying goes, "If you love something, let it go; if it comes back to you, it's yours; if it doesn't . . . hunt it down and kill it." Okay, the ending isn't part of the original saying, but what is important is the need to elevate our relationship with our consumers beyond one fraught with terms and conditions, controls, and small print to one that—warts and all—allows for unfettered, undiluted, and uncensored expressions of love, hate, and emotion in general.

The Real Enemy Is Apathy

In an old blog post on Jaffe Juice,[3] I referenced an article titled "Hate My Brand . . . Please!" It was written by Mike Wagner and referenced the polarizing appeal (or lack thereof) of Crocs shoes and why 'tis better to hate than not to feel at all.

Actually it's not about hate at all but about allowing for and respecting a difference of opinion—or just an opinion. It's that kind of opinion that produces results like this:

> *They've seen Crocs go from selling 1,500 pairs of shoes and a revenue of $24,000 in 2002 to last year's sales of 6 million pairs with total revenues (including shoes, accessories, and clothing) hitting $108.6 million. In May, the financial gurus at Crocs projected 2006 sales to reach over $200 million.*

And if you thought they were a fad, think again: through the third quarter[4] of 2012, Crocs continue to deliver healthy and increasing results.

You see, the problem with the world that we live in today is that we've all become a little numb, haven't we? We take a middle of the road break-even position, avoiding the big win or the big loss as a result. We live in a world of artificially inseminated and falsely perpetuated reality, and when we hear even the smallest whisper of dissention, we put our fingers in our waxed ears, scream at the top of our lungs, and hope to hell that the chief executive officer doesn't find out about our butt-ugly plastic shoes (which might as well be a metaphor for our brand or our marketing communications).

Mike offers these words of wisdom:

Embrace the hate to find your love.

One person's object of desire can be another person's object of distain.

People unite around ugly as much as beauty.

Ugly can be temporary, while people adjust to "your kind of beauty."

Formalizing Advocacy

When it comes to dealing with die-hard crusaders, it is important to resist the urge to control and suffocate these powerful fumes with corporate bureaucracy, legalese, and conditions. Micromanaging has no place here. At the same time—and this is really important—it's equally critical to make sure we don't neglect zealots, whether out of fear (what if they bite?), sensitivity (wouldn't want to tick them off), ideals (it's not in our nature to actually show our humanity), and/or greed (why mess with a good thing?).

I'm a believer that advocacy needs to be formalized (see the action plan in Chapter 15) and incentivized via a combination of monetary, non-cash, experiential, reward, and recognition plans. I am fully aware that there are those who vociferously oppose any form of payment or value exchange, which can be backed into a monetary value. I respect these opinions, although I still disagree with them. I believe that we shy away from that which we do not understand or choose not to understand. For example, a simple smile, thank you, and greeting by name absolutely support my point, and there is actual proof of this courtesy in J.D. Power & Associates' 2013 North America Airline Satisfaction Study.[5] The study reports that passengers who are greeted by smiling airline staff have satisfaction scores 105 points higher than those passengers who never got a smile. Passengers who report airline staff smiling at them consistently report satisfaction scores that are 211 points higher than those who are not seeing a smile.

By my highly unscientific and subjective assessment, I've sold hundreds of Nike FuelBands (a bracelet accelerometer, which measures "Fuel"—Nike's universal currency of activity, calories burned, and steps taken on any given day) based on my absolute love for the sublime piece of wearable tech. Should Nike compensate me in some way? Absolutely they should. Would this compromise my authenticity, integrity, or credibility in terms of advocating on Nike's behalf? Why should it? I'm a customer first and foremost, and that comes before anything. Fears of compromising integrity, in my opinion, are misdirected at the real culprit: opaque and misrepresented marketing and advertising. At the end of the day, it is the customer's own integrity that is in play. Why wouldn't we give him or her the benefit of the doubt and ability to manage his or her own social capital or currency? Furthermore, who is to say that incentivizing advocacy has to be regular and predictable? Why can't it be serendipitous, random, or treated on a case-by-case basis (just like the security checks at airports)?

We have a tremendous opportunity to both formalize advocacy with some kind of ambassador type program *and* implement a series of rewards and recognitions that—to hit this one home—represent things money *can't* buy. Think of first looks, samples, access to executives, invitation-only events, and the like.

By confronting the zealot, a company takes control of its own fate and destiny versus playing a high-stakes game of avoidance in the hopes that the tables don't turn and the unconditional lover isn't left jilted at the alter, ready to unleash hell and revenge on the offender.

This is not an episode of *The Bachelor* people; this is real life!

Pivot, Entrepreneur, Pivot!

In a perfect world, we wouldn't need paid media because we would have a direct pipeline to innovation, creativity, and disruptive ideas.

We are on a crash course for a perfect storm in the marketing and media world, and our vehicle of choice for this unpleasant journey is mediocrity and the status quo. If we are to avoid this unpleasant outcome and our inevitable demise, we surely will need to undertake a dual approach of creativity and innovation. And fortunately, they are joined at the hip.

Survival Demands Innovation and Creativity[6]

Ten years ago, I was ranting and raving about the lack of creativity and innovation in the online space. It's kind of sad and even pathetic that we're still asking the same questions today. From the punch the monkey to Yahoo!'s wooing of traditional creative directors to plop their 30-second spots on its well-trafficked home page (how's that working out for you?), we haven't exactly hit a digital home run, now have we?

It's not too late for an intervention, but I fear that soon enough, it will be unless we inject a good dose of truly game-changing digital whoop-ass into the mix.

My antidote is the intersection of technology and advertising: Mountain View meets Madison Avenue.

Earlier in this book, I highlighted the definition of *creativity* as "productive originality," which is the exact opposite of doing the same thing over and over again, hoping to get a different result. Creativity is the solution to insanity, the remedy to mediocrity and status quo, but that's just half of the equation.

Innovation is similarly defined as new approaches that achieve disproportionate results. Is it a coincidence that this is essentially a synonym for creativity? I think not.

This perhaps underscores that the future of marketing (creativity) is a digital one, a tech-laden one. Brands must innovate to evolve and, arguably, to survive. I believe that the intersection between marketing and startups is one way to mix together creativity and innovation into a powerful cocktail.

The catch perhaps is that innovation is typically associated with product or packaging research and development (R&D), as opposed to marketing itself. It's time to change that.

I always like to quote photographer Diane Arbus, who said: "It's what I've never seen before that I recognize."

Our consumers are the same. They ignore what they've seen before time and time again. They notice the unanticipated. They crave the unexpected, the unpredictable, the surprise, and the delight. They long for the intellectual sparring that comes with an idea that provokes, irks, challenges, or dares them to think or act different.

And they're not insane, although we might be if we don't rethink the way we go to market or the way we utilize the full potential of the Internet and its social portfolio of gizmos and gadgets.

The preceding key concepts present a bold new way forward for brands:

1. Innovation is not a nice-to-have. It is a have-to-have; it is mission critical.

2. Innovation in the corporate world is concentrated on R&D associated with product marketing and related aspects, such as packaging, pricing, and distribution. In other words, the 4 Ps.

3. Marketing itself as it relates to direct-to-consumer relationship building, delivery of utility and/or service, and ultimately engagement is void of creativity or innovation.

4. Marketing's future lies in and through technology.

5. The worlds of technology and marketing are fusing.

In other words, technology-based direct-to-consumer innovation holds the key for a brand's survival, evolution, and growth.

But how?

In the epicenter of technology-driven innovation is the startup. The same startup that once upon a time produced the likes of Amazon.com, eBay, and Priceline. The same startup that produced Facebook, Google, and Instagram. The same startup that produced the likes of Hewlett-Packard, Apple, and Microsoft. GarageBand (contrary to popular belief) is not an application on your Mac; it's the place where many startups were born, incubated, and/or accelerated.

The entrepreneurial spirit is not necessarily a function of technology, but these days technology is so pervasive that it might as well be. Startups face a daily reality check of do or die. Well over 95 percent of them will not survive: They will run out of funding, assuming they get funding at all. They will need to adapt or die. They will need to zig, zag, course correct, create a contingency plan in real time, iterate, pivot, and act very lean. They will have to maximize a shoestring budget in order to become the next big thing or at a very minimum get accepted into Apple's App store. Risk is table stakes, and the price of entry is the only guarantee that tomorrow will look nothing like yesterday. Brands could learn a lot from entrepreneurs, and it begins by recognizing two key points:

1. Brands and startups have more in common than they might think.

2. To truly collaborate, new rules have to be written, new standards defined, new metrics developed, and new timelines embraced.

Brands and Startups Are Joined at the Hip

Every day you die a little. You are one step closer to your death. That's not morbid at all. It's factual. It's reality based. Brands act as proxies for companies that keep them and somewhere along the line, we seem to have forgotten that.

Startups are a lot more fortunate than brands in that survival is very binary for them. Brands, however, seem to mask so much in deferred blame, misguided credit, and denial. A tenth of a point decline in market share can result in hundreds of thousands in profits lost, potential layoffs, and reduced growth forecast ahead.

What's the return on investment of survival? As MasterCard would say, "Priceless!"

Another similarity brands and startups share is their starting point: problem solving. The founders of Uber couldn't find a cab when they needed one in San Francisco, so they started a service that helped commuters efficiently locate rides. The founder of Dropbox once forget his USB memory stick on a bus ride and had to sit through a five-hour-plus ride from Boston to New York City without his work files. Etsy was started to correct a geographic inefficiency of a bunch of talented artists standing on a street corner in Brooklyn hawking their magnificent wares that the world was dying to discover. Brands do the same in every creative brief when they express a business challenge, brand problem, or consumer insight that needs to be tapped into. Unfortunately, instead of solving the problem through the creation of a startup (existing or otherwise), they settle for paid media's off-cuts in the form of advertising.

A third point of commonality is that of transformational change. Startups aren't looking to invent a tweak on an existing model or an incremental modification on a service that already exists; they want to do something that has never been done before. They want to absolutely shatter the ceiling on what is considered standard operating practice. They want to change the existing market or business model for the better. They want to invent an entirely new market. Brands are not (at least at the core) any different. Transformational change is always the prime directive in the form of changing perception, buyer behavior, and ingrained habits, as well as creating the ultimate differentiated, sustainable, competitive advantage (aka obliterating the competition with a patented, ownable, and clear point of advantage). Again, sadly, they settle for a poor fallback option in the form of changing ad agencies, logos, and taglines—and paying top dollar for the privilege of doing so.

Finally, both startups and brands desperately covet and strive for critical mass in terms of audience, users, or customer base; however, there is a big difference between mass media (tonnage) and critical mass (sufficiency, economies of scale, and networked effect of communities).

These days, brands have become enamored with the next bright and shiny object, namely, conducting tests or experiments with startups. Only startups aren't some passing fad, gimmick, flavor of the month, or test tube guinea pig. Collectively, they represent value propositions or utilities that disrupt norms, challenge conventions, and move markets. But they won't get to realize their vision—their proof of concept—if brands continue to hold them at arm's length, dispatching their agency minions to negotiate the impossible "big ideas at scale."

Innovative and unprecedented executions are absolutely doable. They fall apart when brands turn away because the reach isn't there—or, put differently, they can't measure or compare these startlings to incumbent blunt instruments like TV, radio, print, or even online.

My message to brands is very simple: Don't be turned off by some startups' lack of reach. In fact, this should turn you on! You're dealing with the most fertile real estate, untouched and unspoiled by the masses (even your competitors). You have the incredible opportunity to help them achieve their path to reach with your brand dollars, talent, resources, and media. You have the unique chance to join forces with them at the earliest possible stage to cocreate and own that big idea.

Agile Brands

Thinking and acting like a startup—whether figuratively (contingency planning, marketing in real time in the "Age of Improv?") or quite literally (collaborating with startups)—is the realization of the vision and assertion that marketing's future and salvation lies in and through technology, the bridge between Madison Avenue and Mountain View.

In 2013, Mondelēz International (an Evol8tion client) launched its Mobile Futures Program, putting a firm stake in the ground in terms of (1) partnering with startups, (2) investing in mobile (the future of shopper marketing), and (3) committing to innovation, both internally and externally. The first leg of the program was to execute nine pilot programs by nine brands, partnering with nine startups, in 90 days! Figure 9.5 showcases the nine sets of brand managers and their startup soulmates. The program has since expanded to Brazil and plans to continue rolling out globally.

Mondelēz International Mobile Futures (US)

Figure 9.5   Celebrating the intrapreneurs

Hug It Out, Customer, Hug It Out (Retention Expanded)

In a perfect world, we wouldn't need paid media because we would have enough revenue coming in from enough customers who spend more and keep coming back for more.

If you're wondering what all this flipping funnel stuff is about, it refers to a funnel that expanded over time instead of contracting or narrowing. In my book *Flip the Funnel*, I took aim front and center at the traditional marketing and sales funnels and asked why we were spending more than 80 percent of our marketing dollars on people who were essentially strangers (the acquisition or first-time buyer bucket) when in reality, 80 percent of our revenues were coming from existing customers (the retention bucket).

Think about it for a moment: How on Earth could a solid business invest 20 percent of its dollars against an 80 percent revenue contribution? In addition, the 80/20 rule associated with power users amplified this chasm to a fever pitch: When 80 percent of this 80 percent comes from just 20 percent of these customers (and in many cases significantly less), we are faced with a seemingly irreconcilable difference and inconvenient

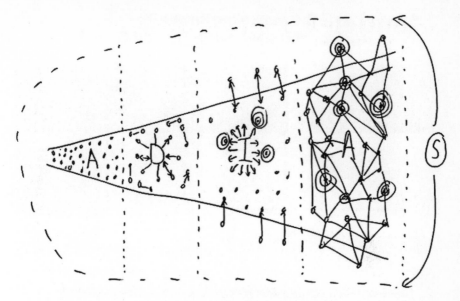

Figure 9.6   The flipped funnel

truth: Two thirds of your revenue is being egregiously underinvested at best and deliberately or even fraudulently neglected at worst. This has to stop—immediately.

In *Flip the Funnel*, I outlined three primary hypotheses to address the flawed traditional marketing and sales funnels, namely:

1. Retention becomes the new acquisition. It is possible, plausible, and probable to build a business from the inside out via cross-selling, upselling, and referrals.

2. Customer service and customer experience becomes *the* key strategic differentiators.

3. The real role of social media is retention.

I also introduced the Marketing Bowtie, which (so I've been told) is the industry's first complete engagement framework that reflects as close as possible the lifetime value of the customer process from preawareness to zealot.

The Marketing Bowtie shown in Figure 9.7 demonstrates how the flipped funnel joins forces with the traditional funnel to address some of

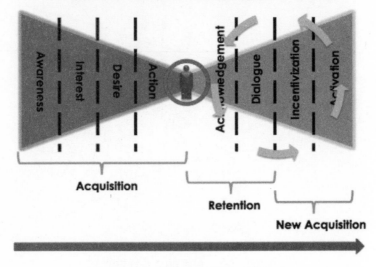

**The Marketing Bowtie™:
Traditional Funnel meets Flipped Funnel**

Awareness · Interest · Desire · Action · Acknowledgement · Dialogue · Incentivization · Activation

Acquisition

Retention

New Acquisition

Figure 9.7   The Marketing Bowtie

the key deficiencies of the latter (open, incomplete, diminishing margin of returns; oversimplified; linear) and, in so doing, reverses the fortunes over time of sustained and/or long-term marketing investment.

The prediction ahead (if the Marketing Bowtie is, in fact, on the money) is one of the most powerful and profound shifts and optimizations in our marketing lifetimes (bigger than traditional to digital, communication to conversation, awareness to interest, or search): the shift from acquisition to retention budgets.

In fact, if you take the generous 80/20 allocation in favor of acquisition/retention (you know the numbers are much more embarrassing) and do the math, you could *double* the amount spent on retention, for example, from 20 percent (unacceptable) to 40 percent (acceptable), by reducing the proportion allocated to acquisition, namely, from 80 percent (inexcusable) to 60 percent (tolerable). That's a 25 percent reduction in acquisition to invest in your customers at *twice the preexisting rate*. It's an 8× differential, which is absolutely in line with what WPP's Sorrell had already conceded was being wasted. So what's your excuse? You can't find the 25 percent? Don't be ridiculous. Get to work!

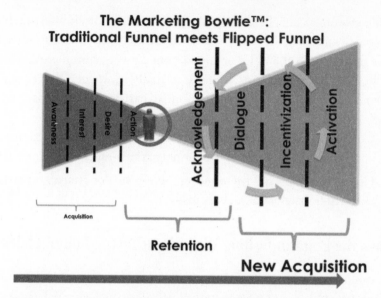

Figure 9.8   The only optimization you should care about: from acquisition to retention

If you think about it (and if you haven't, I have), it is inevitable in a world that continues to become increasingly and exponentially more digital—and therefore more measurable and therefore more accountable—that we will continue to have to produce more with less and more from less. In other words, efficiency is a curse (procurement, Wall Street, and Sarbanes-Oxley led) and a blessing (less waste). It is the latter that interests me and is reflected in the optimized bowtie visual: We will become more efficient at acquiring new customers (largely because of technology) and we will likewise (have to) become more effective at retaining and upgrading our existing ones. It's an efficiency-effectiveness one-two punch second to none, and the spoils of this process will be the new acquisition: new customers via existing ones.

In many respects, this fits in nicely with the Z of zealots as the pinnacle of passion, but it all begins with a deep-seated and cultural ~~commitment~~ obsession with service and experience excellence.

Taking One Step Backward to Avoid Two Steps Backward

The new acquisition (aka new customers via existing ones) is a little presumptuous in that it assumes you're already doing enough to keep your existing customers delighted. Actually, that in and of itself is a stretch, and most of us are mired in the sometimes cathartic and sometimes gut-wrenching task of dealing with the holes or leaks in our existing customer reservoirs—namely, dealing with churn or attrition. Actually, I wonder if that's even rock bottom. Rock bottom would represent one of two doomsday scenarios:

1. Companies carrying on their business blissfully unaware, or worse, in complete denial, of the flipped funnel or open-ended traditional funnel
2. Companies masking the unacceptable levels of churn and attrition with their drug of choice: acquisition

What's the Point in Fishing When Your Net Is Full of Holes?

Gain one new customer to make up for the one lost customer. The result? The misdirected appearance of status quo or business as usual. Step along now. Nothing to see here.

I wonder how many companies default to the paid media trough in order to gorge themselves on the swill of temporal new business instead of addressing the real directive: Plug the holes, fill the gaps, and invest in customers as lifeblood, partners, and credible, able, and influential "salespeople."

Convene, Landlords, Convene (Owned Assets Expanded)

In a perfect world, we wouldn't need paid media because we would have enough access and assets to actually produce revenue.

Your store is an asset.

Your packaging is an asset.

Your website is an asset.

Your content is an asset.

Your trucks are an asset.

Your e-mail list is an asset.

Your employees are an asset.

Your social presence is an asset.

And yes, even your media is an asset.

Only we don't treat them as such. We don't invest in them as such. We don't allocate budget to them as such. And we don't measure (and evaluate) them as such.

What percentage of your marketing dollars do you invest in these assets? We rent media. We own assets.

With such a wealth of resources at our disposal, why do we continue to take the subservient role of tenants when in reality we are sitting on a proverbial treasure trove of branded real estate?

Why do we continue to charge intermediaries with our proxy when we actually have the ability to "go direct," like Dell once said in its advertising campaign? In some cases, we've spectacularly regressed by shunning our own websites in favor of the new drug of choice: Facebook. We've ceded IP ownership, creative control, and the relationship high ground by locking out our customers or hijacking their engagement for a throwaway "like." We've buried our content in the false promise and prophet of 1 billion potential sets of eyeballs and in the process put ourselves under tremendous duress and pressure of being suffocated by the new tsunami of clutter in a turbulent sea of consumer skepticism and the need to share as many photos with as many people as possible. We've set ourselves on the new binge-drinking game of like acquisition, but in doing so, we're broadening the *wrong* end of the *wrong* funnel (Figure 9.9).

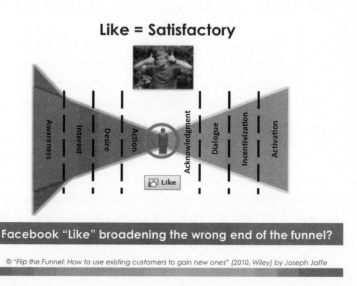

Figure 9.9 Like broadens the wrong end of the wrong funnel

This is not meant to be a Facebook-bashing session. Some of my favorite fake friends are on Facebook. Actually Facebook is probably the first platform in our time and lives (and maybe never again) to amass the kind of reach the likes of which we haven't seen since number 1 chart toppers like the universal dial tone, electricity, and the Union Pacific Railway. In addition, Facebook quite brilliantly delivers against all four forms of media: paid, earned, owned, and non. But at the same time, it exacerbates the problem at hand: our disproportionate investment, allocation, and optimization against these four categories *within* Facebook itself (intra) as well as a percentage of the greater digital—and even integrated—spends (inter).

As referenced toward the beginning of this book, both General Motors and P&G were essentially forced to reverse their paid media positions in Facebook because Facebook loaded the dice to reflect a "no pay, no play" scenario that otherwise would have buried any content deep within the black hole of status updates. Allegedly.

No greed. No feed.

The ability to buy likes and resultant reach provides opportunities for companies to place contextually relevant engagement ads both adjacent to and within a "user's" feed. Personally, I have strong concerns about long-term viability and sustainability, especially amid an extremely fickle consumer base. (MySpace anyone?)

Facebook's sublime earned media dominance is probably its most natural success story and case study. In fact, the naturally sharable and viral nature of "sticky" content, memes, and ideas whose time has come is the oil that greases the wheels of the social media and social networking machine. From stories of tragedy and triumph to petitions to deport Piers Morgan, from the Arab Spring to Irish Spring, we've also witnessed firsthand the power of the people—citizens, customers, humans—the whole shebang.

Owned media (not assets, but media) is the third leg of the beautifully constructed table, with companies able to build elaborate (but gated) communities of interest to house their content, commercials, and sweepstakes programs. With multiple tabs and downloadable apps, Facebook is the world's largest attention mall and it would appear that everyone wants to have a storefront.

And finally, there is nonmedia and its dirty little secret: The real reason why people are on Facebook is to view photos (particularly ones of that 20-something hottie intern). Okay, that was a *little* cynical, but not

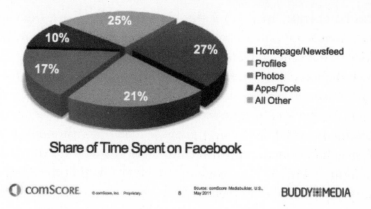

Figure 9.10   Share of time spent on Facebook

entirely untrue. The fact is that most people are on Facebook to connect with other people regarding things that really have nothing to do with buying and selling more washing powder (Figure 9.10).

Revenge of the Brick[8]

In Piccadilly, Circus, London, Audi has launched a concept showroom that completely breaks the mold of the typical automotive dealership (Figure 9.11). The showroom is exceptionally clean, with one or two

Figure 9.11   Concept Audi showroom in London

models on a white floor. No desks. No papers. No chairs. But there are several color-coordinated, well-dressed salespeople, several interactive kiosks, and wall-to-wall giant synchronized TV screens.

Consumers can customize their swanky new S5 convertible using the interactive kiosks and, with an effortless swipe, project their configured car onto the big screen. They can also swivel the car using gestures on the kiosk, and using Microsoft's Kinect technology, they can use their body as a joystick or mouse to take down the roof and watch it roll back in real time. They can also watch the car drive off and come back to rest with surround sound emulating the actual sounds of the car. It provides a truly realistic experience of what it might feel like to drive an Audi S5 convertible.

How on Earth could this experience be delivered online?

There were those who once said (and I'm probably one of them) that brick-and-mortar stores were an endangered species and that everyone would shift to online shopping, customization, and e-commerce. There were also those who said (I was not one of them) that no one would ever move to digital channels to purchase things like clothing, homes, or cars.

As it turns out, they were both wrong.

Could this be the future of retail? A holistic, immersive, physical *digital* experience: one in which human beings still played a key role. The best of all worlds.

I believe the future of brick-and-mortar stores is a bright one if, and only if, it is anchored around a core digital experience and supported by humans.

This is true not only for traditional brands but for pure plays as well. For example, I expect to see an Amazon.com store in the near future, one without a single piece of merchandise in it. Why would you need a book, when everything can be swiped, synced, and swooshed into your Kindle? I expect Barnes & Noble to be out of business if they cannot figure out a way—quickly—to emulate the Audi showroom and in the process get rid of as many dust-gathering books (and space) as possible.

People might continue to window-shop online using their screens as nose warmers, but when they want to actually buy, there's a lot to be said for getting off their rear ends and making the physical commitment to get into a store.

The Coca-Cola Media Company

In 2003, the chief operating officer of Coca-Cola, outspoken Steven Heyer, laid down his manifesto for the Coca-Cola Media Company:

> *Look around you; the Coca-Cola Company has more impressions than any other company on the planet. You see our brand on cafes, concession booths, and hot dog stands. Our brands light up Times Square and Piccadilly Square, but also neighborhood delis and ballparks. People wear the brand on T-shirts and ball caps. They display it on coolers and beach balls and key chains—just about anything you can think of. The Coca-Cola Company in the U.S. spends $1 million on advertising every day that 20 million people see. . . . 30 million people drink Cokes in exclusive Coca-Cola foodservice accounts every day. . . . 20 million people buy Cokes from vending machines every day. . . . 4 million people go see movies sipping on Cokes every day. . . . 25 million people buy our bottles or cans every day. . . . Coke trucks travel over 1 million miles every day. In total, the Coca-Cola Company benefits from 2 billion plus brand communication opportunities every day in the U.S. alone.*

Today, this vision lives on. In Brazil, the aptly named Coke Zero has been running a program where specific regions, local cities, or towns have been highlighted on cans. The campaign has now shifted to people's names. In both cases, the brand released the usual suspects based on popular destinations or names, but it now has turned it over to the crowd to suggest and vote on new names (Figure 9.12). The campaign (if you want to call it that) has been so successful it launched across Europe in the summer of 2013.

Think Z.E.R.O. Is a Pipe Dream?

Consider the fact that Google, Facebook, Amazon, eBay, Zappos, Starbucks, and so on were all built on a platform of word-of-mouth, social buzz, and customer-driven passion. Today, these brands use advertising to sustain their market position, but we're not talking about game changing anymore; we're talking about staying in the game.

Brands know it, whether they want to admit it or not. It's estimated that half of the more than 50 Super Bowl spots in 2012 launched prior to game

Figure 9.12   A Coke Zero can as an "owned asset"

day, flying in the face of the previously widely held belief that commercials should be kept close to the chest. Compare this to only one spot in 2011 (the VW spot featuring mini-Darth) launching prior to the Super Bowl.[9] It's a tacit tell or even explicit concession that even the Super Bowl's reach is *not* enough in terms of registering the kind of numbers, talk factor, and ultimately aggregate impressions needed to justify a $5 million[10] investment in 30 seconds.

Twitter Is the New YouTube[11]

But wait, it gets worse. At a media conference in 2013, I saw several presenters showcasing their television creative—and in particular their Super Bowl spots. And right afterward, they showed screenshots of Twitter reactions, in the form of @comments, retweets, and celebrity endorsements.

I immediately thought back to a time not so long ago (to be precise, before the mainstreaming of Twitter) when brand marketers or their agencies would showcase their television buys with a reference to the number of YouTube views.

I couldn't help but make the same observation and connection with the Twitter references as I did with the augmented YouTube wave. Here it is: There's something wrong with the model if you have to use an ancillary platform to augment and justify a mass medium.

Put simply, it would appear that Twitter has become a crutch to justify and showcase a television buy. In fact, the presentation playbook goes something like this:

Step 1: Show the creative.

Step 2: Show several tweets, verbatim, and possibly some cockamamy graph to reflect a spike or aggregation of so-called earned media.

Step 3: If asked whether the spot actually sold any product or registered significant brand lift, give the confidentiality excuse ("We can't share") and supplement with a healthy dose of unsupported hyperbole ("Put it this way: We're all happy and will be back").

Of course you will. Who wouldn't, when your entire accountability spectrum is fulfilled with a few tweet-shots?

Whether your crutch of choice is YouTube views, search queries, Twitter retweets, Facebook likes, or Instagram followers, I recommend a basic leveling of the playing fields, beginning with the basic concession that when you put a piece of creative in front of an audience of more than 100 million people, some of them are bound to react, regardless of how crappy the brand, message, or creative is.

What I'd like to see is something closer to Newton's Third Law—namely, for every action, there is an equal and opposite reaction—instead of a screenshot of a celebrity tweet.

What I'd like to see is over 100 million tweets. (I'll settle for a click-through equivalent of 0.1 percent at 100,000.)

What I'd like to see is the activation platform results and high-value actions as a direct outcome of the exposure. I'll settle for some benchmark or translation that answers the question "Is that good?"—which is what a company called Unmetric does. (Full disclosure: I'm an advisor to that company.)

If you want to advertise during the Super Bowl, be my guest. But please—pretty please—justify it with traditional media metrics, standards, and practices, as opposed to smearing lipstick on a pig via the social channels.

Oreo-Speedwagon[12]

Okay, other than the word *Oreo*, that title has nothing to do with this section. But that's fitting, because along the same lines, Oreo's 2013 Super Bowl commercial didn't have anything to do with its stellar opportunistic play on Twitter following the now-famous blackout in the Super Bowl stadium. Taking advantage of the situation, the brand tweeted a photo with the tagline "You can still dunk in the dark" (Figure 9.13).

With more than 16,000 retweets and a total paid media investment of zero, you might be scratching your head wondering why it was necessary to spend more than $4 million on a Super Bowl commercial at all. Or why

Figure 9.13   The award-winning Real Time Marketing (RTM) effort from Oreo

Oreo chose to put all of its eggs into the Instagram bucket, as opposed to the seemingly passé Facebook or the positively archaic InterWeb.

Here's what we know: Oreo's Instagram account went from zero (2,000) to hero (almost 22,000) within Super Bowl seconds. Right now it's sitting on 96,000. In a rather brilliant activation, Oreo used its account to invite Instagram users to tag a photo with its handle @oreo, as well as either #cookies or #cream (actually #creme, but I'll come back to that shortly). In-studio designers or sculptors were standing by to create a rendering of the photo using either cookie crumbs or cream.

It began with a photo of a cookied background and cremed date of 2.3.13 and the caption "Are you cookie? Or are you creme? Choose your side and come back Sunday to battle it out, Instagram style" (Figure 9.14). The post has since had 5,145 likes and 6,168 comments. Clearly a lot of people have an opinion about cookies or cream.

Figure 9.14 Launch of Oreo Instagram account

Since then, roughly 150 of these photos have been transformed into cookilism or creamism art (as in pixelism or pointillism, but decidedly more edible; see Figure 9.15).

And then about 48 hours after the whirlwind was set in motion, it all stopped as quickly as it began, with a photo depicting a gallery of all the creations and the words, "IT'S ALL OVER! The final score: 17,060 tags for cookie, 21,050 for creme. Creme wins . . . for now. But there's still lots more coming from OREO, very soon . . ."

If you're doing the math, that's potentially as much as 38,000 photo requests, all things being equal. It's a pretty good rough estimate of engagement or a correlation between "follow" (passive) and "request for cookie" (an active RFC).

So, instead of asking, "Why only a few days?" or "Why disappoint so many eager beavers?" I'll give the company the benefit of the doubt with

Figure 9.15   Tasty artist rendering of a photo

its open-ended "there's still lots more coming from OREO, very soon . . . " but I will be watching very closely and will hold the brand to its promise.

In the interim, to complete the thought leadership sandwich, let's go back to the opportunistic tweet. I'm fairly certain the folks over at Oreo parent Mondelēz International were *not* responsible for the blackout. On one hand, this was déjà vu all over again with the spirit of Old Spice's Isaiah Mustafa living large in a content studio with a team of copywriters, art directors, clients, and suits on sugar highs. On the other hand, this showed the power of thinking quickly, being responsive, and adapting to pop culture in real time.

Why haven't more brands done something similar? Many reasons, including the fact that it's extremely difficult to scale and execute such a move with any consistency and authenticity.

To date, the execution (do we call it a spot? Impression? Activation? Or just plain tweet?) has racked up the following accolades:[13]

- Cannes Lions Awards: Direct (Digital Marketing)—Silver Lion
- Cannes Lions Awards: Cyber (Viral)—Bronze Lion
- CLIO Awards: Social Media—Bronze
- CLIO Awards: Innovative Media—Bronze
- Adweek Project Isaac Awards: Social Media Invention
- Golden Award of Montreux: Viral Marketing—Gold Medal
- Food & Beverage (FAB) Awards: Viral Marketing—Finalist
- Digiday Awards: Best Creative—Winner

More significantly, Dunking in the Dark (not to be confused with Springsteen's "Dancing in the Dark") has ushered in the Golden Age of Real Time Marketing (RTM), at least according to every digital conference, trade publication, or award show. Or has it? Personally, I think it makes for a fantastic drinking game, but my genuine concern is that it is inherently not scalable.

How long before consumers mutiny at brands injecting messaging into every single piece of news, current event, or natural moment of our lives? Even Oreo experienced a reversal of fortune with their opportunist tweet after the birth of George Alexander Louis (see Figure 9.16) and, with it, a fair amount of backlash.

Figure 9.16   Prepare the royal backlash service!

I was recently asked at a conference what I thought of RTM. I replied, "RTM is b*** s**t. Instead of moving at the speed of a tweet, how about just moving quicker and by quicker, I'm referring to quicker than 9 to 12 month planning and execution cycles!"

Will Oreo be back in next year's Super Bowl, but this time without spending a dime on paid media? If so, perhaps they will get to have their Oreo cookies and creme—and eat it!

So You Want More Proof?

Consider these two examples that should be fairly, if not extremely, well known to you. Are these not prime examples of a Z.E.R.O. mentality applied to an otherwise imperfect marketplace?

Dove's Campaign for Real Beauty

Unilever's Dove beauty bar dared to go where no beauty brand had gone before: It took on the role of smoking gun to rail against the very industry it had willingly supported and even built in the past. "They're all lying to you," said Dove, as it delivered a perfectly sublime on-brand message that beauty lies within, so why not take care of that ugly exterior with the creamy goodness that is Dove? Dove's Evolution was a 1 minute 22 second Cannes Grand Prix–winning masterpiece, which may have been supported with ancillary paid media, but at its core it was delivered with node plume by "the people" at a whopping cost of zero (Figure 9.17).

Dove's Evolution was more than just a nontraditional form of earned media. It was a call to action supported by a movement: the Campaign for Real Beauty and a fund designed to touch the lives of more than 1 million girls worldwide girls by 2008. (This target has long since been reached.[14])

Evolution was spoofed, riffed, mashed, and hacked until the "skinny" cows came home. It delivered even more freebie impressions and underscored the proof point that this was not a one-off ad exposure but in fact a meme. It was followed by a second attempt called Onslaught, which was rugby tackled by Greenpeace. Although at the time, this may have scared off some of the Unilever executives from pursuing the same creative

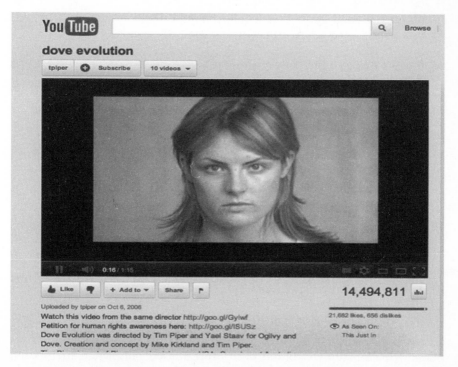

Figure 9.17 Dove's Evolution of Real Beauty

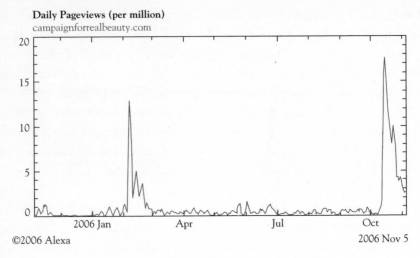

Daily Pageviews (per million)
campaignforrealbeauty.com

©2006 Alexa   2006 Nov 5

Figure 9.18   Impact of Dove's onslaught

approach, it in no way, shape, or form detracted from the realization that zero dollars could equal hero impact.

All press is good press? You decide (Figure 9.18).

As further evidence, consider these results:

- Dove's Evolution (*free* online spot) was more successful than the $2.5 million Super Bowl spot in driving traffic to Dove's Campaign for Real Beauty website (see Figure 9.17).

- The video achieved more than 14 million views.

- Evolution drove more than 30,000 testimonials on the campaign website.

- The Dove Evolution campaign reached almost one-fourth of all Internet users.

A few years later, Dove was back with its Sketches campaign that reflected a woman's self-image versus how a total stranger perceived her (Figure 9.19).

The anthem video is now the most watched brand video in YouTube history.

The campaign took a different approach to make the statement that real beauty is in the eye of the beholder (maybe this time a little less at odds with its Axe/Lynx brand positioning), especially when juxtaposed against the hilarious spoofs that sprouted overnight (Figure 9.20). One thing that didn't change was Unilever's mastery of Z.E.R.O.

Figure 9.19   Dove's sketches

Figure 9.20   The difference between men and women

Hello, Ladies

Arguably inspired by Dove (call it healthy competition rising the—ahem—Tide that floats all boats or even ships), a couple of years later P&G's Old Spice attempted to reinvent a brand associated with your grandfather (may he rest in peace) by using football player and spokesperson Isaiah Mustapha, who, after becoming a viral hit with the original "The man your man could smell like" commercial, began a two-day social media blitz and extravaganza by "replying" via the same video format, treatment, production value, and script quality to a host of celebrities, mainstream, and Internet personalities and influencers who asked him a question or made a comment via their own channels or channels like Facebook or Twitter (Figure 9.21).

These days the only viral phenomena are ugly ones, like United Breaks Guitars, McDonald's Twitter embarrassment during the 2012 London Olympic[15] Games, and a host of Qantas Airlines social media missteps.[16] It's very uncommon to see a brand-led initiative capture the hearts and minds of the populous in such a short period of time, but with a Z.E.R.O. approach and partnership (as Figure 9.22 reflects[17]), it is certainly possible:

Figure 9.21   Hello, ladies!

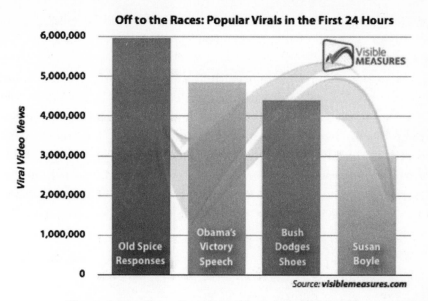

Off to the Races: Popular Virals in the First 24 Hours

*Source: **visiblemeasures.com***

Figure 9.22 Does President Obama use Old Spice?

- "Old Spice Responses" feature Mustafa responding to questions from Twitter, Facebook, Reddit, and blogs in as close to real time as you can get with online video publishing.

- Old Spice uploaded an unprecedented 180-plus clips for its "Response" campaign, which generated more than 5.9 million views and in excess of 22,500 comments.

- @OldSpice followers increased from 10,000 to almost 40,000 in four days.

- Blog coverage increased almost 400 percent in a single day.

It should be noted that it was paid media in the form of the original spot that opened the gambit, but what moved this from monologue to dialogue, from communication to conversation, and resulted in an award-winning Grand Prix commercial that created enduring growth platform was, in fact, Z.E.R.O.

Then there's Red Bull (as will be expanded on later), which has rebuilt its entire brand architecture around Z.E.R.O.—with an army of human billboards exemplifying the fusion of owned assets and zealots.

These are a couple of the more well-known case studies, but there are a host more, such as the ways Microsoft's MSN brand launched Hotmail or Google launched Gmail. In both cases, we would be talking about the R and O of Z.E.R.O., and when you add the I, as in the consumer, you get ROI, don't you?

When Ben & Jerry introduced their special edition Linsanity yogurt flavor (in honor of basketball phenom Jeremy Lin), it became a controversial hotbed due to the culturally insensitive inclusion of "fortune cookie" as an ingredient (Lin is Asian American). This too extolled the virtues of Z.E.R.O. via the E of earned media. The limited edition or trial yogurt was sold only in one store, yet it found its way to myriad news outlets, social media conversations, and water cooler discussions. In this case, moving quickly at a paid media cost of zero was cancelled out by pretty dumb moves.

Whichever way you look at it, these example are just the tip of the iceberg.

Am I Too Small for Z.E.R.O.?

Wait a minute, we hear you say. These are all great examples, but they are all from really big Fast Moving Consumer Goods Companies (FMCGs). I am a small business, an entrepreneur, a business to business (B2B) company, an NGO, or nonprofit. I don't have the resources these guys have. Heck, I don't have resources at all. Our answer: even more reason to pursue Z.E.R.O. Here are some examples that hopefully put your mind at ease.

1. Will it Blend (B2B with small budgets)?

Have you ever heard of Blendtec? Neither had anyone else before CEO, Tom Dickson, let his product do the talking and created a series of videos which demonstrated the industrial blender basically blending *anything* (and I mean, anything). His Blender took out guns, Coke cans, baseballs, and even Glow Sticks. They were extremely topical, current, and relevant. For example, blending (destroying) the iPhone or iPad when it had just come out and was all the rage, or the Vuvusela horn during the Soccer World Cup held in South Africa in 2012.

P.S. In response to all the above, "yes, it blends!"

Today, Blendtec blenders are found in recognizable places like Starbucks, Barnes and Noble, and Dickerson is known to parade the hallways of technology and social media expo halls like the Consumer Electronics Show (CES) held every year in Las Vegas, Nevada, in his mad scientist white lab coat, 100 percent in character to pose for photographs and strike up an interview or two.

2. Amtel Corporation—Semiconductors (B2B with small budgets)

Sander Arts (@sander1arts) is a fellow Dutchman and is the current VP of Marketing of Amtel Corporation, a manufacturer of microcontroller chips. Sander joined the company in late 2012.

He found out that 93 percent of B2B purchases start with an Internet search, and that 70 percent of the buying process is complete before prospects engage with a live salesperson. What do you think he created? A major TV campaign, like Intel does? Not really.

He did create:

o A website per his guidance of the "best in the industry."

o An integrated approach to marketing that spanned all departments (not just marketing).

o Hired three editors to write content for specific target audiences, as well as a social media specialist.

o Started a corporate blog (403 blog posts to date) and social media listening (and responding) via Twitter.

o Created and distributed multiple videos generating over a million views though YouTube.

Per Sander, it's the early days as we write this chapter. But all indicators are positive and show the growth he was hired to bring.

3. charity: water (NGO / Nonprofit with "zero" budget)

charity: water operates with a $0 marketing budget. They don't buy ads online or offline; they don't do direct mail, and they don't issue press releases. Instead, every year charity: water launches a September Campaign where they produce an epic story with a short film and microsite and use the power of the content to spark thousands of campaigns to raise millions for clean water. In 2013, they launched a new video in partnership with the Hubspot Inbound Conference, showing it for the first time to 5,000 people and inviting them all to share on social media. Coupled with online outreach and an uber influencer in the form of Anil Dash, who had a personal connection to Orissa, the region representing 100 villages being funded in this campaign, they had over 100,000 views and raised over $100,000 in just three days!

Do these things sound impossible to you?

Z.E.R.O. Is a Philosophical Mind Shift

Taken literally, at face value and in isolation, we believe the hypothesis that paid media is a luxury, but not necessarily a necessity, holds true. In so many of the success stories of the past couple of decades (conveniently coinciding with the mainstreaming of digital) such as "Will It Blend"'s owned asset collection of YouTube videos, it can and does work. However, at the same time it is just as much a philosophical, conceptual, take always and strategic sea change in thinking that suggests we start with the Z.E.R.O. approach and then—and only then—fill in the gaps with the same old, same old.

The take-always from the case studies are thus four-fold:

1. Everything has its place, and in many cases, paid media has a definitive and distinct role, such as a conversation starter or quick-and-dirty way to reach the masses (in a good way).

2. But equally so, everything should be put in its place. Paid media is not an entitlement, a default, or a right. We would serve our shareholders and ourselves well by remembering that.

3. Paid media, mass media, or even advertising is one piece of the puzzle and should be an equal piece of the puzzle—if not in size, then in terms of strategic contribution. This applies both to P.E.O.N., acquisition versus retention, as well as Z.E.R.O. itself. The implication is simple: Paid media is not necessarily your first move, nor is it necessarily your best move.

4. Instead of starting with the incumbent, end with the "tried"—or is that "tired"—and tested.

Z.E.R.O. is an aspirational journey, not a staccato destination. Every year, we should be firing ourselves and starting again, using the zero-based budgeting versus zero-sum approach to wipe the slate clean to undertake our "blue ocean" voyage.

We may never reach the Ponce de León of zero paid media, but if you are on the bus, believing the argument that the old paid media model is slowly pricing and disengaging itself out of the market, then it doesn't hurt to try. And most likely it would serve as a perfect tonic to corporate health and longevity compared to the foolish notion of immortality.

No one lives forever. Just look at history.

The Z.E.R.O. Action Plan

The question Maarten gets the most from the community of global marketers who are members of the World Federation of Advertisers, whom he works with daily, is "I understand I need to do something, but *what* should I do?" In this book, and especially in these last chapters, we have tried to make that *what* tangible.

Joseph began his career on the brand side and then transitioned into and out of the agency quagmire, whereas Maarten worked on the agency side before moving over to the dark side. From our combined tenures on both agency and brand marketer sides, we've picked up enough best and worst practices to triangulate a list of 10 action categories, designed to bring Z.E.R.O. to life, both holistically (zero paid media as the new marketing model) and individually (zealots, entrepreneurship, retention, owned assets).

To set up the 10-point action plan, we'll introduce one more acronym (can't promise it's the last one, but it is meaningful): C.O.S.T. (cultural, organizational, strategic, and tactical).

C.O.S.T. is a simplified (almost to a fault) change management continuum that fairly clearly offers insight into corporate growth and acceptance as it relates to marketing change. It was introduced by Joseph to explain digital adoption and has proved relevant for everything that has followed thereafter: social, mobile, and even customer service and experience.

C.O.S.T. essentially describes the phases or stages of a company's approach to various new, emerging, and/or growing sectors. At the lowest point of the evolutionary hierarchy is tactical, followed by strategic, orga-nizational, and finally cultural.

Most companies overfocus on tactical implementation and execution. And increasingly and exponentially so, they underfocus on strategic, orga-nizational, and cultural integration and activation. Most companies exe-cute tactically against a nonexistent strategic framework, plan, or vision.

Tactics in search of strategy
Solutions to nonexistent problems

In the marketing realm, this is absolutely true for pretty much every "next big thing" that began with the digital wave and continued through social, mobile, and whatever came before and after. Can you say "virtual worlds"? Or how about SoMoLo, which essentially attempted to cram everything into one nonsensical world.

I fondly recall IBM's brand commercials circa 1997[1] (life before life after the 30-second spot):

Silver-haired C-suite executive reading the Wall Street Journal: *Says here that the Internet will revolutionize business as we know it . . .*

Younger executive in the room continues reading his paper and says nothing.

Silver-haired C-suite executive continues: Says here that the Internet will be like nothing before it . . .

Younger executive in the room continues reading his paper and says nothing.

Silver-haired C-suite executive continues: Says here that companies that don't get on the Internet will be left behind . . .

Younger executive in the room continues reading his paper and says nothing.

Silver-haired C-suite executive continues: WE NEED TO GET ON THE INTERNET!

Younger executive in the room finally responds: Why?

Silver-haired C-suite executive concedes: It doesn't say . . .

On so many levels, this has been déjà vu all over again with respect to each wave of a bright and shiny object: from having a Facebook presence to branded apps, from virtual worlds to Twitter. The results more often than not are the kind of gems that speakers, consultants, and authors eat up for breakfast and put into books like these.

Consider BlackBerry's Facebook post that asked people about their new Super Bowl commercial and received a barrage of comments or responses that were nearly all completely negative: "I'm shocked you can even afford a Super Bowl commercial!"

BlackBerry's (dis)Connect

Everything begins with strategy and from there parallel paths diverge in separate directions:

Strategy informs tactics

Strategy facilitates organizational design and process

Strategy inspires cultural change

What follows is a collection of what we believe is a combination of cultural, organizational, strategic, and tactical triaged recommendations that are actionable, practical, and tactical. They are conceptually resonant and pragmatically relevant. We challenge you to implement them. We urge you to pay attention to them. We beg you not to ignore them.

Some of them may sting a little, but it is nothing compared with the pain that may follow if the bottom falls out of the paid media model as we know it.

Don't try everything at once, but do try to take the medicine we have prescribed. Some of it is hard, as it will challenge long-held beliefs and thinking. But we guarantee you that your brands and your company will be better off if you do.

CHAPTER

10

Culture and Talent

A quick search on Google on the day that I write this reveals that there are about 134 million results when looking for "Change Management Quotes" (delivered in 0.35 second). Although I did not perform a scientific evaluation of all of them (actually, of any of them), I would venture to say that most focus on the difficulty of changing a company at all or changing just one aspect of a company.

Apparently, change is hard.

At the same time, there are many smart people in business, and in marketing specifically. Do you think Mark Zuckerberg is one of them? I think so, and not just because he managed to create something that a billion-plus people seem to like.

As he has evolved from being a smart kid to a smart entrepreneur to a smart global chief executive officer (CEO), he has demonstrated his insight and foresight in many interviews. One of my favorite Mark Zuckerberg quotes is, "In a world that's changing really quickly the only strategy where you're guaranteed to fail is not taking any risk and not changing anything."[1]

And this brings us to what is most likely the biggest obstacle to change in any company: you and the people you work with.

Arguably, Facebook moves fast whichever way you look at it. The most obvious evidence that they have moved fast is their user base. But in order to keep that user base engaged and the competition out, they need to invent, reinvent, and iterate at a pretty fast pace. This is what their motto, "move fast and break things," is focused on.

Obviously, Facebook comes from a self-confessed hacker culture and is a high-tech company in the digital world. This makes it a little easier to embrace a change culture compared with nontech companies. Or does it?

For years, Nokia ruled the global mobile phone market. And then the Motorola RAZR, BlackBerry, and Apple came along. And then Google's Android, Samsung, HTC, and many others. What happened at Nokia? What happened at BlackBerry? Sony at one point owned portable music and had the highest reputation in high-end TVs. Kodak is (was) obviously a technology company. How did they all drop the ball so badly? Apparently being a tech company does not necessarily translate to easily adapting to change.

How come the engineers, marketers, insights analysts, and other departments weren't able to grasp what was happening or convince their management of the need to move in a different direction? How could management not see the numbers, look at the trends or even the writing on the wall, and put two and two together?

How come IBM could reinvent itself from a PC and other assorted hardware maker to a global, high-end digital consulting behemoth, while Hewlett-Packard tried about five different directions before ultimately returning to what they were to begin with?

Why did Yahoo!, AOL, MySpace, or (if you are reading this in 2025) Apple at one point fall from their perches? The answers are obviously multifold, but I think it is a safe bet that company culture was very much part of it. These companies probably all had company missions/visions that talked about innovation, change, diversity, and growth. But at the same time the culture at these places led to inertia or complacency. It stalled them, blocked them from viewing over the fence, or stifled ideas that were a little beyond their comfort zone.

First, and this might be controversial, let's talk about hiring practices but this time in the context of business culture. Many companies pride themselves in having a very specific culture. "Cost cutters," "brand builders," and "technology married with humanity" are examples of company DNA that informs the kind of culture you may find within. Often the senior leadership reflects the kind of culture that will be successful within that company (especially if the company founder is at the helm: the Mars Brothers, Rupert Murdoch, Steve Jobs, Adi Dassler, Mark Zuckerberg).

The authors have worked in many different cultures around the world. We have dealt with English, Spanish, Japanese, German, Chinese, Portuguese, and even Flemish speakers. We have had bosses, business partners, and clients who were male, alpha-male, gay, and female. And none of this matters.

It is our belief that you should not hire outside of your comfort zone. How many times have you heard conservative companies saying they want to bring in rebels? Or steady-as-you-go companies want to bring in entrepreneurial-minded executives. It rarely works. There are countless examples of highly visible failures, and probably many, many more examples that played out below the radar. "We have decided to part ways due to differences of opinion regarding the strategic direction of XYC." Yeah, right. We hated John because he was so "different" (which is why we hired him in the first place).

What you *should* do is hire very smart people who are a good fit. And then you should expose them (and yourself) to ideas. The ideas should come from within and from outside. We share our ideas for this in the action plan on tenure (see Chapter 11).

So what other simple things could you implement to help your company become more comfortable with change?

Learning by Doing

This is probably one of the things I feel most passionate about because it has served me so well over the years.

I have always said that in order to learn, you need to experience it (whatever it is) yourself—firsthand, hands on. Just do it. If you Google "Maarten Albarda" you will find more than 16,000 results. "Joseph Jaffe" garners over 6.7 million results, but then again his name is far more common.

("Says *you!*" says Joseph Jaffe)

This does not happen by accident. We are out there. I sign up for pretty much any new platform or digital service available, so I know what it is like. How can I explain to my boss what Pinterest is if I have never been on it, created a board, and pinned some content, let alone looked at the thousands of boards available?

How can I credibly discuss whether Foursquare is an option to be considered as part of a strategy if I have never checked in while out on the town? Is the 6-second Vine the new 30-second spot? Is Montaj the new YouTube? Is Klout useful? Is it easy to check prices online using the PriceCheck app while shopping in Walmart? What makes Tumblr popular? (I'll defer to Marissa Mayer on that one!)

There is only one way to find out, and that is to immerse yourself. Again: Just do it.

Many senior leaders tell us, however—usually somewhat defensively and sometimes with a dismissive air—that they don't have time for all that stuff.

But here is the thing: Your consumers do. How can you not be involved and actively interested in their world? How can you judge plans or make or approve investment decisions, strategies, and brand direction if you are disconnected from what your consumer spends an enormous amount of time on?

And no, being on LinkedIn and reading the *Financial Times* or *Wall Street Journal* on your iPad does not count. Well, not enough anyway.

"Okay, so you want me to tweet?" asks the CEO with dread and trepidation. Few CEOs (or other C-suite executives) are active on social media, through blogs, Twitter, or otherwise, according to a CEO.com report, but should they?

My standard answer to this question is an emphatic, *no!* Most CEOs have no place on Twitter (or any other social network for that matter) unless they want to be on it as an individual (just like "normal" people). There are few industries or personalities that warrant an active, business-related reason to tweet. Figure 10.1 shows Maarten's Reasometer to determine whether a CEO should tweet.

The Twitter Hall of Shame is littered with failed and ridiculous examples of CEOs and other business luminaries who tried their (forced by corporate communications?) hand at sounding authentic and sharing their innermost thoughts only to find themselves the target of unwanted backlash or ridicule. You're a sitting duck for being memed or hashtagged, and if you don't know what that means, steer clear!

But *do* get involved. Set up accounts and use social media, but ensure you understand walls and security and privacy settings. It is not unsafe, unless you treat it as unsafe. Try Instagram, Vine, and Tumblr; read blogs; create a Pinterest board; and try whatever is the hot thing at the moment of you reading this book in the future (as we write this in May 2013, they

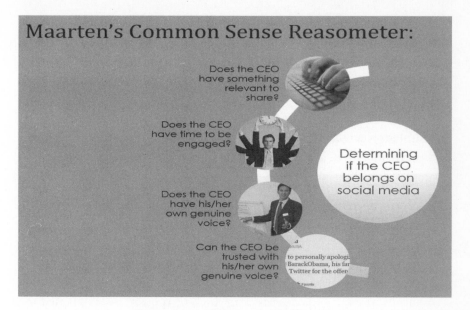

Figure 10.1   **Maarten's Reasometer**

are likely not any of the examples we gave here). Use your mother's maiden name if you have to, but do learn by doing. Then and only then will you be an informed person when your marketing team and/or agency proposes any of these platforms to you as part of a brand business plan.

Trusting Your Brand to a 20-Something Intern Is a Recipe for Disaster

So you just had a brain wave: If these young folk are so involved with all this stuff, why not get a war room set up with some digital natives and let them connect with those people who seek brand interaction. Perhaps they can tweet in my name, too?

Have you ever heard of or watched any of these TV shows: *Boys and Girls Alone, The Baby Borrowers,* or *Kid Nation?* You're probably better off if you didn't. Each show's premise was that children were left in charge of adult tasks.

In the case of *Boys and Girls Alone* (Channel 4 in the United Kingdom), it was kind of *Big Brother* for kids, where a group of children between 8 and 11 lived by themselves. There was proper supervision, but all decisions were made by the kids. *Kid Nation* (CBS in the United States) was sort of the same but with more emphasis on seeing if children could form a functioning society without adults. Finally, *Baby Borrowers* (BBC 3 in the United Kingdom; NBC in the United States) focused on late teens (ages 16 to 19 in the United Kingdom; ages 18 to 20 in the United States), who took responsibility for a baby, followed by a toddler, followed by a preteen, and ultimately a teen. They took on full parental responsibilities to show-case parenting ain't easy.

Neither is parenting a brand: orchestrating and managing a conversation that should build and maintain the reputation of a carefully developed brand. As with CEOs' Twitter feeds, there are many examples of brand reputations being harmed or train-wrecked through inexperience, insensitivity, or downright immaturity:

- Accidentally sending a tweet from the brand account when you meant to send it from your own, which by the way has happened too many times to mention (Figure 10.2)

- Getting upset with a consumer complaint, fair or unreasonable, and letting them hear it (Figure 10.3)

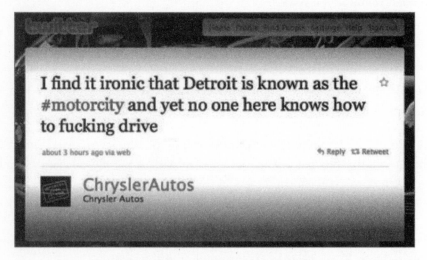

Figure 10.2   Chrysler Twitter Fail

The list goes on.

There is nothing wrong with wanting to communicate in an authentic voice, and there are some really good examples out there (Best Buy's

Twelp Force, most U.S. and some European airlines, etc.). But these come from carefully staged and managed accounts with trained professionals at the helm.

Displaying posts 1 - 30 out of 49.

Mike Shepard My husband and I just went to your theater to see Shutter Island.
First off, the year is 2010 and your establishment does not accept cash cards or credit cards. We did not have enough cash on us and neither did your ATM. If you run out of cash by Saturday evening you should have a higher allotment of cash. Since most people expect to use their cash card, the ATM, I'm sure, is utilized frequently. Frankly, get with the time. I know you are charged for transactions on a card machine but frankly your customers would be better served. How many customers do you lose because they don't have cash or check (since 90% of establishments don't accept checks anymore).Thankfully, we had friends who had 1 check on them. We would have had to go to the bank to get cash to see a movie. Should we charge you for time and gas?
Secondly, after the first 10 minutes a staff member came in and announced that there were 8 people who should not be in that movie. She proceded to check tickets of paying customers trying to enjoy a movie. She also brought in the ticket clerk to see if she would recognize the 4 remaining people who did not leave after the announcement. This ruined the first 30 minutes of the movie. Frankly, we lost the first part of the plot and new characters. I did not pay 18.00 to have a distracted experience. Are 8 people worth a theater full of refunds? Why not wait until the movie is over and check people leaving? Why not pause the movie? I expect a refund, but only by check card. Oh wait, sorry, we are all out of check cards. Get the point yet? I would rather drive to White Bear Lake, where they obviously know how to run a theater than have this experience again.
Sarah
Taylors Falls
February 21 at 3:36pm · Report

Mike Shepard Response from the Vice President of the company:

Sarah,

Drive to White Bear Lake and also go fuck yourself. If you dont have money for entertainment, get a better job, and don't pay for everything on your credit or check card. You can also shove your time and gas up your fucking ass. Also, find better things to do with your time. This email is an absolute joke. We don't care to have you as a customer. Let me know if you need directions to white bear lake.

Steven
Steven J. Payne - Vice President
Evergreen Entertainment
929 Old Highway 8 NW
Suite 200
New Brighton, MN 55112

Phone - (651) 636-1417
Fax - (651) 636-1418
February 21 at 3:38pm · Report

Figure 10.3   Evergreen Entertainment Facebook fail

Do you have a consumer hotline? Chances are that these people are your best bet for an authentic brand or company voice. They already field questions from consumers on every topic imaginable and have playbooks and answers at their fingertips that have been perfected and honed over the years.

In other words: Subject matter experts already exist in your company. Use them if you think your company or brands deserve a voice. They will do a whole lot better as brand advocates than a 21-year-old—or you.

Jaffe's Response: Although I agree with pretty much everything Maarten said (after all he was my client once upon a time and I did undertake this journey with him), I do want to add that there is no ageism at play in all. A young employee is extremely capable of interacting directly with the outside world—if and only if—that person is well trained, able to exercise sound judgment (mature), and empowered to either make independent decisions or contact management accordingly. Clearly, this is the exception rather than the norm.

CHAPTER

11

Tenure

Before we tackle compensation in the following chapter, we need to address another human resources–related topic: tenure. It ties back to the business and economic reasons for the perfect storm, where we described the short-term-ness of business today.

Remember Dave from Chapter 4? The average length of any one of his positions within one and the same company was 1.7 years. It will come as no surprise that we will advocate for a slow-as-you-go approach to career development as opposed to this kind of moving on up.

We recommend that businesses implement a variation of the following rules:

- Any job assignment should last three years at a minimum.

  This is the no-brainer rule. Year 1 is the year you do everything for the first time. President Obama took 100 days to get to know his job when he was first elected, and so should you. Then get to work.

  In year 2, you can call the plans your own. These are the 12 months where your impact will be felt, as it is all driven by you.

  And finally you get to year 3, when you reap the rewards of your cunning plans and we can truly judge the business impact you have. This is the year you also begin to plot your next move. Repeat until retirement.

- If the assignment takes you to a foreign land (or a completely new industry), add one or two years. This makes sense because not only are you trying to make the business your own, but you are also navigating a new culture and business environment.

- Build targets and incentive objectives that are realistic to either the first, second, or third year.

Continuity Bonus

How about incentivizing people that transition into a new role for actually implementing the plans that his or her predecessor put in place? We spoke about how so very often people who are promoted into new roles start by throwing out all the old plans and fire all the agencies for good measure as well. Although this might be the right thing to do when you become, for instance, the new chief marketing officer (CMO) for Kodak, Twinkies, Blockbuster, or Nokia, more often than not you won't find yourself in such an urgently broken scenario.

A Royalty Bonus for Innovation

Some companies already offer royalty bonuses for people in the innovation department, but why not offer a bonus for truly innovative marketing ideas? Or why not foster a culture of entrepreneurship from anyone, anywhere within the extended organization and its expanded ecosystem?

Obviously you need to spell out the criteria beforehand and ensure that your corporate culture actually wants (and endures) the risk taking that comes part and parcel with innovative ideas. Have the ideas judged by a panel of experts, perhaps including one or two external panelists (from your agency? from a university? two somewhat talented book writers?).

An Imitation (Stealing) Bonus

Ensure people look to what might already be available from other brand teams or what has been tried before. We are not referring to a straightforward copy/paste but to the slightly more enlightened copy/adapt/paste. You will want your marketers to take the inspiration or core of the idea and make it their own so that it is relevant for their brand and market.

You will be surprised what might be worth stealing. Think, for instance, about apps or games that have been developed for some of your brands in different markets. If you don't have any idea regarding what has been developed across your portfolio, then you should build a digital asset management (DAM) system (discussed later in this chapter).

Another way to expose a large group of employees to smart ideas is to organize an internal awards model. I have seen this successfully implemented at quite a few companies and agencies. Marketers submit entries in different categories (not too many to keep the awards both special and manageable), and a jury judges them according to predefined criteria.

One category should definitely be "Best reuse of an idea" or something similar, for which marketers can showcase how they copied/adapted/pasted an idea from somewhere else.

Imitation bonuses create a number of benefits:

- They drive innovation ideas to more markets and brands.
- They create a culture of innovation acceptance and motivation in your company.
- They are great corporate moral boosters.
- They serve as equal or better incentives in comparison to a pay raise.[1]
- They are not too expensive.

You could choose to host the whole thing online, which makes it relatively cheap to do. You could also consider flying the nominees to the global headquarters or an annual global meeting you are probably having anyway for a final shoot-out. Then, you could record the whole thing and make that part of an online video series to drive the message of innovation culture throughout the organization.

To manage the entries into a manageable structure, all the entries should be submitted in the same simple format called SAR (situation, action, result). Literally, the report is three pages, with one page for each topic: The *situation* describes the impetus for the *action*, which of course describes what was done. The most important part, the *result*, presents data and learnings about what happened after the action was implemented.

Marketers and agencies tend to make descriptions longer, fluffier, or far too detailed in a belief that this ensures their ideas are taken more seriously. To be honest, who has the time for any of that?

(Jaffe: "And as a judge of one of your award shows, I second the motion!")

So, by forcing people into the concise SAR format, they must think, "What precisely convinces the people judging the ideas that theirs is the best?" Allow them to add any manner of backup they want (a place where they can put all the fluffy stuff) but enforce SAR and judge on that. Success is ensured. Plus, the SAR format is easily tagable, which will serve your DAM system.

Build an Electronic Repository of Plans, Learnings, Creative Work, and Results

It is time to invest in a knowledge management system: a repository that holds all past and present plans and a database of learnings and results versus brand business objectives. It should also contain all significant creative work in a DAM system.

Doing this will not only help you with each personnel change, but it will also create a "one and only" place for all approved plans and creative work. This has enormous business benefits.

As we all know, many marketers suffer from the "not invented here" syndrome. In reality, almost anything in mainstream marketing that you need for a particular brand in one market has most likely already been done at least once in one of your other markets.

If you truly want to be a savvy, cost-effective marketer, screen what your brand is doing across markets against what your direct competitors are doing.

Inspiration can come from anywhere. Here are two quotes that support our desire for you to take inspiration: "Good artists copy. Great artists steal" (attributed to Pablo Picasso, but also famously used by Steve Jobs in the mid-1990s). If you don't steal, the following anonymous quote might come to haunt you: "I hate people who steal my ideas before I think of them."

The second reason you need a DAM system is that it will save you money on production and possibly on costly litigation. It will save costs as all members of the marketing family will have access to what exists and might be available for reuse in the system (especially if you attach a record for image and music rights along with an expiration date).

Regarding that litigation issue, in a prior role, I once received a phone call from an agent representing a certain model. He wanted to send us a very large bill for using a poster that included said model in a major German airport. I had no idea what he was talking about. After a swift investigation, I learned that this poster had indeed gone up in the airport, but not by us in the marketing department. Instead, a well-meaning local trade marketing representative grabbed the poster opportunity in his sales territory when it offered itself. He simply went online, found some artwork, and had the poster made locally.

Obviously this was well intended, but ended up costing a lot. Lesson learned: We built a DAM system that allowed agencies to upload creative work at low resolution so it could not be used for reproduction. We also granted access to sales and trade marketing reps so they could use the database with their clients from their laptops and could order appropriate artwork, thus ensuring it would be both cleared for usage and represent the appropriate campaign message.

Jaffe's Response: With the average tenure of the CMO doubling, hopefully this will set into motion a ripple effect that brings more stability and continuity to organizations. This—coupled with a desperate need to stop the constant musical chairs of the "reorg"—are vital in order to allow some momentum to build and for ideas to be given more time to pass their 100-day marks. One final point: Talent retention is another critical component that must be addressed. Attracting talent is hard enough; keeping it is even harder. With the constant lure and pull of Startup Nation, brand managers are always one step away from defecting to greener pastures. Who needs a gold Rolex when you can get a Pebble on Kickstarter! Companies need to recognize and reward ingenuity and promote from within.

On the human resources side as it relates to recruitment and training, the learning curve is both steep and decidedly fluid. When 50 *percent of the marketing roles* recruiters are looking to fill *did not exist five years ago* and job titles like brand textologists, Facebook friend agents, or Twitter curators are in play, brands need to make decisive steps to reinvent, rather than increment.

CHAPTER

12

Compensation

In this chapter we will cover the thorny subject of paying and getting paid. As we outlined in the chapters covering business and economic reasons for the perfect storm, there are serious disconnects surrounding our current compensation practices and the new reality that marketers find themselves in.

At heart, we are firm believers of Jim Rohn's observation that "You don't get paid for the hour. You get paid for the value you bring to the hour." With this in mind, we concluded earlier that marketing executive and agency pay is tied to out-of-date performance indicators such as TV commercial pretest scores and the number of social media likes or fans.

The other side of the coin, and perhaps the more important one, is that we should perhaps first think about how we are going to pay consumers for their currently active role in the marketing plan.

Consumers

If you believe in the *Flip the Funnel* model, then you agree that the journey continues, or really starts, with the consumer who is on board with your brand. That is where the puck is and where your Z.E.R.O. budget should be.

Flip the Funnel recommends shifting some (if not most) of the massive budget spent on acquisition toward retention and new acquisition through existing customers. As we have stated, in most marketing plans today, especially those from fast-moving consumer goods brands, acquisition easily eats up more than 80 percent of the consumer connection budget.

Given that consumers now have the means to make their opinions heard, their intentions known, and their experiences shared, it is imperative that marketers listen—not just by joining the social media conversation but by truly listening to what the new consumer-driven marketing paradigm might offer as a brand building opportunity. It is time to add some Flipped Funnel A.D.I.A. (Acknowledgement → Dialog → Incentivization → Activation) to your Traditional Funnel A.I.D.A. (Awareness → Interest → Desire → Action).

So how should you incentivize consumers? How do you pay them (back) for their loyalty and their readiness to wear your brand as a badge and as an extension of their personality on social media, such as Instagram, LinkedIn, or YouTube?

The lazy marketers' answer is visible every day in your inbox or your newsfeed through sponsored tweets and posts: "Like me for a chance to win," "Share this with 10 friends for a chance to . . . ," "We care so much about you we would like to use all your personal data to send more uninspired marketing messages your way, so please install this app." Okay, that last one was made up. But it basically is what the lazy conversation marketer is saying.

There are better examples.

Walkers Chips, or to name them correctly by their British English name Walkers Crisps, is a UK brand competing in a crowded field of brands and flavors. Its idea was as simple as it was genius. Why not crowdsource new flavors and reward the people whose line extensions are voted as the winning new flavor with a stake in the profits? And thus "Do me a flavor" was born. It was so successful that it has been repeated for a number of years and exported to the United States (under the Lay's brand).

Starbucks crowdsourced innovative ideas for any and all aspects of its business—and so the splash-stick for on-the-go cups was created.

For a number of years, U.S. snack brand Dorito's has crowdsourced its Super Bowl spots.

Heineken beer launched its Ideas Brewery to invite crowdsourced innovation from consumers.

The list goes on.

Employees

We are big fans of pay for performance.

I have witnessed firsthand how a well-structured compensation and bonus system can work miracles for employees. I have also been part of companies who were the kings of vague annual employee targets, of even vaguer evaluations, and of people who got a bonus and promotion based on personal relationships and being the like of that year. Guess which type of employer made bigger gains in delivering business results and shareholder value?

This is not going to be a section just for human resources managers. It is, however, very clear that if you decide to move your marketing organization into a different direction of always-on, AIDA + ADIA, and consumer-centric marketing, it is also time to change the way you evaluate, compensate, and incentivize the people responsible for these activities.

The tricky part is how to do that. The answer is, "It depends." It depends on what your brands and business are trying to accomplish. It depends on what challenges were affected by clever, effective, innovative, and cost-conscious marketing. It depends on the scope of the marketing department (for example: if they don't have a say on pricing, then don't withhold bonuses due to market share losses attributable to price increases). And so on.

Also, your measurement and tracking must inevitably be beefed up. You will actually have to make an effort to get data for the objectives you are trying to affect. If those data do not exist, publicly or bespoke, then you will need to make the investment to track and measure them going forward. Or you will need to change the targets associated with bonus eligibility. After all, "What gets measured gets done."

It also means taking seriously the process of brand and business target setting. How many of us have sat in postbuy meetings or brand plan after-action-reviews and the verdict delivered upon looking back was "That was great, so let's do it again but then bigger."

I cringe when I hear this, because this statement is usually not based on any solid data and analysis. Doing it again as well as bigger are two decisions right there. How about, "Let's do it again, but smaller"? or "Let's not do it again, and here is why"?

In a prior life, I was part of a marketing team that launched a promotion in which the winner would get a slot in our up-and-coming new

TV commercial. We were looking for the new face for the brand in that particular market. We devised a clever 360-degree campaign that covered all touch points, including a televised final candidate "shoot-out" that was broadcast on one of the national TV networks and where the viewers could find details about how to vote for the penultimate winner. Sounds like almost every TV talent show today, right?

Well, this was well before the deluge of shows with online and text voting. We were truly ahead of the curve. And so came the time to evaluate the event. Was it a success? Absolutely. The brand, which was relatively new, gained strong recognition for what made it different from other brands, the promotion attracted strong participation on the back of which we gained new listings and volume, and the TV network was quite happy with the ratings for the show.

In all, it was time to say, "That was great, so let's do it again but bigger!" And guess what? We didn't. Why? Because our initial success generated a whole raft of me-too promotions that were played out in a variety of different media, some of which included a televised final and all of which included a form of voting. We felt that, even though the entire thing had been very successful, a repeat would enter a very crowded field that would make standing out more difficult and would potentially harm our brand image as that of an originator and innovator.

So when you hear, "That was great, so let's do it again but bigger!" please look at the data and what you learned.

Of course, this also serves as further evidence to set appropriate targets for both the marketers on the project as well as their agency partners.

Partners

As with employees, incentivize your agencies on what you really want them to do. But before you hand out handsome agency bonuses, consider how you pay them to begin with.

We all agree that agency commission is out of date, and if you are one of the few who still pay your agency that way, you are probably number one on Sir Martin Sorrell's annual Hanukkah list.

At the other end of the spectrum of agency compensation is what the Coca-Cola Company introduced and presented publicly in 2009, called value-based compensation. More about this in a moment, but first, let's get some basics out of the way (especially for all you procurement-loving people):

Rule 1: Agencies Are Businesses and Should Be Allowed to Make a Profit

This is a revolutionary idea for some advertisers but is really a no-brainer. All agencies run costly operations, and the biggest cost is their people. It is those people you are hiring as a client, so you should pay the agency fairly for their time and efforts. Pay the basic cost and then allow them a profit margin that is based on performance.

Rule 2: Agencies Should Not Be Allowed to Profit from the Client's Significant Investments in Media, Digital, or Production

This is a huge point, and it has made headlines all over the world in the past few decades. It started with La loi Sapin in the early 1990s in France in an effort to root out so-called media surcommissions or bonifications.

For those of you who don't know what those are, it basically means that agencies or agency groups negotiate an additional volume bonus across all of their client billings with a media owner or other partners/suppliers such as production houses, print companies, and so on.

Let's say I have three clients: client A has a budget of $30, client B has $20, and client C has $50. As an agency, I am obviously negotiating on behalf of each of my clients relative to their volume, and client C should get a better deal than client A or B. But agencies or agency groups now also negotiate an additional percent for placing the total volume with a media owner, which goes back to the agency in cash or media space. Advertisers (and, for instance, La loi Sapin) contend that each client should (must) get their fair share of these additional benefits.

The reality is very different and murky.

For instance, what if the media space given as bonus space to the agency as a result of combined billings ends up on clients' media schedule and the client is charged for it as a "normal" media space at the client's cost? It is invoiced as such and thus creates an additional income for the agency.

Obviously, if the bonifications are received in cash, some risky creative bookkeeping is required on the agency side.

Since La loi Sapin and subsequent laws in other countries were introduced, as well as increased self-regulation, the rules have become tighter and the game of generating "additional agency income" has become more difficult. But with the advent of independent media auditing and smarter clients in general a few scandals have emerged that have have exposed some of the more unsavory dealings, showcasing that with even the best rules and regulations, even the biggest name could be guilty somewhere at some point. The pressure on delivering the numbers is simply too high.

Most global companies doing business in the United States must now be compliant with the Sarbanes-Oxley Act. One scandal related to Sarbanes-Oxley was the McCann-Erickson debacle, which came to a head in 2005 and resulted in a $550 million restatement for their parent holding company Interpublic Group. About $60 million was directly due to media agency volume bonifications not being shared with clients.

There was the case of Carat in Germany, where bonifications led to the fall of chief executive officer (CEO) Alexander Ruzicka. He ended up with an 11-year prison sentence in 2009 after being found guilty on 86 counts of fraud. Carat had to completely open their books to one of its clients to showcase how much money the agency had made on the back of the client's budgets. In this case, individuals enriched themselves on top of enriching their businesses.

Given how small the number of public scandals is, one can only assume there must be a lot more to discover, as well as many cases that were perhaps settled quietly.

Why do media surcommissions and bonifications happen? Because many advertisers want to have it both ways. As explained, they demand that their agency offers the best people, the smartest tools and systems, the most complete data, and the ability to magically deliver things well past official deadlines. And all of this must be provided at the absolute lowest cost, for example, less than perhaps 1 (one!) percent of the media billings and a profit margin of close to zero (this is not the zero we are advocating in our book!).

Why is this bad? I am sure you can think of many reasons yourself, but it obviously hampers the agency's ability to deliver impartial advice. Because the bonifications come with commitments to the seller, there is pressure on the agency to ensure the seller is well represented in the proposals for its advertisers. This allows the agency to score a bonus by hitting or overshooting the commitment.

There aren't many reasons to feel sorry for Sir Martin Sorrell from WPP or Jeremy Buhlman from Aegis/Dentsu (have you seen the pay packages of Sir Martin and Buhlman-san?), but this business conundrum is one that is a truly tough challenge. I have been in a position in which I had to negotiate a deal with an agency and I was uncomfortable with what we were trying to accomplish. Yes, our cost would go down, but would it be reflected in either the quality of the work or in encouraging the agency to be "creative" in finding alternative sources of income? Have you ever been in a pitch where the outcome was a higher agency cost compared with what you were paying the incumbent?

In the spring of 2013, both Procter & Gamble (P&G) and Mondelēz announced they were seeking significant increases on the payment terms they require from their media agencies. Mondelēz International is going the way of AB InBev with 120-day payment terms, whereas P&G is going with 75 days. This change means advertisers are asking their media agencies to bankroll the advertiser's media costs and fees for a longer period of time (up to 120 days).

There are agency group CEOs who have simply said "no" and walked away from the billings. This strategy is acceptable as long as there are enough advertisers who still pay in more commonly accepted payment terms like 30 to 45 days. But I am sure many more advertiser chief financial officers (CFOs) and heads of procurement are getting together to compare their current payment terms with P&G, Mondelēz, and AB InBev.

At the same time, plenty of major agencies have already agreed to the clients' demands for more time. This fact should actually worry advertisers. If an agency is capable of bankrolling P&G's media dollars for 75 days, or Mondelēz's for 120, then clearly money is being made somewhere and somehow for that to be an acceptable business decision. Is that money being made to ensure they can operate a viable business, or is it adding to the agency groups' financial riches?

So what is the chicken and what is the egg in this scenario? Are advertisers rightly lengthening their payment terms because agency groups are enriching themselves via media deals that are difficult to trace and only partially passed back to the clients? Or are agency groups forced to do such deals because advertisers keep squeezing their margins while increasing their demands?

This is why rule number 1 in this chapter is number 1. If you allow a modest but fair profit and then still find the agency with their fingers in the till, you have every right to call for a pitch, a refund, and a prison sentence.

Rule 3: Advertisers Should Pay Agencies on Time and for the Work That Was Agreed upon as the Deliverable

This is another big one. First, agree on fair and transparent payment terms. What will be delivered at cost? What work will be done with a profit margin? What are the criteria for the agency to earn agency profit? Once that is agreed upon, pay your agency partner on time. You demand on-time payment from your suppliers, don't you? Well, then . . .

Similarly, expect a higher bill if your briefings are always late and the deadline given on Friday is for the following Monday. Likewise, consider whether the delivery date for the creative work was officially yesterday for the broadcast next week and you somehow won't be able to get the green light from your boss until tomorrow, or if you want the media placement schedule to be changed after the deadline for when the media closed.

Somehow, most agencies make all these miracles happen. But it happens at a cost (and we are not even talking about the cost to your reputation as an advertiser if you are a repeat no-pay offender). So pay for what it took to get the job done. It is only fair.

Rule 4: Pitches Should Not Be Paid for and Should Not Occur Willy-Nilly Each Time You Don't Like Your Current Agency's Latest Proposals—or Each Time There Is a New CMO or Brand Director

Don't get me wrong: Client-agency relationships turn sour, just like some real-life relationships. But very often it is (again, just like in real life) because one or the other in the relationship has become complacent, bored, or distracted by that fresh new thing they stumbled upon the other day.

My mantra is and always has been that from a business cost and continuity perspective, it is better to repair than to replace. Sure, if it is really broken (Danone and Carat in Germany), then it is time to call for a new agency, but in most cases, it is much better to address the people issues (usually) at the heart of the potential break up and make changes there.

The hidden cost of a pitch typically comes the first year after you have changed agencies. This is because your new agency will have to do everything that year for the first time, and no matter how wonderful everything was in the pitch presentation, the real world is often quite a bit more challenging.

Rule 5: No Matter How Hard You Try to Explain It to Me (and Trust Me, Many Have Tried), Your Agency Overhead Can Never Be More Than 100 Percent

Again, agencies should be allowed a modest but reasonable profit. But whatever the costs are to run said agency, if it constitutes something you can charge your clients for, the total should always add up to 100 percent. Nothing more. Period.

So now that we have some rules, let's examine the best way to compensate your agency: value-based compensation (VBC). As the name suggests, VBC compensates for value delivered. VBC is unlike an hourly model, which creates compensation based on time spent. To explore this concept, let's use the previously mentioned Coca-Cola model, which the company publicly shared[1] through a variety of platforms in 2009 and in whose creation I played a supporting role (with full credit to Sarah Armstrong, who did all the heavy lifting).

VBC requires creating a set of definitions for things that add value to the business, such as level of strategic importance of the brief. This practice suggests there should be a difference in 100 hours spent by the agency on developing the annual plan versus 100 hours spent on the development of shelf wobblers in supermarkets. Not only is the first of higher strategic value to Coke, it also would require a different set of people, who would be classified as more valuable and therefore warrant a higher price tag.

This approach is by no means easy, common, or without potential controversy. But, in essence, agencies agreed with Coke that it would lead to fair compensation and an opportunity to charge appropriately for those things that are costly.

It also forces a behavior change at the advertiser. If low-value agency tasks end up taking more time than the value-creating agency tasks, there is clearly something wrong. I bet it is any one of the bad behaviors as described in rule 3.

Jaffe's Response: I feel so strongly about this action item. First, I always think of the M&M's characters and how the agency that created them should—to this day—receive royalties or residuals for this idea. I'm not sure if the agency that created them is still the agency of record. I can't even find that out based on a Google search. Second, I think it's important to both reward and punish agencies for exceeding and failing to meet the bar, respectively. Having skin in the game is important, and I have no problem with an agency having to put a chunk of its compensation (over and above its cost plus overhead) at risk against mutually agreed-upon realistic goals. However, this is only if the client in turn agrees to assign a target and a stretch target against which a bonus over and above the original fee will be paid. Let's call these 10 percent and 25 percent, respectively, as placeholders.

CHAPTER

13

Budget Setting

O nce every year, most major marketing departments go through the excruciating but important process of setting annual budgets. They typically follow either a calendar year or a fiscal year. In Chapter 3 we outlined some of the current (bad) practices when it comes to budget setting.

In this chapter we will set out some markers to achieve the goal of this book, which is to at least drive the third-party media investments down in favor of investments in your non, owned, and earned media. At best, and in our perfect world, we would accomplish having the paid media investment at zero.

Here is our first piece of advice. Do not kill your third-party, rented, paid media space. Do not go cold turkey. You will surely shock the system, and you will surely fail. As we have discussed throughout this book, you and/or your organization are probably not ready for it—nor are your agencies or the media owners. The only one who is, is your consumer, but you will have to make the journey in stages rather than in one fell swoop, because that fell swoop would turn into a foul flop if taken too swiftly and without preparation.

So what are some of the things that you can do?

First, we recommend setting a three-year gradual evolution plan. This will allow you to not only shift your budget but also shift your company, your brands, your agencies, and even your consumers to the new you.

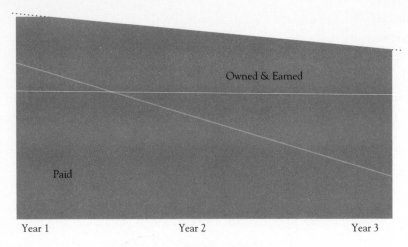

Figure 13.1   Budget shift over time

Figure 13.1 illustrates how your budget allocation will (should!) shift over time.

As you can see there are two outcomes:

Drive down your paid media dependence.

Drive down your overall media investment.

The first goal is the hard bit; the second will happen automatically if you are successful at the first. Do remember that we are not advocating reducing your overall investment in consumer-facing touch points: we never said "zero marketing" or "zero advertising." But a reduction in costly touch points in favor of more modestly priced touch points is inevitable (and desirable) because you are shifting from expensive, rented, third-party touch points such as TV or out-of-home to social media and your own website, for instance. The cost reduction is not a goal, but it could be a most welcome by-product (ask your chief financial officer or the procurement guys if you need confirmation).

This shift makes total sense from the point of view of your consumers. The digital opportunities to get close to (location-based) engaged consumers (social media) at any time of the day (mobile, network, broadband, cable) are just too good to be true. Ignore them at your peril.

But just as we are not advocating a reduction in your overall connection spend, we are also not advocating a shift from analog to digital or from off-line to online. In fact, the only thing we recommend is to change your budget setting mind-set from being brand- and campaign-driven to being consumer-driven.

We outlined in Chapter 3 how current budget setting practices basically perpetuate the status quo of your media mix. And because you are reading this book it is clear you are unhappy with that system. The only way out of the budget quandary is to start with the consumers:

Who are they?

Where are they?

What do they spend time with?

How engaged are they with what they spent time with (casual gaming versus reading the *Wall Street Journal* versus watching the Super Bowl in a pub)?

Do you have permission or even a requirement to be where they are (watching *The X Factor* on TV versus actively searching for BBQ sauce stain removal)?

This means that from now on, budget split is no longer an objective but an outcome. This is a major shift you will have to make in your thinking. Here are a few simple (but very difficult) budget setting/briefing rules you should start to implement:

Budget Setting Rule 1

Do not include any type of budget split in your brief, not even an approximation. Instead, brief the agency on what the budget split should be on the basis of their best consumer analysis and subsequent connection strategy and plan.

Budget Setting Rule 2

Do not base your budget on what you spent last year (increased by *x* percent for media inflation). Always give a realistic total budget. Then apply rule 1.

Budget Setting Rule 3

Do not ask for ideal plans. This is an enormous waste of time, as we all know that the ideal budget never, ever happens. Again, always brief by giving a realistic budget. If you know you are facing a tough 12 months ahead, it might make sense to have the agency prepare a schedule through which

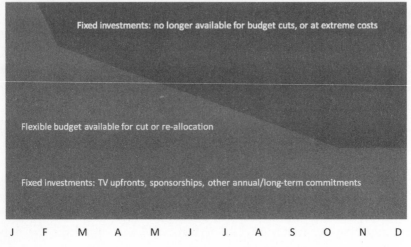

Fixed investments: no longer available for budget cuts, or at extreme costs

Flexible budget available for cut or re-allocation

Fixed investments: TV upfronts, sponsorships, other annual/long-term commitments

J   F   M   A   M   J   J.   A   S   O   N   D

Figure 13.2   Fixed versus Flexible budgets

you can see what parts of your budget are flexible versus fixed throughout the course of the year. Make sure everyone who needs to make budget decisions (for example, finance, procurement) is very aware of these realities when signing off on the budget. It might look something like Figure 13.2.

Budget Setting Rule 4

Be sure you include "mandatories" that you know will need to be included. If you signed a sponsorship deal, if you made a multiyear commitment, or any of these types of things that need to come out of this budget, include them in the brief. I can't tell you how many rebriefs and replans I have had to make because it was not communicated that about 30 percent of the budget was going to be used for activity X, but we forgot to tell you.

Budget Setting Rule 5

Identify your 70/20/10 (or 60/30/10 depending on risk appetite). Most people know of this allocation from the innovation approach that Eric Schmidt pioneered at Google: 70 percent of time allocated to core business tasks, 20 percent to projects directly related to the core business, and 10 percent dedicated to projects unrelated to the core business. This last one allows the company to find blue-sky opportunities without losing focus on the core business.

We recommend allocating your connections budget the same way:

o 70 percent to deliver your core connections (for example, video, including TV and other key media that deliver your audience in large numbers)

o 20 percent to connections that are not must-haves but that are great to enrich, deepen, or contextualize your campaign (for example, touch points that are 100 percent on target or on topic but are not make or break for the campaign)

o 10 percent to connections that you have not used before or that are unusual or experimental in nature (for example, placing chicken soup in the cold medicine aisle or a cereal with strawberries in the produce section; see Figure 13.3)

Figure 13.3   Honey Bunches cereal in context

Budget Setting Rule 6

When you cut, cut from what you have a lot of. This seems like a huge open door, right? Yet, time and again when a budget needs to be trimmed it seems like there is only one sacred cow: TV. Why are you prepared to cut everything else before you touch TV? If you follow our allocation process as outlined in this chapter, it is time to reverse this practice once and for all. Cut TV first because that is probably where the largest budget sits. It is also the video medium with the highest waste outside your core target audience and the medium with the lowest average engagement score as compared with all other video media.

If you follow these budget setting rules, you will also find that, at long last, you are learning from your 10 percent budget allocation experiments and can decide whether they merit a larger or ongoing role in your future mix. The objective is of course that some of the "10 percent experiments" make it into the 20 percent or 70 percent allocations. If you always cut everything but TV, you will never be able to debate the merits of these new connections and create a first-mover advantage and knowledge for yourself vis-à-vis your competitors.

Now let's tackle the most challenging part of the budget journey: the new role of TV. To do that, we must ban the word *television* from connection plans (previously published as a blog post on Maarten's *Connection Planning Perspectives*).

In case you have not noticed yet, there is a battle going on in the living room, and it is not about who holds the remote. (Okay, there is that battle, too.)

It is, of course, the decades-old battle for TV viewers. The TV in its most primitive form was invented in 1925 in Scotland, a logical place given that the only other diversion at that time in Scotland revolved around anything to do with sheep. In the 1950s Procter & Gamble moved its soap operas from radio to TV, and the rest is, as we know, history. GRPs ruled.

Today, the viewer battle has become a lot more complex and now includes TV networks, cable networks, satellite networks, online networks, individual producers, and assorted other players, such as events and sports owners.

Companies such as Netflix, Amazon, and Hulu are broadcasting original content to lure viewers. YouTube has launched more than 150 content channels and rules them with an iron delivery fist: Content makers must deliver viewers to be featured (and make money); if they don't, they're out.

And even the viewer can get into the game, as we have witnessed in the first successful attempts at crowdsourced TV content through Mobcaster, a Kickstarter-type service for TV/video content production.

What has this done to TV viewership?

As we have shown earlier in this book, the surprising, and perhaps sad answer, is "pretty much nothing."

Why is that? It's because the real growth is in time spent online, especially with social media.

It is clear from Figure 13.4 that online "anything" is eating up an enormous and growing amount of time. The problem is that a lot of digital "activity" is difficult to classify: video content is viewed through a variety of platforms, such as Facebook, Pinterest, and Flipboard; reading a book, newspaper, or magazine happens on a Kindle or other e-reader. So how do we measure these views, or that reach? Do consumers even classify (and should they care?)? Should online time be classified as social media

Weekly Time Spent with Media among U.S. Adults, 1995, 2003 & 2012			
% of total	**1995**	**2003**	**2012**
TV & DVD/video	73%	55%	45%
Radio	1%	23%	15%
Internet	1%	7%	12%
Mobile & phone calls (e.g., landline phone)	10%	1%	9%
Digital audio	–	–	7%
Newspapers	4%	6%	4%
Magazines	7%	4%	3%
Books	3%	3%	3%
Playing video games	–	1%	2%
Writing letters	1%	–	–
Using computers	1%	–	–

Source: MAGNAGLOBAL, "Media Economy Report: The Ultimate Mobile Deep Dive," January 8, 2013
Note: numbers may not add up to 100% due to rounding

Figure 13.4   Weekly time spent with media

activity or video viewing? Reading a book, or e-reading? Good luck figuring that out if you think it matters. One thing is certain: Video viewing is big (Figure 13.5).

So where does that leave TV advertisers? Here are our points for consideration:

1.   *Don't depend on TV to deliver your audience.* This is especially true if you want to reach a younger audience, but it is more and more true for

Internet Users in Select Countries Who Have Downloaded, Recorded, or Stored a TV Program or Movie*, by Device, December 2012

% of respondents	Laptop/netbook	Tablet	Smartphone
Argentina	25%	4%	9%
Australia	15%	5%	7%
Brazil	31%	8%	10%
China	56%	26%	34%
France	21%	4%	6%
Germany	15%	4%	6%
India	44%	12%	22%
Japan	11%	4%	7%
Malaysia	61%	18%	24%
Mexico	36%	8%	14%
Russia	30%	7%	6%
South Korea	20%	9%	33%
Sweden	17%	4%	7%
Turkey	55%	9%	17%
United Arab Emirates	60%	19%	24%
UK	15%	4%	6%
US	19%	7%	11%

Source: Motorola Mobility, "Fourth Annual Media Engagement Barometer" conducted by Vanson Bourne, March 19, 2013
Note: ages 16+; *via a subscription service

Figure 13.5   Internet users in select countries

any audience. From the data we presented earlier, it is clear that most audiences are shifting significant amounts of their time to online viewing or using an online-connected device to accompany their viewing. You probably need to be where they are (if you can find a meaningful or at least nondisruptive and respectful way to inject yourself into that activity).

2.   *Change your mind-set.* A major shift you need to make in your thinking is this: TV is the icing on the cake in your media mix, not the scaffolding that holds everything else up.

To reach your consumer, especially any audience younger than 40, your first budget port of call is online. We advocate a basic layer of search before you do anything else—year round. This means you will need a search destination in the form of a search algorithm–friendly website and a Facebook page (in China, choose the equivalents).

Figure 13.6 is an eMarketer chart showcasing that there are many options to find a video viewing audience.

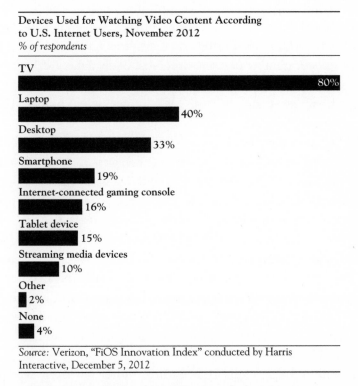

Devices Used for Watching Video Content According to U.S. Internet Users, November 2012
% of respondents

TV — 80%
Laptop — 40%
Desktop — 33%
Smartphone — 19%
Internet-connected gaming console — 16%
Tablet device — 15%
Streaming media devices — 10%
Other — 2%
None — 4%

Source: Verizon, "FiOS Innovation Index" conducted by Harris Interactive, December 5, 2012

Figure 13.6   Devices used for watching video content

Now that we have a picture of where our viewers might be online, it is time to start building a video budget mix. And this is no different than planning an old-fashioned TV schedule. You're looking for eyeballs, and assuming you are a mass-distributed national brand, you will have a lot to choose from.

Buying online eyeballs can be a very cost-effective way to extend video reach. You will be able to afford significant amounts of well-targeted and time- and content-relevant eyeballs.

As mentioned, online video comes in many forms, and depending on who you are, what you are trying to communicate, and when you are trying to do this, you should pull together your mix of channels, day-parts, content mix, and so on.

See? That sounds remarkably like old-fashioned TV planning, doesn't it?

Just like with TV, there is a prime time for video viewing as well, and when that is depends on your target audience.

If, for instance, you want to reach people with a lunch offer from Subway, you would select a different time of day for your ad versus trying to reach people with a family phone/Internet/mobile bundle offer. It is time to forget the whole first-, second-, or third-screen debate. Different screens are first depending on the end user's time and place. If you're on a train or bus, your number one screen is most likely a mobile device. If you want to watch the Super Bowl, Oscars, or Champions League with your friends at home or at the pub, the TV is probably still number one (but not the exclusive) screen.

To add more complexity but also further opportunity for better targeting (and therefore higher relevance and engagement) we should dig a little deeper into the platforms used to watch your content (Figure 13.7). This will help in selecting both the appropriate reach vehicle and the kind of message you should use (content, meet context!).

Ultimately, you should mix time of day with the viewing platform the consumer is using to decide which form of content makes most sense: long form? Call to action? Entertaining or informational? And so on.

3.   *Change how you buy.* After all of this planning, it is time to start buying. Here the options are also multiple and again should depend on timing, your audience, the type of message, and the time, place, and device it will be seen on.

Some might be anxious that online video is—even worse than TV—a medium that is easily avoided, clicked away from, or even

Devices Used to View Digital Video among U.S. Digital Video Viewers*, by Type, March 2013

% of respondents	Online TV (n = 495)	User-generated content (n = 724)	Original professionally produced video (n = 441)
Laptop	58%	58%	50%
Internet-connected TV	47%	13%	27%
Desktop	39%	45%	39%
Smartphone	28%	36%	26%
Tablet	28%	26%	23%
iPod touch	14%	11%	13%

Source: Interactive Advertising Bureau (IAB), "45 Million Reasons and Counting to Check Out the NewFronts" conducted in partnership with GfK, April 29, 2013
Note: ages 18+; *who watch a given type of video monthly or more

Figure 13.7   Devices used to view digital video

ignored. The data suggest otherwise: click-through and completion rates are healthy, and let's be honest, what is the completion rate of a TV commercial with potty breaks, popcorn breaks, or any other diversions and interruptions occurring in the living room (or bedroom)? (Figure 13.8)

But if you are seeking "guaranteed deliverys," online video offers one additional and unique benefit that makes it almost criminal *not* to buy: Most online video networks and sellers now offer, at a manageable premium, the option to pay for only those people who actually completed the entire video. In other words, if your video is 30 seconds long, you don't pay for anyone who has not watched the complete 30 seconds. I challenge you to try to negotiate similar conditions with your traditional TV networks. It will never happen.

The industry is quickly shifting from opportunity to see to guaranteed delivery. From average reach to "signed, sealed, delivered." From Gross Rating Points (GRPs) to actual impact. Certified. And the added benefit is that more and more of these viewers have registered profiles on the platform they are viewing your video on, meaning you are going to

Completion and Click Rate of U.S. Online Pre-Roll* Video Ads, by Industry, Second Quarter 2012		
	Completion rate	Click rate
Food and drink	78.18%	0.48%
Business and finance	77.79%	0.82%
Entertainment	75.50%	0.75%
Automotive	73.95%	0.77%
CPG	73.03%	0.51%
Computing/tech	72.66%	0.80%
Health and lifestyle	72.34%	0.84%
Travel	69.41%	0.71%
Telecom	67.51%	1.20%
Retail	60.47%	1.12%
Consumer electronics	53.22%	0.56%
Total	71.65%	0.71%

Source: VideoHub, "Performance Replay Report: Q1 2012," October 1, 2012
Note: *includes both pre-roll and interactive pre-roll video ads

Figure 13.8   Completion and click rate of U.S. online pre-roll video ads

know quite a bit more about them than age and gender, which is about as detailed as most TV ratings get.

Case in point, AB InBev decided to test online video as an alternative to TV. In Germany, for example, the core target of young adult males for Beck's beer had always underdelivered against TV. By switching to online video, the results were staggering: Not only was the gap plugged, but aided ad awareness increased, as did recognition and the brand's key performance indicators, such as favored brand and brand love. And, by the way, it cost a whole lot less.

Based on these results, the next year the brand shifted 20 percent of GRPs to online video.

(Note: Full credit should be given to Reckitt Benckiser, the first ones to pilot this approach at scale in the United States.)

When all is said and done, your video mix will look something like the budget shown in Figure 13.9 (hypothetical).

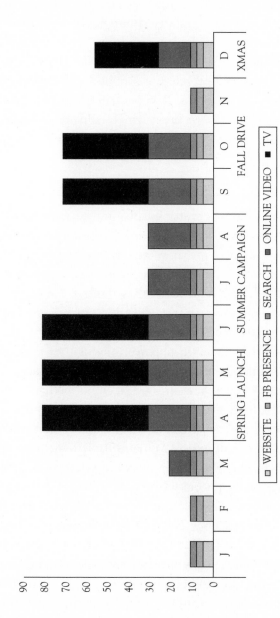

Figure 13.9   Hypothetical budget allocation over a year

As you can see in Figure 13.9, we have applied the principles of an ongoing Web, search, and social presence and used online video for all major campaign periods. TV is the heavy-up medium only, scheduled when eyeballs are needed in extralarge (nonprecise) quantities. TV makes up less than 50 percent of the budget and is used only when it is deemed necessary, which is during the key campaign periods. This means that waste is now limited to less than 50 percent of your budget, finally putting to bed John Wanamaker's famous quote, "I know half of my budget is wasted; I just don't know which half." You know which half, and as you evolve your marketing approach, it may even become zero over time.

Jaffe's Response: That was pretty specific and extremely meticulous. I hope I won't be tested on it afterward. I do want to add one more point to the how we plan and how we buy one-two punch. I believe we need entirely new budgets that go beyond new connection points themselves. I'd recommend three of these budgets (or budget allocations). The first is an innovation budget dedicated to rapid prototyping and active experimentation. Next, I recommend a speculative budget designed to pounce on opportunities as they present themselves, not dissimilar from real-time marketing as a subset of content strategy (see Oreo's Dunk in the Dark), but perhaps a little less contrived. Think football superstar Gareth Bale being photographed in a Nando's store and the possibilities of aligning "left wings" with a "left wing," or baseball legend Mariano Riviera mentioning (multiple times) at the All-Star Game the word priceless. In May 2013, McDonald's utilized its speculative budget by giving Cleveland, Ohio, kidnapping case hero Charles Ramsey free food for a year. Finally, I recommend a contingency budget that is designed to be able to pivot mid-campaign and in real time. When Howard Stern criticized Katie Couric for offering up a measly $500 prize for a talent competition on her show, she stumbled her way to $1,000 amid laughter from the studio audience, instead of knocking the prize up ten-fold to $5,000 or higher. Brands need to have a budget to address missteps mid-campaign but also be able to build on successes and aspects of the campaign that resonate especially strongly with audiences.

CHAPTER

14

Measurement and Insights

How often have you heard Einstein's famous measurement quote: "Not everything that can be counted counts and not everything that counts can be counted"? Yeah, same for us.

In its elegance it is also absolutely right and highly appropriate for this chapter.

As we outlined earlier, all things are not good in measurement land. We highlighted the problem of how we still measure and track the brand marketing objectives of senior executives through out-of-touch metrics. The problem with out-of-touch metrics is not only that using them perpetuates out-of-date connection plans (TV, anybody?) but that it affects how marketing and agency executives are incentivized.

And all of this is happening in a world that has allegedly become more measurable than ever. Digital data and the digitalization of all media have allowed for real-time buying, real-time tracking, real-time optimization, and real-time dashboarding.

More Data, More Confusion[1]

We have all heard of Moore's law, right? According to Wikipedia, Intel cofounder Gordon E. Moore concluded in a 1965 (!) paper that the number of components in integrated circuits had doubled every year since their invention in 1958 thus doubling their power, and he predicted the trend would continue for the next 10 years. The only thing wrong with his prediction about the doubling of computer horsepower was the "10 years" part. The law otherwise still holds true today.

Yes, big data. It is now used (and abused) so much that the term delivers 1.5 billion results through a Google search. If we narrow the search to "big data marketing," the results are still a portly 251 million. That is a lot of data about big data.

But has it been helping marketers to date? I don't think so. In fact, the opposite of helpful seems to be true. So I humbly present Maarten's law of marketing data and understanding (Figure 14.1).

Although I think the picture is clear, here is how I have put the law into words: "As the amount of marketing data increases, the marketer's understanding of where to look and what to deduct from all available data decreases at an equal rate."

According to a white paper published by IBM and 9sight Consulting in October 2012, big data and marketing are a huge opportunity just waiting to be tapped. All you need to do as a marketer is become comfortable with things like the Hadoop ecosystem and process-mediated data. And don't forget the important steps of data virtualization and agent-based modeling. Got it?

The obvious promise of the *big data vomit* (a technical term I borrowed from data guru D. J. Patel, formerly of LinkedIn and now at Greyrock— Twitter handle @dpatel) is that marketing becomes seriously measurable,

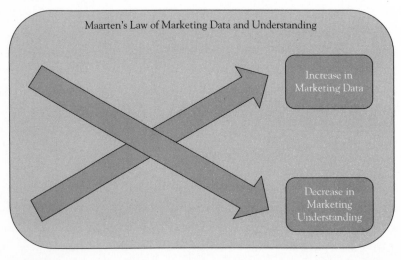

Figure 14.1   Maarten's law of marketing data and understanding

predictable, and driven by return on investment (ROI). As a result practical and useable insights should increase. In theory, I believe this to be true. In reality I am speaking with many large Fortune 500 marketers and their agencies and they are all as bewildered as you and I are.

So let's examine the facts first: How much data is there?

In 1995, Craig Jolley stated that one weekday edition of the *New York Times* contained more information than the average seventeenth-century Englishman would encounter in a lifetime. In that same year, Jack Trout and Steve Rivkin stated that more information had been produced in the preceding 30 years than in the 5,000 years before that. And this was 18 years ago. There was no *i*-anything yet. Mobile phones were meant for making phone calls.

Today's data stream has dramatically increased. Here are some data points I found on a blog from Marcia Connor: In one day, 144.8 billion e-mails are sent (and they seem to be all in my inbox!), 340 million tweets are sent, and 72 hours of YouTube video are uploaded. The list goes on and covers only digital media. Add to the list your car, refrigerator, toilet, and very soon your glasses and wristwatch.

The Marketer's Data Insights World

As a marketer, life used to be easy. To evaluate the sturdiness of your media plan, all you needed to do was to look at the number of GRPs the TV plan generated. What GRPs *were* wasn't quite clear to you, but no doubt, more meant better. Perhaps you also looked at the number of radio spots and outdoor locations booked for your campaign. Again, more was probably better, so that was your benchmark.

The truly enlightened (or dorky) looked perhaps at cost per thousand (CPM), cost per GRP, or (for the really advanced) share of voice (SOV)/ share of market (SOM). Not to repeat myself, but the yardstick again was more is better, with the exception of CPM or cost per point (cost per GRP), where the opposite was true.

The scary part is that it seems that for most marketers, time has stood still. The only difference is that instead of GRPs, we apply the same more is better rule to click-through rates, number of fans/likes, time spent on a website, or page views. And less is more is true for any cost measure (especially agency remuneration).

The Marketer's New Data Insights World

And now you have heard of big data and the promise of uber-measurability and ROI (Figure 14.2). IBM, Salesforce, and Adobe promise to make sense of it all. Do they? And even if they do, will you be able to follow along? The data (*sic!*) in the chart below seems to suggest otherwise.

So you can't follow and probably won't, because you're not a statistician or a data analyst. Chances are no one in your marketing department is either. So it is time to strengthen your department by including someone who is capable of that (unless you want to leave the informed decision making to IBM, Adobe, Salesforce, etc.).

One thing you must do is engage and immerse yourself in the data. Find as much motivation to look and learn as you do from looking at your latest EBITDA, market share, or sales figures. Because really, can you afford not to have an ongoing dialogue with the people in the know? Can you afford not to spend at least a few hours every month to understand what is driving consumer media behavior in your key targets? And vice versa, can you afford not to be in the know about how the brand is doing?

What happens if you don't? I am predicting perfectly optimized plans and a brand that is tanking.

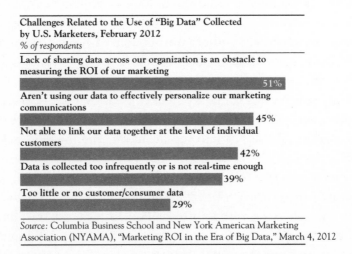

Challenges Related to the Use of "Big Data" Collected by U.S. Marketers, February 2012
% of respondents

Lack of sharing data across our organization is an obstacle to measuring the ROI of our marketing — 51%

Aren't using our data to effectively personalize our marketing communications — 45%

Not able to link our data together at the level of individual customers — 42%

Data is collected too infrequently or is not real-time enough — 39%

Too little or no customer/consumer data — 29%

Source: Columbia Business School and New York American Marketing Association (NYAMA), "Marketing ROI in the Era of Big Data," March 4, 2012

Figure 14.2   Challenges related to the use of "big data"

Often, in big marketing organizations or departments, different brand managers are responsible for different parts of the analysis; for example, one is in charge of tracking media (can you say junior brand manager?) and another is in charge of Nielsen or digital data. Decisions are based on budget needs and not brand consumer value. This strategy seldom delivers the most optimal solution for what the brand needs.

Typically, budget need–driven decisions lead to cuts in all touch points except TV. Why? Well, refering back to Chapter 13 on budget setting, we know that the marketer making budget decisions trusts the TV creative the best, as it was tested (one-number score through the roof, remember?) and because nobody ever got fired for supporting TV in the marketing plan. It is what we believe works, and the dealers/retailers love it, too, so there. Cut everything else.

Our recommendations are, unsurprisingly, as follows:

- Address the data situation.
- Hire people that understand data and can deliver insightful analytics.
- Don't rely on Excel as your data management solution.
- Equally, don't rely on Excel as your plan management tool.

With regards to the people component, I believe that we are entering the Marketing Analytics era. The 60s through the 80s was the era of the Mad Men, also known as account managers. The 90s was the era of the Media Men (the rise of the media shops as a spin-off from agencies).

The first decade of this century was the era of the Digital Men. So I predict that the next era will be for Homo Analyticus. I would hire a few!

You may also want to invest in setting up a dashboard. "But I already have 15 of those," you say. Let me guess: dashboards for Nielsen, social media listening, search, Salesforce data, Web traffic, and a bunch more—all reporting very useful but isolated outcomes from individual pieces of the puzzle. And all are very likely reviewed by different people in your team, perhaps even different functions (marketing, sales, digital, insights, and more).

None of these are dashboards. They are scorecards, trackers, and other data sets at best, all very relevant in their own right and all great inputs into your big data solution. But where we go wrong is that (1) we call every collection of data a dashboard, and (2) we throw everything and the kitchen sink onto the dashboard. So let's first establish the official definition of *dashboard* according to Dictionary.com:

dash•board [dash-bawrd, -bohrd] n.

1. *(In an automobile or similar vehicle) A panel beneath the front window having various gauges and accessories for the use of the driver; instrument panel.*
2. *A board or panel at the front of an open carriage or the like to protect the occupants from mud or dirt cast up by the hoofs of the animals drawing the vehicle.*

I recommend forgetting the mud and dirt definition, although if you see mud and/or dirt on your dashboard, it might be a metaphor indicating that something is wrong with your plans.

In more recent years, I have started a dashboard renaming crusade. To ensure clarity and simplicity, I am pushing for one, and only one, dashboard. The-thing-we-call-dashboard, actually Dashboard with a capital D, is the tool that reports how our brand business is doing, in as real time as possible, and shows only the most important data.

A former colleague of mine, who is also a pilot, likened this Dashboard approach as follows: A pilot sits in his or her cockpit with a bewildering array of dials, indicators, buttons, screens, and the like. However, to ensure the plane is still flying right, there are only a few key indicators that need to be tracked continuously. If I remember correctly they were the speedometer, the altimeter, the compass, the indicator for the rudders for direction, and the one for the engine's health in general. Oh, and the coffeemaker.

Obviously, when something malfunctions, a pilot wants to know early on what's happening and to a great degree of detail so he or she can take corrective action or switch to alternative solutions. This means the pilot doesn't just want to know that engine number two has a problem; the pilot wants to know if it is a fire, an oil leak, or just running low on gas. Each scenario requires a different course of action.

Sound familiar? At most times, you will want to track the general health of your brand:

- Are we growing at pace (speedometer)?
- How are we doing versus key identified competitors (altimeter)?

- Where am I headed next, and is all set appropriately for that direction (rudders)?

- Are we growing in the right direction, that is, with the right target, in the right geographies, with the most profitable pack/price combination, and so on (compass)?

- Is all well with my marketing engine: budget, connection strategy and plan, creative content, and so on (engine health)?

- Am I awake (coffee!)?

Figure 14.3 is a schematic of how I see your Dashboard functioning. This is obviously hugely simplified, but I think it gives you the general idea.

As a senior leader (aka "the pilot"), most days you need only the top bar of this Dashboard. If something does not look right, each of these areas should offer a double-click option to delve deeper into the data.

If you are a subject matter specialist, you still need to understand the big brand marketing results picture. I have witnessed many times

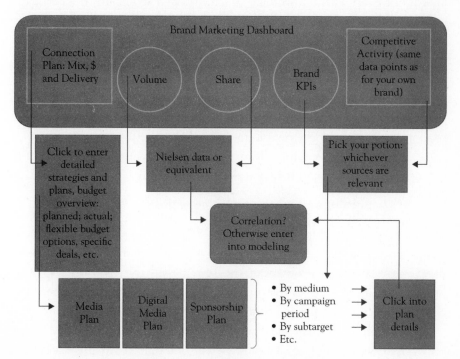

Figure 14.3   Brand marketing Dashboard

that the agency's media department, or even the in-house media or digital specialists, are completely in the dark regarding what's driving the brand's success, or they are unaware of specific brand challenges. They blissfully optimize their plans and deliver stellar output results only to find budgets are being cut or plans are changed without a true understanding of why.

Output results are data points such as reach, frequency, TV or other media GRPs, click-through rates, website or social media page time spent, unique visitors, cost per thousand reach/clicks, search data, and all the other very important checkpoints that indicate the technical details of the plan are all in good order. The subject matter specialist should track all of these and optimize as best as possible during the campaign.

As a subject matter specialist, you need to be able to go deep and detailed when needed. You need access to and will probably use all manner of detailed data to ensure that your part of the investment delivers what is needed.

But do yourself a favor: Don't call any of these data collections a dashboard, not even with a lowercase d. Call them a scorecard, tracker, data point, postbuy, after-action review, or anything else appropriate. That way, when someone says, "According to the Dashboard, we seem to have a problem," everyone knows where to look—and not at the other data collections.

Most important, institute a shared review culture. Data is dumb. The smartest data are useless unless they are jointly reviewed at regular (not too long) intervals by the people responsible for the plans.

Let's look at an example from the U.S. presidential election campaign of 2012 (partly published earlier on Maarten's *Connection Planning Perspectives* blog).

Like everyone else in the United States, my airwaves were flooded during the U.S. presidential election of 2012 with—surprise!—political advertising. Candidates, PACS, Super PACS, unions, issue groups—everyone was trying to outshout the rest. It was the election with the biggest media price tag in history. An estimated $6 billion was spent on campaigns across the United States.

In the end, there was a clear winner, which makes this case history so easy. There was always going to be a clear outcome (with the exception of Florida): two brands were competing for the highest office, and one would win. So what did Team Obama do that made the win so emphatic, and why did so many predict a close race when there really wasn't one in the end?

1. *Smart data beats an out-of-date and out-of-touch model.*

The *New York Times* reported how the Super PAC investors licked their wounds the day after the elections. Despite their massive investment, they had not won any of the contested political races they invested in, including the number one job.

Major contributors to Super PACs have been identified as people associated with big brand names such Home Depot, TD Ameritrade, and the WWE. Others are associated with multibillion-dollar hedge funds, other investment companies, and various other industries.

It is fair to say that all these investors, without exception, were (are) extremely successful businesspeople and entrepreneurs. They built or even created industries, conglomerates, and brands and delivered incredible wealth for their share-holders and themselves.

So how is it possible that these very smart businesspeople failed to ask, or actually demand, that for their money they get the best, state-of-the-art data analytics and ROI measurement available?

They didn't. They decided to invest using the old model from prior campaigns instead of trusting something like Nate Silver's smart modeling. According to Wikipedia, Nate Silver is an American statistician, sabermetrician, psephologist, and writer. He developed PECOTA, a system for forecasting the performance and career development of Major League Baseball players, which he sold to and then managed for Baseball Prospectus from 2003 to 2009.

In 2007, using the pseudonym Poblano, Silver began to write analyses and predictions related to the 2008 U.S. presidential election. In March 2008 he established his own website, FiveThirtyEight.com. The *New York Times* eventually took him on, incorporating his blog and model into its political coverage. Silver scored almost 100 percent accuracy in the elections of 2008, 2010, and 2012. Silver has since moved back into sports.

And herein lies the first lesson for business, especially with regard to connection planning.

If you and your business are still measuring your marketing ROI by using your old model and ignoring the new possibilities (out of convenience or lack of understanding), it is likely that your brands will become Romney, especially if your competitor brands are Obama.

2.   Clogging the airwaves with traditional TV ads does not work (anymore). Didn't we know this already?

Team Obama invested using a very different connection strategy than did Team Romney. Team Obama had a clear deliverable ("register 1.7 million voters, of which the majority are minorities"). They had a daily Dashboard, going both wide (for the leadership: the pilots) and deep (for the subject matter specialists: from ratings for spots on TV to how many doors had been knocked on the day before), and in as real time as the data would allow.

They also spent twice as much as Team Romney in digital, according to data from Re-Targeter.com.

In short, they managed their campaign by making maximum use of not only a wide palette of connections but also all that data and insights could offer today.

3.   Meanwhile, Team Romney and the Super PACs were pumping out negative TV ads.

The final lesson here is that negativity does not pay and is not a strategy but at best a flawed tactic. Yes, here in the United States (and many other markets around the world), we do see comparative advertising. But no brand ever takes it to the degree that apparently politicians or Super PACs believe is necessary to convince us they are the right choice and the other is by the wrong choice (and by *wrong*, they mean that the other is, at minimum, a despicable, lying, deceitful, scheming, dodging, and/or flip-flopping socialist).

As bitter as the Coke versus Pepsi or Android versus Apple wars ever are, they never resorted to the level of mudslinging U.S. politicians deem appropriate. Even these warring brands recognize (and demonstrate) that, first and foremost, there needs to be a brand idea that people buy into. Dissing the other is not a brand idea that leads to results.

So the biggest difference in the 2012 presidential election was that in the end, ideas won over negative messaging. That is good news for marketing. In Z.E.R.O. terms, the election result is further proof that the bullhorn method (massive TV ads) is dead and that highly targeted, dynamic strategies in medium and message are the only way forward.

And for this chapter, it proves that smart measurement and use of data, in the hands of smart people, can lead to big results. Big—and predictable!

Jaffe's Response: As I've often said, if you want to get the right answers, you have to ask the right questions. Visualizing real-time metrics and measuring anything that moves in real time is valuable only if you react and respond *in real time*. Companies like Dell are doing stellar jobs in terms of their Social Media Command Center, which is a visual masterpiece. It has even created a new revenue stream by implementing this tool at other companies. Listening without responding is the corollary to analysis paralysis. Pretty dashboards (lowercase d) are like the glut of infographics adding more noise instead of signal. What is really required is to find an intricate balance of timing—both in terms of when to measure and when to act. And if you are struggling with this, you will be relieved to know there are medical remedies and treatments for premature optimization.

CHAPTER
15

Use Existing Customers to Gain New Ones

I recently presented to a room filled with senior marketing executives. One executive who shall remain nameless, representing one of the large financial services/credit card companies, asked me this question: "What if we don't have enough customers? What if we are losing existing customers because of [insert some ridiculous excuse here] and therefore need to replace them with new [insert some ridiculous adjective here like *younger, hipper, richer, poorer, blacker, whiter, thinner, fatter, you get the drift-er*] ones?" In my head I was throttling this person, trying to shake some sense into that out-of-touch head. Outside of my head, I politely indicated I would ever-so-gently push back and challenge that assertion.

Any churn or attrition whatsoever is unacceptable. Industry averages and norms are nothing but numbers or percentages. We deal with human beings, and there should never be a reason to lose a single customer—not ever. I was once taught to treat every customer like my best customer—and my only customer.

Granted, the funnel (traditional or flipped) may sprout some leaks from time to time, but if you're questioning whether you have enough customers to begin with or are concerned they're not getting any younger, isn't the real issue at hand a failure to activate?

The central premise from *Flip the Funnel* is that retention becomes the new acquisition, and in doing so, companies can grow from the inside-out, acquiring NEW customers via EXISTING ones. Retention thus moves from an end unto itself to a means to an end. In other words, through (1) upselling,(2) cross-selling, (3) increased frequency, (4) increased recency, (5) content creation, (6) conversation, and (7) referrals, the funnel truly flips and, in the process, customer count, word-of-mouth, revenues, tenure, loyalty, and the bottom line increase.

I wonder how much of *that* was going on with the company in question.

Z.E.R.O. asserts that a brand does not need new customers via traditional acquisition channels led by paid media because there are enough existing customers who are able to deliver against objectives 1 through 7, which of course includes bringing in new customers in the process.

As a sidebar, this does not exclude companies launching completely new products or service lines (after all, there is already an installed base within the extended ecosystem) or even completely new companies launching from scratch (you don't have a Rolodex?) using an initial influencer open or closed beta test as the nucleus for future growth. Nor does it exclude smaller companies with smaller bases: everything and everyone has to begin somewhere. Come to think of it, wouldn't the plethora of success stories from the past decade or two (Skype, Amazon, Instagram, Facebook, Google, Zappos, and the list continues) all qualify under these "exclusions?"

Now here comes the call to action (as this is an action plan after all):

1. How many of pathways 1 through 7 are you currently executing against?

2. How well are you executing against them? Are we talking lip-service, superficial check-listing or something more substantial?

3. How much are you investing? Or put differently, are you investing enough?

4. And if the answer to question 3 is no, to what extent are you considering optimization scenarios to invest sufficiently?

5. And in the spirit of closing the loop, how well are you identifying and consequently tracking and plugging the leaks, that is, attrition,

churn, defection (passive: to alternatives), switching (active: to competitors), and atrophy (just fading away with nary a fight or struggle to retain)?

To take a massive leap backward, it is time you consider a set of chasms so huge—virtually uncrossable—that it would make Jim Collins turn in his grave (and he's still alive!).

Chasm 1: Based on the percentage of total revenue that comes from your existing customers (repeat: returning customers), proportionately how much of your marketing budget do you currently invest in them?

Chasm 2: Of that same revenue contribution, proportionately how much of that marketing budget do you spend against your power users, the heavy buyers, the heavy talkers, the heavy buyers/talkers? Do you even know? And who and where they are?

Chasm 3: Of the percentage of new business generated via existing customers through referrals, reviews, and/or recommendations, to what extent are you recognizing and rewarding, formalizing, amplifying, or activating?

Perhaps I'm not making myself clear. Why on Earth are you wasting money on strangers and neglecting your most valuable customers, rather than taking advantage of those customers who are basically doing your job for you—better (efficiently, effectively, credibly) than you could ever do it?

How much business that comes from your existing customers are you falsely taking credit for, calling it ROI (return on your paid media investment) when it should be called ROA (return on nonpaid or nonmedia advocacy)?

Two-Way Street

Think about it: Every single time you ask your customers to tweet or share any nugget of content with their network, you are essentially asking for a freebie. And if you don't provide something back in return, this is tantamount to manipulation, coercion, greed, and shortsighted selfishness.

On the flip side, why not offer a simple thank you, a retweet, a keychain? Or via universal currency, provide the ability to truly activate against the three-C model of content, conversation, and (re)commendations.

The Basics: Cross-Sell and Upsell

What six words added instant profits to McDonald's bottom line?

Would. You. Like. Fries. With. That?

This simple phrase is just that: simple. And yet, it is a lot more complicated to implement consistently across the board. Ultimately, it is a function of training, and it shouldn't be a stretch for a cashier to utter those indomitable six words (they used to be, "Would you like to supersize that?") or even improvise with a repertoire with two to three key phrases. And yet it is.

In April 2013, the *Wall Street Journal* ran an article titled "McDonald's Tackles Repair of 'Broken' Service." Amidst disappointing earnings, McDonald's is turning away from the paid media promise of "We love to see you smile" and toward the delivery on the promise of "If we don't smile ourselves, how on Earth do we expect you to?" In other words, it is returning to ground Z.E.R.O.—its stores, its people, its owned assets put to the retention test. Perhaps if McDonald's completed the framework by flexing its entrepreneurial muscles to work with a startup that allows customers to snap photos of smiling (or snarling) employees, it could fast-track a path to producing true zealots.

The real point here is to focus on existing customers as a source of incremental (new) revenue. Chapter 16 will focus on the holistic customer experience, which itself is built or spun around one absolutely critical truism: The most powerful moment for any given brand is the Point of Purchase (what I call P.O.P., which also stands for Place of Purchase and Proof of Purchase). It is the moment at which two worlds collide. In the form of the traditional and flipped funnels, aka the Marketing Bowtie. Instead of taking a shortsighted approach to making a quick buck from a sterile transaction, focus on maximizing that purchase potential and recognizing its influence in terms of how it affects future revenue—both direct (same person) and indirect (different people).

Apple of My Eye

Apple's retail stores are a modern-day miracle. At a time when brick-and-mortar stores are flailing and struggling to deal with the very real threat of eradication or extinction, Apple is expanding and conquering its rivals with premium real estate investment. Apple retail stores are marvels to behold, a blue ocean of blue shirts (as opposed to Best Buy's Blue Shirts) that almost outnumber customers. The store is completely fluid in that every single inch of retail space is available for consultative selling and, ultimately, transacting in the form of virtual cash registers (an iPhone app). Apple's Genius Bar offers a host of *free* services, but so help me, I've never walked into an Apple store for free advice and *not* walked out having purchased something.

Apple is the king of maximizing value from existing customers in the form of a vertically integrated masterpiece of an ecosystem that empowers consumers by making it simple to buy and simple to use. By creating products that not only do good but *look good*, Apple has also built in a very powerful referral network that lets the product do the talking.

Prime Time

Amazon is another company that truly understands the power of using existing customers to gain new ones in the form of increased frequency.

Free shipping is a practice this retailer has seemingly perfected; however, it did not sit back and wait for the market to duplicate or emulate based on incremental tweaks to the status quo—for example, lowering the threshold for basket size. Instead of scraping the bottom of the barrel, Amazon set its sights on the shipping companies that (very successfully I might add) set up an artificially created expectation that packages simply had to be delivered the very next day for an exorbitant cost. And while Barnes & Noble was experimenting with same-day delivery service— another cost premium for the customer—Amazon introduced Prime. With an annual fee of $79, Prime members enjoy unlimited two-day shipping for any purchase amount. Prime's genius was three-fold:

1. By lowering the minimum purchase, Amazon made it easier to transact as many times as required.

2. In doing so, Amazon gave itself the perfect opportunity—through a combination of big data goodness, personalization, customization, and customer service—to upsell its customer. (*People like you who purchased* X, *also purchased* Y.)

3. An upfront payment of $79 goes straight to Amazon's bank account to earn interest.

Prime has also become a platform through which to deliver a ton of digital content via Amazon's Kindle devices.

Inside-Out Marketing

We all know the data that show how much less it costs to retain an existing customer compared with the costs to acquire a new one. All things being equal, every transaction is not equal, especially if it comes from an existing customer versus a new one. Not only does it cost less, it most likely will yield more in terms of basket size or transaction value. There is no beginner's luck when it comes to converting a prospect into a customer when competing head-to-head with a loyalist or zealot. And yet, here we are neglecting ours in the form of underinvesting in their patronage.

What would you say if I told you that it also costs less to acquire new customers via an existing one compared with acquiring new ones via existing means (read: paid media)? What if I told you it costs one-third the amount you're currently throwing at strangers in the wind? To be perfectly honest, I haven't proven this definitively. It is anecdotal at best and wishful at worst, but in your gut you know this to be true, don't you?

For starters, the weapon of choice in the referral-based sale costs absolutely nothing—zero.

Second, consider the credibility of a referral that comes from a customer—a real customer, even if a customer with an incentive.

Whichever way you slice it, a customer-driven referral contains a healthy mix of authenticity, influence, credibility, and persuasiveness, more so than any equivalent recipe of Kim Kardashian, her cabal of paid celebrity spokespeople—or paid media.

Third, consider the fact that new customers via existing customers are almost never considered cold leads. They are warm to the touch, especially if initiated by the prospective buyer looking for assistance, help, advice, or even inspiration. Pull-based referrals—or supercharged inbound leads—are automatically opt-in ones. They are not based on the incumbent interruptive model. Rather, they are built on an incredibly solid and stable platform of permission-based "requests for proposal"—a need to know basis where prospective customers have the "need" and existing members of a customer-centric ecosystem or community have the "know" or "know how."

How can you possibly hold a candle to this path compared with any legacy system of haste, waste, and sketchy snake oil pitchmen?

> Your employee is your most credible spokesperson. Your customer is your most influential salesperson. Honor these two fact-based statements and you will truly leverage the power of inside-out marketing.

Silent versus Violent

Perhaps the biggest misnomer as it relates to the power of existing customers is that a *loyal* customer is a customer for life. Lifetime value of the customer is about as commonplace as a sighting of the yeti. It's an aspirational high ground that would make some sense if any of us actually cared to the take the high ground, ever. The faux pas doesn't stop there. We ignore our best customers in favor of wooing strangers. You would be surprised how many times I'm told by senior marketers that there's no value in doing anything explicit, overt, or formal to engage the 20 percent of customers responsible for 80 percent of the revenues. Or in more cases than not, that number is way south—maybe 10 percent or 5 percent of a customer base commanding the lion's share of revenue.

"Why should we do anything with these customers? We have their business already. It's not as if they're going to spend *more* with us?"

Maybe not. But if you neglect or upset them, they could go away—quickly—and make it their business to ruin you, literally. Remember the chapter on zealots? There's a fine line between giving someone space and letting them fall into gross neglect. Likewise, there's a fine line between listening and monitoring our customers' conversations and stalking them.

But there's a third perspective worth pointing out here. It draws from the thinking that most customers fall into what's called the silent majority, and it is only the vocal minority that tends to monopolize the share of customer sentiment. Nowadays, I think you could make a very compelling argument that this has been flipped on its head, but perhaps not. A 2013 Pew Research Center study found that "postings on [the] social site Twitter may be a misleading barometer of the opinions of the public at large"—in other words, outrage exists in a bubble or pockets of bubbles.

A 2012 IBM study[1] found that shoppers referred from social networks such as Facebook, LinkedIn, and YouTube generated only 0.34 percent of online sales on Black Friday, a decrease of more than 35 percent from the year before. Twitter literally contributed nothing (0 percent) to the revenue. (As an aside, this once again emphasizes the point and differences between paid media and nonmedia and a media versus asset suite upon which to own and build.)

So let's focus on the silent majority for a moment and recognize *their* influence. Recognize every single impression created when an existing customer is in contact with a prospective customer—be it serendipitously (*"Hey, is that thing any good?"*), prospect-generated (*"Anyone know any good plumbers in the Westport area?"*), or fan-generated (*"I am loving the new American Airlines Boeing 77W business-class seats"* as per Figure 15.1).

Why wouldn't we figure out how to harness, scale, formalize, activate, and/or monetize this? That's rhetorical. We would. We should. We must.

At the end of the 2010 tax season, tax giant Intuit did something incredibly simple and cheap (as in zero cheap): It embedded a Facebook like button into its award-winning and best-selling tax preparation software,

Figure 15.1   The new business-class seats on American Airlines' Boeing 77W

TurboTax. And so when a presumably happy customer had completed his or her taxes and—hopefully—was well on the way to receiving a refund from the government, he or she had the ability to like that experience and thereby share the good news with his or her, on average, 150 friends. More than 100,000 chose to do just that, which translated into 15 million earned media impressions. Of those humans (we sometimes forget who is on the other end of the tin can), 500,000 clicked and 100,000 became new TurboTax consumers. A 1 percent click-through rate, which in and of itself is miraculous, generated 100,000 new customers via existing ones. For pretty much zero money spent, an owned asset innovation focused on customer-centric advocacy activation. Actually, Z.E.R.O. is much more succinct!

Are You Lazy, Stupid? Pick Two.

I recently went on my first cruise with my family. I am now technically known as a *cruiser* (not really sure how I feel about that). We ended up choosing Royal Caribbean's *Liberty of the Seas* and, for purposes of this anecdote, let's give credit to my wife, Sarah, who did a great consultative sell. I wanted to share the news with my kids and get them excited for the vacation ahead. Royal Caribbean's website was horrid in terms of educating or motivating. Very few video and interactive experiences were available, so I turned to YouTube. There I found an equally horrible experience with poorly tagged, poorly produced, and fairly boring videos. Nothing official from the liner as far as I could see. I ended up producing a 3-minute clip using a very cool app called Montaj! (And with full disclosure, I am now an advisor and investor.) This video—in my opinion—obliterated anything created before. I even used Flo-Rider's "Good Feelin'," which is the same track Royal Caribbean uses in its commercials. Take a look for yourself and see if you agree: http://www.youtube.com/watch?v=WDa4JyhIad4.

So was Royal Caribbean listening? I couldn't tell you. If they were and chose to do nothing about it, they're lazy. And if they weren't even aware this was created at all, they're incredibly stupid.

You're welcome!

These situations are really the norm, rather than the exception, although the moments of truth to actually do something about them are somewhat time-sensitive and therefore fleeting. I'm certainly not saying Royal Caribbean should have approached me with an offer to purchase my content, but a simple thank you would have been nice. Perhaps a small discount for my friends, fans, and followers?

Do I need to make the point again? I hope not.

Maarten's Response: Trust me, the flipped funnel idea is huge! It single-handedly challenges one of the biggest marketing staples that has been around forever. The idea to invest more behind existing consumers was probably always a good idea, but in today's always-on marketing economy, it is finally coming into its own.

I would never advocate flipping your current 80 percent acquisition budget to 80 percent retention. But I would advocate a significant shift. More important, however, is the mind shift: Attend to your existing pool of consumers before trying to grow the pool by spending huge amounts of money on opportunities to see, average frequency, gross rating points, or any other spray-and-pray tactics. Did you notice, by the way, how imprecise our old-world measurement terminology is formulated? "Gross" rating points is the worst one. There is a probably reason for that!

CHAPTER

16

Customer Experience Becomes the *Key* Strategic Differentiator

Differentiating Your Brand with Customer Experience

Your product, service, or brand is commoditized. And quite possibly you don't even know it. But it is.

Think about it. What really differentiates you from your competitors? What separates Delta from American (besides bankruptcy protection—past and present, respectively)? What separates Avis from Hertz? What separates Hilton from Marriott? What separates Colgate from Crest?

The sad truth is that we exist between a rock and a hard place, desperately trying to stand out from the crowd or break through the clutter using old, tired blunt objects of yesteryear (paid media and traditional forms of marketing communication).

To be clear, nothing should ever replacing making great products that literally sell themselves through referrals, recommendations, reviews, testimonials, and of course, happy, loyal, returning, and new customers. But what happens when there are too many great products that don't necessarily have enough on the table to clearly separate themselves in the hearts, minds, and pocketbooks of their intended audience?

In a commodity-driven market, there is only one thing that differentiates—and that is price. Whether you're buying wheat, pork bellies, or coal, price is the universal currency that governs the market and the connection between buyers and sellers. While you may not be in the salt or sugar trade, I would argue that you might as well be. And in fact, it's a worthwhile exercise to strategize as if you were competing in a cutthroat industry where perfect information and full-blown transparency create a very narrow transactional operating framework.

Chicken and Customer Service

I began my career working for a fast-food chicken company in South Africa (Figure 16.1). The company commanded a premium price compared with the competition, and as the poor marketing schlub who had

Figure 16.1   Nando's Chickenland: The Taste of Portugal

to face resistant and skeptical franchisees, I had to constantly answer the recurring concern or complaint about the price being too high.

I once performed an exercise with the franchisees where I asked them to put a price on the following:

- How much would you pay for a high-quality product (chicken)?
- How much would you pay for a great-tasting product?
- How much would you pay for consistent delivery of that product every single time (moist versus dry; undercooked versus overdone)?
- How much would you pay for great service (smiling cashier, etc.)?
- How much would you pay to buy into a great brand experience (feel good about associating with a company that is cool, shares your values, is in touch, etc.)?

When I was finished with the exercise, I asked them to add up the amounts and almost all of them without exception came out with a number that greatly exceeded that of the purchase price. "That, my friends, is the expression and perception of value," I said. "Two people can pay the exact same price for the exact same product; one feels like they got the deal of the century, and one feels ripped off." I helped the franchisees understand that although value was in the mind of the beholder, *they* were in control and able to influence almost every single one of the inputs into that equation.

To be sure, it's tough to get your mind around an intangible and often ephemeral ingredient in a potentially potent and game-changing recipe of leadership, differentiation, and success through customer experience. But it is possible. And it is mission critical.

Or take the entire trend of *showrooming* and how people are walking into brick-and-mortar stores like Best Buy to research merchandise and then using their Amazon.com PriceCheck app to compare prices and, in some cases, order the item online right there and then. Try as we might to mystify the act of purchasing consumer electronics with a variety of add-ons, confusing features that require explanation, necessaries (necessary accessories), and the like, at the end of the day it is either Walmart or Amazon that wins.

Unless of course you're Apple, which—although feeling the effects of increased confidence and competition from its competitors like Samsung in the form of disappointing quarterly earnings announced on January

23, 2013—still continues to command a premium price for an otherwise dumbed-down product.

Yes, competitors are looking to steal Apple's lunch with cheaper imitations, and combined with the chaotic effects of Moore's law and accelerated product development cycles, they have overtaken as measured in market share. But without Apple's service and experiential leadership, this would no doubt be happening at an exponentially accelerated rate.

Price is a necessary evil that rules supreme in a commoditized world, but it can be overthrown in a differentiated world.

Branding and Brand Building No Longer Differentiate

The central premise here is very simple: People will pay a premium for brands that matter. From Tiffany to Nike, from Audi to Starbucks, from Ritz-Carlton to Howard Stern. Premium pricing is less about luxury brands, although it is easy to associate price and quality together. Or price and consistent delivery of a superior experience. Or price and the expectation of something that is less about a feature and more about a feeling.

But this is where things get muddled up. The model used to be a one-trick pony that pivoted around using advertising to build up and create something larger than life. This is no longer the case.

Outliers of the four Ps (product, pricing, place, and promotion) seem to stand out only as anomalies nowadays; they are exceptions to the norm of mediocrity and status quo. From Tesla (product) to TOMS Shoes (pricing), from the infrastructure of the efficient matchmaker between limousines/cabs and consumers Uber (place), to Red Bull's content-driven blitz (promotion).

Standing out from the crowd these days results from acts of contraction or contrition, such as Amazon *cutting* television ads in order to promote free shipping and service to customers.

Creating a separation between product (what it does, what we buy) and brand (how it makes us feel, why we buy) is not enough anymore to create sustainable and monetizable distance. Moreover, the tools in our arsenal are no longer effective to accomplish this.

On my weekly jog around Fairfield County, I was listening to the BeanCast Marketing Podcast,[1] in which host Bob Knorpp spoke about a brand's messaging being a *reflection* of what former Forrester analyst and current director of social media at Prudential, Augie Ray, referred to as a brand's experience—namely, the intersection with the brand's people, product, and service. I decided to build on Knorpp's metaphor of a reflection (quite literally) to reinforce the fact that brands and branding are nothing more than just that, a reflection. They are in no way real. Brands were always meant to be nothing more than a proxy or symbol for a sum total of profound and meaningful indicators of real value.

Let's not forget that.

At Evol8tion, we created a methodology called P.B.E.C., which stands for product, brand, experience (the current chapter), and community (see Chapter 19 on ecosystems) as a four-phased approach to an evolved marketing model. We argue that functional or emotional benefit is not enough; a company needs to be able to implement and offer experiential and communal (community) layers as well. The Nike example that will be discussed later brings this idea to life.

The good news is that there is a solution, and a very viable and actionable one. It is the combination of listening, formalizing advocacy, and customer service 2.0^2 into a pragmatic and implementable customer-experience-led action plan as a front-office, dynamic, proactive, strategic, and game-changing corporate imperative.

Who Owns the Customer?

Before expanding on the service and experience component, perhaps it is worthwhile to analyze the customer part of the compound phrase.

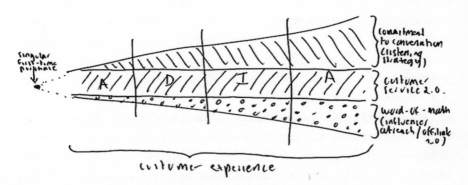

Figure 16.2   Dissecting customer experience using the flipped funnel as context

It would appear that too many people are still enamored with the bright and shiny object that is social media and the lion's portion of mindshare and budget in this category is heaped into the Facebook bucket. Tactics in search of strategy don't exactly provide the kind of competitive advantage or strategic differentiation alluded to earlier. In fact, brands seem to be locked in a juvenile battle of who can acquire the most likes, fans, or followers. One of the early adopters in this category, Starbucks, did this quite literally by buying likes in the form of offering free pastries. Personally, I have no problem giving such items away to loyal customers, but we all know that this wasn't exactly a retention-based initiative at all.

At the same time, there has been an organizational land grab for the social media category. Public relations (PR) enjoyed first-mover advantage (and arguably still does), although other departments such as human resources, marketing, and, of course, customer service, have equally laid claim to this space. On the vendor side, advertising agencies, digital agencies, PR shops, and a handful of social media specialists have thrown their hats into the arena in order to service the space—and more recently, an entirely new cluster of companies in the quickly mainstreaming SaaS (software as a service) genre. Salesforce.com, Adobe, Oracle, Eloqua, and ExactTarget (a client) are just a few.

With this competitive scrimmage in play, the debate rages on as to who owns social media, but perhaps the ultimate question should be, "Who owns the customer?"

If it's true that marketing is everything (at least according to Regis McKenna) and that "everything communicates" (Sergio Zyman at Coca-Cola in 2001), then isn't it equally true that customer service and customer experience are everything? Whereas the former states that anything that touches a *consumer* directly or indirectly should be the property of the chief marketing officer (CMO), then the latter would hold that anything that touches the customer directly or indirectly should be the property or domain of the chief customer officer or chief experience officer.

Of course there is another scenario, namely, that the chief customer officer does not exist, because all customer service reports to the marketing department. Perhaps, but I'd like to believe that the corollary is probably more likely to occur, namely, that all marketing ladders up to the customer experience group. This probably will not happen in our immediate future, but that doesn't mean that it's not correct and shouldn't happen.

I recently met a former CMO of a Fortune 500 company for a coffee in the high-end Italian food market/mall chain Eataly in Manhattan. We found refuge from frigid winter weather at one of the many standing tables and proceeded to have coffee, followed by cheese and wine. A crabby waiter approached us as we were mid-sip and not so subtly offered to escort us to a table out of his section. Apparently, we weren't part of his personal gratuity inner sanctum. I explained to him that this was my first time in Eataly and my first impression wasn't exactly encouraging me to come back any time soon. He didn't really care. He was no Ritz-Carlton team member, empowered to be able to spend independently on a guest in need. He had no vested interest in the overall health and wellness of the very company keeping him in business. After he grudgingly left us, I brainstormed some new-age solutions such as being able to just pay him the equivalent of his gratuity in order for him to leave us in peace for an extra 10 to 15 minutes.

At the end of the day, if too many *people like me* don't return to Eataly, neither will he.

Everything Communicates, Everyone Communicates

Just like the sum total of all touch points with a brand form the overall perception of that company, so too is the case with the sum total of all encounters, transactions, or interactions with that company's people.

Suddenly Eataly got a lot more expensive.

First Impressions

You don't get a second chance to make a good first impression, but you certainly do get a second chance to make a good second impression.

In 2009, I celebrated my 10-year anniversary being an American Express customer.

I celebrated alone.

How do I know it was a milestone anniversary? From my card, of course. It plainly states that I am a cardmember since 1999. Sadly, I must have missed my fruit basket or Blue Mountain e-greeting card. Perhaps it got lost in the vortex of "an opportunity lost is an opportunity cost."

Ironically, Jim Bush, executive vice president of world service at American Express, said something as profound as, "This is a people business powered by technology," and yet the financial service giant gets tripped up in the simple act of giving thanks.

No doubt implementing is much tougher than articulating, but it's a lot better than the alternatives. Amex announced in January 2013 that it is laying off 8.5 percent of its workforce. Coincidence? Unfair comparison perhaps, but a cheap fruit basket can speak so much louder than the number crunching of annual percentage rate revisions.

Contrast this with the Four Seasons in Atlanta. I visited the hotel some time ago on business. When I checked in, I was greeted with a "Welcome back, Mr. Jaffe," even though I hadn't been there in about a year. When I got to my room, I was welcomed with a beautiful dessert tray (I still remember the chocolate-covered strawberries) and a hand-written card stating it was my tenth visit there and the hotel manager appreciated my business.

Where do you think I'll go to next time I'm in Atlanta?

Price Transparency with an Experience Twist

In 2012 at South by Southwest the interactive festival in Austin, Texas, I visited a pop-up store for Nike, which was built around the launch of their new FuelBand. I waited in line for about 30 minutes to enter the store. Eventually a personal shopper (let's call him Lance) met me and walked me into the store. He measured my hand to determine the right size, adjusted the band accordingly, set me up on Wi-Fi in order to download the Nike FuelBand app, helped me set up a profile on the in-store screens, and then checked me out directly from his handheld station with my credit card. Bright lights flashed, a disk jockey spun some tracks, and the store felt like an endless rave party. I thanked Lance and walked out of the store with the FuelBand attached to my arm (like a convict, so to speak). Only once I had taken 100 steps (according to my band) did I realize that I hadn't even checked the price. Didn't even think about it. Had no clue what it was. Didn't care.

That Is Customer Experience at Its Finest

And now back to Starbucks—the place that charges you more than $4 for a hot cup of water flavored by freeze-dried beans and served up by a barista (imported from Brooklyn). When it comes to customer experience,

Starbucks is somewhat bipolar. And this identity crisis almost definitely comes from multiple departments within the corporation that may not always cooperate, collaborate, communicate, and, most important, share the same compensation schemes and incentive structures. Starbucks used to be the place where you could come and hang out, conduct a job interview, or let someone go; it was an oasis for students, freelancers, and the creative class. It even began to offer free Wi-Fi for those with Starbucks cards, a brilliant idea from an advocacy standpoint.

And then something happened. Some Starbucks stores gave with one hand (offered free Wi-Fi to all) and then took away with the other (covered all the power outlets). It made no sense: Incentivize the stranger or casual visitor and, in doing so, punish the loyal advocate customer. The message sent out was a confusing and disenfranchising one: *We don't trust you to do the right thing.* We don't believe that the more time you spend in our stores, the more you'll spend. And either way, we'd rather turn over our tables and keep the turnstiles moving (understandable, but shortsighted).

Enter Tsiferblat (or Clockface Café, in English). Started in Moscow, Clockface Café turns the Starbucks model on its head. At Clockface, you pay for time and coffee but Danish are free. In many respects, it's a shared workspace, but on another level it's dialing into the real insight as to why Starbucks grew the way it did; it was *not* because of triple grande no-foam soy lattes, but in fact because of the Starbucks *experience*. That is what differentiated Howard Schultz's concern, and if his bean counters continue to cut costs by limiting the time someone spends in its stores based on that person's laptop's battery life, they may be cutting off the very lifeblood of the business.

A final example comes from AT&T (and it has a happy ending). AT&T was never known for its customer service; if anything it was known for its lousy customer service. Its customers were reluctant ones, trapped into a contract or a legacy relationship based on the inability to change one's cellphone number. And then legislation was handed down that allowed people to keep their numbers but change their provider. Probably—and arguably—it was also the catalyst that contributed to a reinvention and cultural commitment toward customer service. Today, AT&T stores resemble Apple stores (big stretch but the first step is the hardest), with employees walking around with iPads and checking out customers on the floor.

AT&T customer service agents on the phone are now more like hotel concierges or consultative specialists than salespeople. If you're disconnected (which sadly happens a lot on AT&T phones), they'll just call you right back. I recently called AT&T and an agent helped migrate me to the new mobile sharing plan that ended up saving me almost 50 percent of my bill. Afterward, I was asked to take a survey, which I agreed to. The first question was this:

How likely are you to recommend AT&T to a friend on a scale of 0 to 10?

Sound familiar?

Of course, *I* know this was net promoter score (NPS). And it's not the first time this has happened, which is why in the past I knew exactly what I was doing when I gave them a 7, or perhaps it was a 6. I suspect more and more consumers will do the same over time, namely, understanding their clout (or Klout) as it relates to the impact of a negative review, critical testimonial, ambivalent point of view, or noncommittal referral, if not hacking the NPS application programming interface (API) altogether.

As it turns out, I gave AT&T a 10. They earned it, and they fully deserved it.

It also turns out that I've since told a bunch of people about this positive experience and how much *they* can save on this mobile sharing plan, which—although Machiavellian-like in its construction in order to gently nudge me to give up my grandfathered unlimited data plan—made total sense.

Connecting the Dots

A 2012 joint study by Forrester Research and Heidrick & Struggles highlights that only 14 percent of organizations have the same unified and integrated view of the customer (Figure 16.3). Which bucket do you think American Express fits into? How about Nike? And what about AT&T?

Customer Experience Is the Difference between Good and Great

As choice becomes more complex and confusing, as the marketplace continues to fragment and clutter, and as consumers become more discerning,

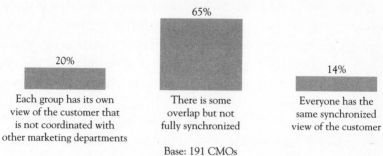

"How would you describe customer-facing employees' view of the customer?"

65%

20%

14%

Each group has its own
view of the customer that
is not coordinated with
other marketing departments

There is some
overlap but not
fully synchronized

Everyone has the
same synchronized
view of the customer

Base: 191 CMOs
(percentages do not total 100 because of rounding)

Source: Q3 2011 Forrester/Heidrick & Struggles Global Evolved CMO Online Survey
Source: Forrester Research, Inc.

Figure 16.3   Who owns the customer?

critical, and empowered through knowledge, the wisdom of crowds and self-service, there is only one thing that will separate the wheat from the chaff: customer experience.

I believe that customer experience will become *the* key strategic differentiator and in doing so, will become a top three (if not the top) imperative from the office of the chairman down to the line worker. It's both exceptionally simple and frustratingly complex as it involves a perfect balance between common sense (the easy part) and cultural transformation (the damn near impossible part), but it is doable and it is mission critical.

How critical? Consider that a whopping $83 billion is lost each year in the United States thanks to poor customer experiences, according to a 2013 IBM report.

So regardless of the side from which you approach this, the *why* should be painfully or blissfully obvious. The good news is that the *what* and *how* are both possible via advocacy programs, ambassador, or prosumer Initiatives, voice of the customer, customer service 2.0, listening strategies, crowdsourced feedback mechanisms, and many more ripe and ready processes, designed to *flip the funnel* and turn retention into the new acquisition.

Maarten's Response: We have always assumed that simple things like a smile matter. Now, at least for the airline industry, we *know* how much it matters. I have no reason to believe it matters any less for any other business where consumers meet your product through intermediaries such as retail personnel, tellers, mechanics, technicians, and so on, every day.

I own a Mophie battery pack for my iPhone. They are lifesavers, doubling the battery life of my iPhone. One day, my Mophie broke: The charger plug would simply not go in anymore. I was ready to go and replace it and rather flippantly put a photo on Facebook of my broken Mophie and a piggy bank (we have dozens of them as my wife Valerie collects them on our world travels). I did not link or hashtag Mophie in any way.

A few hours later, out of the blue and lucky-for-me before I went to the store to replace my Mophie, I was tweeted by Mophie's service desk. They told me that if the device was less than a year old, my Mophie was still under warranty. A few direct tweets later and I had everything I needed to send the broken Mophie back and receive a brand-new one.

So here is why this whole experience is awesome. First, Mophie is clearly proactively listening, and learned of my dead Mophie without me reaching out to them. Second, the company problem solves in real time. Third, Mophie solved my problem, even when I wasn't even asking for help—I merely shared my dependence on my Mophie and my need to replace it. And finally, none of this could have happened in a world without social media.

Obviously, before social media, I could have probably called an 800 number or sent a letter. Weeks if not months would have passed. But now, in the span of three days and a feeling of constant direct contact and care, a problem was solved, but even more important, a brand reputation has been solidified beyond simple brand appreciation.

Ask yourself whether your brand or company could pull this off. Do you have the listening, the customer support, the staff training, and the logistics in place to proactively problem solve within a short period of time? And while doing so make brand friends for life?

I already loved my Mophie, the device. I now love Mophie, the company. And I am telling you about it. That is powerful stuff!

CHAPTER
17

The Innovation Imperative

T
he world has changed more in the past 24 months than in the 24 years before it." Those words (or something to that effect) were said by one of Madison Avenue's media visionaries, David Verklin. Verklin once ran Carat, a rather large media agency. He left to head up an interactive TV startup called Canoe Ventures, which was well funded, well backed by top-tier corporations like Comcast and executives like Comcast chairman Brian Roberts, well advised (I had the pleasure of being the guest speaker at an advisory meeting containing some of our industry's rock stars, such as global chief marketing officer [CMO] for General Electric, Beth Comstock, the Coca-Cola Company's Wendy Clark, and the Association of National Advertisers' Bob Liodice, to name drop a few) and ultimately, ill fated. Canoe capsized and sank and Verklin joined Iron Mike Tyson in Bolivia. (It has since resurfaced as a lean, mean mini-me version of its former self.) Smacks of the story of the scorpion and the frog, doesn't it? We're in 2013 and still can't or won't get behind a broad-based initiative to help save paid media through the power of digital.

Since those "24 months" that Verklin referred to, I feel like our space has been reinvented several times over. Actually I know it has. This quote comes from circa 2007, when the iPhone, YouTube, Facebook, and Twitter were nothing but germs of ideas and/or new products.

Innovate or Die

The original promise of digital was to level the playing fields. Make the big look and act small (IBM) and the small think and act big (Blend Tec). Some figured it out. Most did not. Most attempted to replicate the tired old business models of reach-infected paid media instead of truly disrupting the status quo, creating transformational change, and ultimately creating sustainable competitive advantage that comes from big, hairy, audacious goals; bold thinking; and brave risk taking.

Pfffttt. That's the sound of the wind deflating from our sails as we look back on our absolutely pathetic track record. Score round 1 to the challenger—10–9. The second act or round came in the form of social media, where the power seemed to shift from predigital (corporate dominance) to postdigital (consumer dominance). Once again, we failed to capitalize on the opportunity at hand, namely, meet our consumers halfway on a *level playing field* and listen as intently and intensely as we talk. Score round 2: 10–8 to the challenger (with a standing count after an unfortunate speed wobble due to poor handling of a public consumer issue). Round 3 is mobile's turn to change the rules once again. Only this time, it's not about a power shift but rather a complete power overhaul. Content served up in bite- and byte-sized appetizer portions (sorry, couldn't resist; won't happen again). Real-time immediacy from real locations. Remember the idea of right consumer, right place, and right time? Check. Check. Check. Only it's the wrong message, assuming that we even have the opportunity at all. Round 3 goes to the challenger, 10–8. This time a knockdown in the form of inactivity or anemic attempts (43 percent of users reported being disappointed with branded apps). Which brings us to the final round (at least in this painful extended metaphor) representing emerging media, or what I call the known next big thing. From virtual currency to virtual worlds, makers to 3D printing, and wearable tech to augmented reality, we are standing on a vertiginous precipice that could bring game-changing results for our businesses and brands—or put us out of business. Is it the KO or throwing in the towel that finally seals our fates?

In a 2012 study by Forrester Research and Heidrick & Struggles and as depicted in Figure 17.1, the number one skill that CMOs indicated they need to improve was "technology savviness."

My friends, you'll need to be a lot more savvy if you want to realize Gartner's prediction that *by 2017 the CMO will spend more on IT than the*

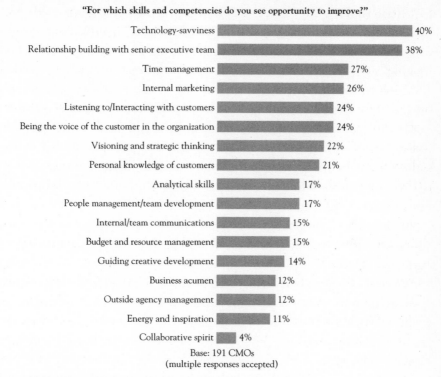

"For which skills and competencies do you see opportunity to improve?"

Technology-savviness	40%
Relationship building with senior executive team	38%
Time management	27%
Internal marketing	26%
Listening to/Interacting with customers	24%
Being the voice of the customer in the organization	24%
Visioning and strategic thinking	22%
Personal knowledge of customers	21%
Analytical skills	17%
People management/team development	17%
Internal/team communications	15%
Budget and resource management	15%
Guiding creative development	14%
Business acumen	12%
Outside agency management	12%
Energy and inspiration	11%
Collaborative spirit	4%

Base: 191 CMOs
(multiple responses accepted)

Source: Q3 2011 Forrester/Heidrick & Struggles Global Evolved CMO Online Survey.
Source: Forrester Research, Inc.

Figure 17.1   Technology savviness leads marketer skills wishlist

chief information officer (CIO), which is not to say it won't happen; it's just that it will be someone else sitting in your corner office making it happen, if you get my drift.

The Next Big Thing or the Next Big Thing for *You*?

The following is an article I wrote[1] to make the innovation imperative appear a little more grounded and pragmatic. Changing the game is fantastic, but change that happens too quickly can be as damaging as change that takes too long to materialize. This book is certainly designed to be a dagger through the heart of lethargy and incumbency, but radical and extreme moves can be equally harmful—especially when not tied to core business principles, practices, and indicators.

"What is more interactive: a coloring-in sheet on a McDonald's tray table or a Web banner?" That was the (rhetorical) question a planner I used to work with once posed and it really stuck with me, especially when looking at the utterly dismal portfolio of online creativity back in the day.

I took that statement and riffed it when giving keynote presentations on life after the 30-second spot with the following points: You can be nontraditional with traditional media, and you can most certainly be traditional with nontraditional media. In this case, nontraditional in the former would be synonymous with bold, creative, original, unique, disruptive, or innovative, while traditional would be akin to boring, predictable, uninspiring, bland, and mediocre.

As an aside: If you could only pick one of the categories to describe your digital investment, which would most accurately represent your story and body of work?

When it comes to partnering with startups, big brands really have two choices: limp in with incremental tweaks or tests designed to emulate or replicate traditional paid media campaigns, or attempt to test a hypothesis designed around something unprecedented for the brand, company, or even industry.

Clearly, there's a little bias in my phraseology, but before I expand on the fork in the road, I think it's important to distinguish between absolute and relative innovation. We're all too familiar with the bright and shiny object syndrome and for some reason, we'll turn our backs on something that could be extremely meaningful only because it's not the next big thing as defined by a social media expert, ad trade, or conference.

In other words, a platform or sector that's old-hat to a fickle and faddish industry could be new and potentially disruptive to you. This category probably covers yesterday's news such as blogs, podcasts, or even virtual worlds. In some cases, it could even include e-mail or search marketing. This is your opportunity to apply nontraditional rigor to traditional platforms.

On the flipside, when it comes to emerging platforms, apps, or startups that are bringing exciting new business models or revenue streams to the table, challenge yourselves to bring the same level of risk, exponential thinking, and nontraditional ideas to the table. For example, if you were Ford and you were partnering with Uber, instead of sponsoring the app or buying an iAd, why not plug your new Ford Fiestas into the ecosystem and provide subsidized rides to users, Air bnb style!

A hypothesis is typically attached to an experiment and the ability to prove or refute it represents two sides of the same coin of success. Perhaps the proof positive is a Win with a capital W, whereas the refuting of the hypothesis (aka failure) is actually positioned (and rightly so) as a win with a lowercase w.

In my book *Join the Conversation*, I wrote, "Marketing is not a campaign; it's a commitment." I believe we can use this same philosophy when evaluating partnering with startups. Are we in it for the long haul, or just to mark another tactic off our short-term checklist? Are we experimenting or testing? Are we managing risk or mitigating it? Are we winning to fail or failing to win?

Provided our motives or motivations are prioritized appropriately, either absolute (doing something that has never been done before—by anyone—and by definition, attached to a hypothesis that has a 50/50 chance of working) or relative (less grand, but equally potent insofar that "new to the brand" or "new to its customer base" brings another set of benefits and upside) innovation may hold the key to your brand's evolution.

Innovation Continuum

In many respects, I'm talking out both sides of my mouth. I'm telling you that you need to innovate or die. And I'm also telling you to stop worrying about the next big thing, because the next big thing is now.

Case in point is the innovation continuum that I created for my company, Evol8tion, to use as part of our training materials, but also as a means to conduct a pretty illuminating workshop and self-assessment exercise designed to produce an innovation score and with it, a benchmarking journey with specific and measured milestones and deliverables.

Ask yourself these questions as they relate to the innovation continuum in Figure 17.2:

1. How do you stack up and score across the individual categories—digital, social, mobile, and emerging?
2. Are you spending enough? Are you getting enough (results)? Are you doing enough (innovation)?

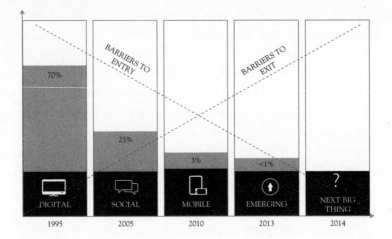

Figure 17.2   Innovation continuum

3. How does this continuum score compare to your consumers'? Your competitors'? The industry at large's?

4. Have you attempted to connect the dots to create some kind of strategic vision, architecture, framework, and foundation?

5. Have you accurately assessed the existing and potential barriers to entry and exit that come from first-mover advantage, deep engagement, real-time optimization, and, ultimately, staying the course (long-term commitment)?

If the answer is no to any of these questions, why? Why are you sitting around waiting for someone else inside your organization, or worse outside of your organization, to do it instead of you? A startup? A competitor? A startup that becomes a competitor? A startup that ends up being acquired by a competitor?

Are you hoping that you can wait it out? Are you hoping it will go away?

The ability to think holistically about innovation has the effect of insulating you from the fads that come and go, while at the same time keeping the residual goodness.

Fads = Jaiku, Pownce (Twitter)

Residual goodness = real-time customer service

When it comes to collaborating with startups, for example, doesn't it make more sense to frame the search for the perfect startup partner as a creative or experimentation or business brief as opposed to "we need to do something in mobile" or "here's a cool startup we should work with"? Instead of positioning startups as the next big thing, isn't it more accurate to recognize that startups are yesterday, today, and tomorrow? (ESPN and CNN were startups once.) Are they digital, social, mobile, and/or emerging? They're technology embodiments of entrepreneurial flair and a deep-seated passion to disrupt the status quo, reinvent a business, solve a problem, correct an inefficiency, and/or transform a market.

The Stakes Have Never Been Higher: Natural Selection and the Evolution of the Marketing Species

We spend so much of our energy splitting decimal points on short-term metrics associated with short-lived, paid media campaigns, instead of looking at the bigger picture. And surely the biggest picture of all is stayin' alive?

If you're a brick-and-mortar retailer, that's the table stakes right now. It's complete reinvention to avoid extinction. As mentioned earlier, there are some makers out there showing glimmers of hope, such as Audi. That said, this is not a short-term fix. I don't know whether it would constitute collusion, but I wonder whether every single retailer should consider joining forces to come out with a "crowd-wisdom" solution to the economics associated with real estate, distribution, shipping, and, yes, paid media accountability. Or perhaps a single retailer will take the initiative by the horns and outinnovate everyone else. Perhaps, but it won't be JC Penney.[2]

In April 2013, JC Penney—or JCP, as the company is now affectionately known—ousted chief executive officer (CEO) Ron Johnson after just 17 months on the job. Yes, *the* Ron Johnson. No, not Ron Jeremy. Ron Johnson—The Dude! The guy they hired from Apple; the guy responsible for Apple retail stores and the Genius Bar.

It turns out that not even Johnson could turn around a failing ship in the form of JC Penney. Although some argue that it was *because* of Johnson that sales continued to plummet, consumers continued to migrate to competitors and the stock price continued to fall. Or if not, certainly these downward trends were at the very least accelerated or exacerbated by Johnson's tactics, such as:

- Eliminating the coupons and discounts that were once "ignored by 99 percent of everyone" in favor of everyday lower prices. JCP ran 590 promotions in 2011, and the idea was to reduce these to just 12 (coincidentally the same number of months in a year).
- Replacing long-time agency Saatchi & Saatchi (the original purveyors of the brand as a lovemark).
- Introducing the new logo, which fit somewhere on the Tropicana-to-Gap continuum of "huh?"
- Arguing with Martha Stewart (she is an ex-con, after all).

The numbers don't lie:

- Same-store sales were down a whopping and record-breaking 32 percent in the fourth quarter of 2012.
- As of February 2013, JCP's stock price was down 46 percent on the year.
- As of April 2013, it hit $14.50, down from the $42.68 when Johnson took over.

How did this happen? After all, Johnson was the Apple guy. And before Apple, he worked at Target. And during his reign, he hired Michael Francis, the CMO of Target credited with the tremendous success story that is Targé, or Cheap Chic.

On TheStreet.com, Rocco Pendola made the comparison between Johnson and former Yahoo! CEO and current pathological liar Scott Thompson in terms of misrepresenting credentials. Or, to quote George Costanza, "It's not a lie . . . if you believe it." Pendola was referring to Johnson's taking credit for the Apple retail miracle, when allegedly it was the outcome of Steve Jobs's pixie dust transfer. In other words, Johnson was just executing Jobs's vision and strategy.

To be quite honest, I'm deeply conflicted. I'm not really sure how to interpret Johnson's departure, but one thing I know is that it isn't good—for anyone. It certainly feels reassuring to be able to pinpoint one single justification for the horror show—for example, the major pricing shift—but the reality was a combination of both internal and external factors that, truthfully, are endemic to the entire brick-and-mortar retail space and experience, as much as they are "inside" one particular brand.

And change takes time, damn it. Probably longer than 17 months, but certainly not when hung out to dry with gruesome numbers. This wasn't a colonic as much as it was a hemorrhage.

The real mismatch here was a cultural disconnect, which put the iconic brand into a tailspin, where they just couldn't seem to do a thing right. Case in point, go and do a Google search for Hitler and JC Penney!

It's disappointing that JCP has since regressed to hiring back its ex-and-now current CEO and reverted to its old pricing strategy of discounts, discounts, and discounts (in that order.)

Risk Is Relative

We're all familiar with the great Bill Bernbach quotation that safe advertising is the riskiest advertising of all. It's a classic and timeless saying, but it's also fairly irrelevant in today's dynamic, turbulent, disruptive, and ever-changing times.

Bernbach knew all the way back when advertising was largely unchallenged in terms of its efficacy that to be different, one had to mix it up and challenge the status quo.

A similar prophet was management guru Peter Drucker, who said "to defend the past is far riskier than creating the future." He might as well have been talking about advertising itself (good, bad, or ugly). He might also have been talking about technology-led innovation, embracing startup collaboration, or investing in digital, social, mobile, and/or emerging platforms.

Drucker also said, "How do you predict the future? You create it." It seems to me that the road map to survival is very clearly laid out in Bernbach's and Drucker's blueprint.

Safety is an illusion.

Status quo is the enemy.

Your fate is in your hands.

Risk is relative.

As I was recently reminded that risk itself is measured in financial terms and specifically monetary loss. So how is it possible that we can attempt to put a financial cost on something we've never done before, that has no precedent, and could very well produce the exact opposite effect—namely, a disproportionate, positive business impact.

Risk is often confused with fear (hat tip to David Spark)—fear of the unknown, fear of change, fear of uncertainty, fear of failure.

Although there are no guarantees for success, isn't it also true that the greatest risk is the one not taken?

Why is getting a brand to do a small calculated test or experiment like pulling teeth? Where is the measured financial risk? (It doesn't exist.) Where is the known probability of failure? (There is none.) Or more specifically, where is the extreme and unwavering belief that the only viable outcome is success? (There is none.)

Isn't it time we started creating the future, where the only risk is the one associated with the opportunity (financial) cost of defending the past?

#FailFail[3]

Perhaps such fears stem from our inability to embrace the concept of failing.

A lot has been said about the need to embrace failure as a natural and healthy part of business life (and personal life). In the world of David (startups) and Goliath (corporations), there's no question who has the edge in terms of adopting and integrating failure into operations.

Fail fast has become part of the startup vernacular, thanks to Lean Startup and the Lean Startup Machine philosophy, which revolves around the ability to continuously, quickly, and cheaply pivot in order to exponentially evolve. Good, fast, cheap—why not pick all three? In truth, this shouldn't be a shock to sluggish corporations, who have long practiced the dark arts of direct marketing or at the very minimum, "Test, learn, evolve."

How is it that startups can take risks, pivot, fail, and still find success? Why can't brands do the same? Where's the disconnect?

In this day and age, where millennials are growing up with the concept of failure being about as foreign as the U.S. Congress actually agreeing on anything, there is an epidemic of sorts when it comes to establishing practices that encourage people to take calculated bets or educated gambles—put simply, be risk takers.

Innovation is one of the most overused terms and misunderstood areas of interest right now, but it's all very superficial and anemic in terms of investment, commitment, and prioritization. Within corporations, small blips of hope are present in the form of people with the word *innovation* in their titles, but they are few and far between. They are reincarnations of digital evangelist, social evangelist, or mobile evangelist. They are cheerleaders without portfolios, overdosing on enthusiasm but flatlining on influence.

The money still sits at the brand level, stewarded by frogs slowly boiling to death in their own lethargy, fear of change, and refusal to embrace failure (of course, you are the exception).

So why not set up a risk budget? Or an innovation budget? Or even a failure budget?

As I once heard from Google's former chief of innovation Alberto Savoia, while there's no point in rewarding widespread failure, there's equally no point in punishing it.

Don't get me wrong. I'm not saying you should disregard the importance of being accountable to tangible, measurable, and valuable results. Return on investment (ROI) is still the absolute cornerstone of great marketing. For every $1 spent, at least $1.10 should be earned in exchange.

That said, what is the ROI on survival? How do you put a price tag on evolution? Survival of the fittest? Competitive differentiation?

"Fail Fast, but Succeed Faster" was the title of an October 2012 article in *Forbes*. It should be our corporate marketing mantra in 2013 (and beyond).

Tackle a new year, with new challenges, complexities, and disruptive technology-infused trends. It's time to get off our butts and make something happen. It's time we recognize that failure is an inevitable part of the success formula in an incredibly dynamic and unpredictable business climate.

Fail Fast or Fail Smart?[4]

In the world of startups, everything is about failing fast. It's a price of entry, a badge of honor—even a cultural imperative—inspired by the entire Lean Startup movement.

The practice of being able to conduct quick, cheap, and relatively painless tests, experiments, or research exercises in order to gain invaluable insights, feedback, solutions to hypotheses, and the like, becomes vital in order to rethink, close the loop, and ultimately pivot or change course based on integrating the new lessons into the model.

Perhaps it isn't fair to expect companies to have to emulate startups in their speed to market. Learn from them—sure. Triangulate and triage based on the behavior of fast-growing small business—why not? But having to shock the system in order to be something they're not is an identity crisis at best and a psychotic break at worst.

I'm not suggesting that we should walk away entirely from the very worthy and important process of speeding up business optimization, especially in a world where consumers are moving at the speed of change. However, it might be better to take a slightly different path in order to end up with the same, if not better, outcome.

Instead of failing fast, why not fail smart? Instead of speed to market, why not focus on speed to learnings: invaluable life lessons about how to move more nimbly in this fast-changing and volatile business environment.

To get there, we need prior agreement on outcomes and the management of expectation of all parties involved and their connected constituencies (read: investors and bosses of startups and brands, respectively).

Failure is really only failure when it becomes an absolute. Along the same lines, smart failure is what I would call good mistakes—the ones you make fast and cheap and are able to pivot from for use in future programs. (Note: The assumption is that you will go back and do it again.)

These mistakes are also the ones you make before your competitors, and the ones that your competitors will be making when you are long gone and miles ahead.

Or as I told a room filled with senior marketers, "The best way to keep innovating . . . is to keep innovating!"

Hey, Fatso, Time to Lose Some Weight

The preceding anecdotes all speak to the idea of a lean brand. With homage to Eric Ries and his Lean Startup cult (we put the cult in culture), we can take a leaf out of the very bottom of the bottom-up economy in order to reinvent our bloated top-down corporate selves.

We may never succeed in the lofty goal of turning our organization into a lean startup, although Intuit cofounder Scott Cook considers his company as both a 30-year-old startup and, these days, a series of lean startups within a larger organization. But what about converting our brand to a lean brand—a brand that lives in the age of improve; that adapts, pivots, course corrects, and iterates; that thinks and acts in real time; and that fails fast *and* fails smart?

A lean brand has the ability to present layers of context and organizes itself based on principles of diversity and inclusiveness. A lean brand finds balance and equilibrium between paid and nonmedia, between production and human budgets, and between technology and talent. Is Starbucks not somewhat of a lean brand when it optimizes its financial resources into loyalty programs, crowdsourced intelligence, and closed-loop marketing via "My Starbucks Idea"? Is Oreo shedding unwanted pounds (sterling) by trading in its own efficient (as in zero cost) content?

Lean brands have solid muscle and minimal fat. Whereas muscle represents substance, fat symbolizes waste. Another metaphor? Not so much. This is about acknowledging the cultural commitment to entrepreneurship and with it the entire suite of beliefs and tenets (fail fast, fail smart, etc.). It's a purpose-driven existence that has tangible and measurable impact on the bottom line (zero impact, if you will) without becoming completely wishy-washy by waxing lyrical about the importance of ideas, the power of storytelling, or standing for something (without actually naming anything or following through).

A lean brand delivers—and even overdelivers—against the innovation continuum. Spending enough. Doing enough. Getting enough. However, the lean brand balances the technology commitment with talent—fostering an intrapreneurial spirit and formalizing a solid two-way partnership with entrepreneurs, hackers, developers, designers, makers, engineers, and investors.

Making it Happen

This is an action plan after all. Whether you are Mondelēz International with their Mobile Futures Program, PepsiCo with their PepsiCo10 initiative, or even Domino's Pizza, who quite bizarrely introduced Pizzavestments in August of 2013 (see Figure 17.3), where they offered up to 30 startups $500 gift cards to "fund" their startups (or at least subsidize their all-nighter comfort food cravings), doing something is the imperative here. Something always trumps nothing. Especially in a world where lemons (failing) are a natural and necessary step in the path towards lemonade

Figure 17.3   Domino's Pizzavestment

(think: Instagram for Kodak). I actually challenged Domino's CEO, Patrick Doyle, to sit down and meet with me and offered to match his entire company's investment ($15,000) from my own personal funds. I'm still waiting for his call. . . .

At Evol8tion, we define this engagement continuum as containing three scenarios: acceleration (help evolve and advise the startups), pilot programs (proof of concept), and/or investment (or even acquisition). We invite you to check out www.startupsforbrands.com for inspiration and guidelines in terms of getting started in the innovation category.

Taking Stock

Your innovation homework is to find the right balance between the next big thing now, the next big thing for *you*, and the unknown next big thing. Simply put, (1) maximize the potential and value for all the opportunities that you glossed over, lost interest in, determined to be yesterday's news or "failures," or, even worse, trust the opinions of others (agency, influencers, journalists) rather than yourself; and (2) find the right mix of technologies, platforms, and/or approaches that work for your brand,

and specifically, the challenges and opportunities in hand. In other words, write a strategic brief. Finally, trust the services of an external partner—or many—whose job it is to discover and discern the next waves of trends, growth, and opportunity, and help qualify and quantify timing, orders of magnitude, and potential impact on the organization.

Invest in both the *intrepreneurs* within and the entrepreneurs outside of the organization. The former will save your body (or head count) and the latter will save your soul.

Who knows—you may very well play an integral part in transforming your own company, brand, and surely yourself into a startup that is both agile and dexterous to fully capitalize on all those new budgets hungry for smart dollars.

One More Thing

Be the Ball. Or, rather, Be the Tray Table.

Innovation is a mind-set shift. A cultural commitment that is key to transformation and long term viability (survival). It is equally as possible to be innovative with a bus shelter or billboard as it is with a website, Instagram account, or augmented reality mobile app. By the same token, it's—sadly—fairly probable to be traditional, boring, underwhelming, and expected with a Facebook page, Twitter account, or startup pilot program.

Technology is an accelerant. A catalyst. An amplifier. But it is not a crutch. It is not a magic bean. Or a magic wand. And it is not always the answering.

Maarten's Response: We have talked a lot about testing and innovating in this book. It is the only thing that will keep you alive and your competitors at bay. Spending time with startups was the most illuminating experience in truly learning my about innovation at the speed of the digital era.

Please do me a favor (and we have stated this before): Do not limit your innovation to your product lineup. Innovate throughout,

(continued)

(*continued*)

up, down, all over. One of my most confusing titles, but at the same time most awesome, was that of director of communication innovation. I was at Coke's headquarters in Atlanta and carried that title for three-plus years. I had to explain it many times (and my mother still doesn't fully understand what I did) but at the same time it made total sense. And I was proud to be in that role.

CHAPTER 18

Become a Data Junkie

I'm not a "data guy"—whatever that means. I suspect you're not a data guy or gal either. Not many people are, and of these people, they're generally lower level or junior by title. Guess what? They will most likely end up being your boss, and sooner than you think.

Truthfully, we are all data guys or will need to be if we are to survive and thrive in the increasingly digital, connected, and social world in which we live, work, and play. Those of us who bet our careers on it will almost inevitably win.

The Geeks Will Inherit the Earth

I made this bet all the way back in 2004–2005, when I predicted that a scrawny, pocket-protecting, overbiting, Band-Aid-repaired glasses–wearing geek would win the Grand Prix at the Cannes Advertising Festival. Although I wasn't being literal (heaven forbid), I was quite serious about the importance of data in the formula of success in a world where creativity is codependent on insights fueled by data. Remember that word: *fuel*. It's coming back soon enough.

In 2013, cannes introduced an innovation category. Will 2014 or 2015 herald in the Data Awards?

Data Is Ground Z.E.R.O. of the New Marketing Model

We operate in a world of unprecedented clutter, where we are completely suffocated by an increasingly claustrophobic mix of noise and meaningless metrics (see Chapter 14). The very backbone of the paid media model is hopelessly outdated and inaccurate and fails to incorporate a suite of new variables associated with a postdigital world. Case in point: Executives still reference the fact that consumers are watching more TV than ever before, without making the subtle (insert heavy sarcasm here) distinction between content and commercials (ads). These same business leaders conveniently omit that their entire planning and pricing methodologies are based on "potential" reach. Even the hallowed Super Bowl is reported as delivering over 100 million viewers, but truthfully, how many of these actually watched *your* commercial—let alone remembered it the next day or ultimately acted on it? Most companies still benchmark their progress against the flawed traditional funnel and barely pay any attention to the postpurchase or flipped funnel scenario.

Your Consumer Is Waldo

I feel both vindicated and violated in going back to the keynotes I used to give in 2006 on life after the 30-second spot. On one slide, I had an image of Waldo from the *Where's Waldo?* books (Figure 18.1). I made the point that attempting to "find" our customers was as futile a search as one for Waldo and his posse (Wenda, Wizard Whitebeard, Woof, etc.).

In reality though, data transform this treasure hunt into a no-brainer (Figure 18.2).

If a company is able to (1) expand, (2) unify, and (3) integrate both outgoing and incoming consumer contacts into its operating structure, the result is as close to one-to-one marketing as we could ever hope for.

If consumers tweet using your "brandle" (brand handle) or hashtag, are you able to immediately identify them as customers, qualify them based on their loyalty (internal) and influence (external), and pull up a live, real-time history of *all* their interactions with the company (via phone, mail, e-mail, Internet, social media, in-store interactions, and any other contact points)? If you answered yes, you're a stinking liar.

Does that sound like a tall order? Are you kidding me? If @jaffejuice tweets @AmericanAir about anything, does American Airlines immediately make the connection that @jaffejuice = Joseph Jaffe, Executive Platinum AAdvantage Member? It should. It's not hard. All it takes is asking customers to provide their Twitter handles. Hell, they could even

Figure 18.1 Where's Waldo?

Figure 18.2 There's Waldo

Figure 18.3   Tweet exchange with @AmericanAir

Figure 18.4

go medieval and ask for this information via e-mail, with an offer of 1,000 meaningless miles as an incentive.

To their credit, they replied to my innocuous tweet after only 10 minutes (Figure 18.3).

So I tested them again by upping the ante (Figure 18.4).

Crickets.

Connect the Dots. Win a Prize

Connecting the dots is the name of the game. Whoever does it first and can make a meaningful connection from a meaningless sea of numbers and binary zeroes and ones is in an enviable position to truly connect with customers.

British Airways have spent almost a decade trying to corral all of its passenger data from over 200 sources into one database to create a customer-service experience transformed by data (that will deliver) personalization to passengers in a way that impresses, them rather than spooks them.[1]

Big Data. Big Dummy

Data is meant to inform, empower, and enable us to make incredibly smart decisions governing consumer insights, attitudes, behavior, actions, and sentiment. As introduced in Chapter 14 on measurement, we're dumber than ever before; but now that big data is the rage, we've just become bigger dummies.

People will rise to the levels of their own incompetence. Data helps expose our ineptness.

As I'm one of the dummies, I turned to my fellow "twits" for help in defining *big data*. Here's the pick of the bunch:

@sammotea: More data than an organisation knows what to do with. Entirely subjective term.

Actually, I heard a good definition as well: *Big data refers to when there's so much data from machines that you need more machines to make sense of it all. #awesomeness*

If you think about it, many of the definitions for *big data* are fairly ephemeral and conceptual. Perhaps it should read, "too big for you." Remember the American Express anniversary example? I wonder to what extent big data is really just a red herring. To be sure, there is a lot of data, and data is growing all the time. But big data is a moving target that we may never hit. We're always behind and chasing the elusive million-dollar big idea, which is buried somewhere in the bottomless pit of big data.

What We Need Here, People, Is More Cowbell

Or, in the absence of cowbell, we can thankfully turn to the plethora of data visualization tools, technologies, and platforms that are helping us make sense of all the swirls, streams, and feeds.

Nike Is a Technology Company

Nike has become a data junkie following the release of FuelBand. Every single day it collects invaluable information about me, from me, and on me. Sometimes, I share the data with my friends, fans, and followers. Some days, Nike even responds to me directly. Almost every day since I purchased my FuelBand, Nike has been tracking me, with my permission and blessing. When I became a FuelBand Millionaire (more than 1,000,000 Fuel Points), I got a tweet from them (Figure 18.5). Um, gee, thanks!

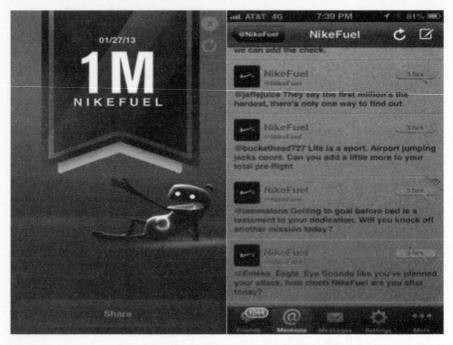

Figure 18.5   Nike is paying attention

I once heard someone ask: "Can you imagine how much money they'll make when they sell this data to marketers?" Are you crazy? Why on Earth would Nike *ever* sell this proprietary, mission-critical data to anyone, ever? The real question is, "What is it going to do with all that data?"

I'd like to see Nike take this to the next level by offering special deals, promotions, and experiences solely to FuelBand Millionaires. Perhaps it could open up its stores 15 minutes early to anyone with a FuelBand. Is it really a stretch to make the assertion that Nike is a technology company? That's what Digiday's Jack Marshall wrote in a March 2012 article.

He Slimed Me

In the same presentation in which I made the *Where's Waldo?* analogy, I also showed a video clip from one of the great movies ever made. No, not *Gone with the Wind*, *Casablanca*, or *Citizen Kane*. No, not *Highlander* or *My Cousin Vinny*, either. I'm talking, of course, about *Ghostbusters*. In the movie, there's a scene where Dr. Peter Venkman (played by Bill Murray) gets intimately acquainted with Slimer at the Sedgewick Hotel:

Raymond Stantz (Dan Aykroyd): Venkman, I saw it I saw it I saw it.

Peter Venkman (Murray): It's right here, Ray. It's looking at me.

Stantz: He's an ugly little spud, isn't he?

Venkman: I think he can hear you, Ray.

Stantz: Don't move. It won't hurt you.

(Venkman gets Slimed.)

Stantz: Venkman! Venkman! Venkman, what happened? Are you okay?

Venkman: He slimed me.

Stantz: That's great. Actual physical contact. Can you move . . . ?

Venkman: I feel so funky.

Stantz: Spengler, I'm with Venkman. He got slimed.

Spengler (Harold Ramis): That's great, Ray. Save some for me.

I always thought this exchange was a sublime analogy for our relationship with our consumers. It captures our fears—of the unknown, of contact, of having to deal directly with the "ugly little spuds." The reality is they can "hear" us using the various social media channels. There is a reassurance that this "first contact" won't hurt us, followed by the "funky" feeling of "actual physical contact." I call this residue, or the modern-day equivalent of Hansel and Gretel's crumbs. Consumers leave behind a ton of crumbs and residue. We need to pay attention, connect the dots, and roll in the deep—get ourselves dirty and rub all that residue over our marketing bodies. That's what happens when "data get sexy," as my brother from another mother, Mitch Joel, says in his new book, *<Ctrl> <Alt> <Del>*. That's when the geek gets to win the award and you get to win the prize.

Starbucks has put the sex back into data with its mobile app, which uses a trio of customer experience (Chapter 16), innovation (Chapter 17), and data (Chapter 18) to create a sublime loyalty-based ecosystem (Chapter 19) that *flips the funnel* using elementary gaming mechanics. For some reason, I keep buying my friends coffee, not because I like them, but because I want to earn stars (see Figure 18.6) and upgrade my status from Green to Gold!

Figure 18.6   **Starbucks star bucks**

Long-Term Metrics and Milestones

There's another part of the data equation—the measurement and metrics side.[2]

What is the definition of data?
The sun rises at 5:38 AM.

What is the definition of information?
The sun rises in the east at 5:38 AM and sets in the west at 7:45 PM.

What is the definition of knowledge?
If you ever get lost in the woods, follow the path of the sun across the sky to determine your direction.

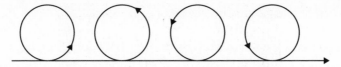

Figure 18.7 Continuous closed-loop improvement and processes

What is the definition of *wisdom?*
Don't ever get stuck in the woods.

Data is a means to an end, not the end itself. The means and the end are points on a continuum, if you will: They represent a journey. It is in part a continuous, never-ending journey, but it also consists of several "closed loop" processes (see Figure 18.7) and opportunities to "test, learn, and evolve"; adapt, improvise, and improve; and optimize and pivot to a higher form of marketing engagement and relationship.

Reframing the Conversation

The Z.E.R.O. model makes a pretty impassioned case for a change in marketing vision. Maarten and I did our best to explain why change doesn't happen quickly enough, if at all. We hope we made a compelling argument in terms of extracting and highlighting the various internal and external reasons why we struggle with adapting to the new marketing reality and what the dire implications might be if we continue to fall further behind our consumers.

In many respects, the common theme here is time, and our disconnect or mismanagement in terms of moving at the same rate and pace as our consumers in the inexorable march of technology-infused change. The great irony is how slow we move, and yet how "fast" we hold ourselves accountable in terms of short-term goals and short-term metrics.

It is a sort of purgatory that comes from a legacy of direct marketing and the pressures of quarterly earnings that come from Wall Street or venture capitalists for public or private companies.

The Art of Change

Very simply put, we need to find the balance between changing too slowly and changing too quickly. To help you on this quest, I suggest introducing three new phased sets of metrics designed to better manage expectations along the journey:

1. *Medium-term metrics:* If immediate gratification (such as the click-through) is short-lived and lifetime value is a mirage, how about setting up appropriate medium-term metrics that are themselves markers, milestones, or beacons to both reassure we are on track and, if we're not, help triangulate a prescriptive and realistic path back to our road map? The medium-term metric is essentially a series of interim forecasts not dissimilar from mile markers in a marathon race that advise whether it's time to pick up the pace or slow down to smell the roses. Examples include members of an advocacy program, app downloads, tenured customers, or subscribers to an e-mail list. The key here is that going from zero (the bad kind) to hero in one giant step is as much a chasm as it is a lofty, seemingly unrealistic goal.

2. *Long-term sales:* We often talk about short-term sales and long-term relationship in mutually exclusive terms. They are polar opposites in terms of their time frames, but how about building a bridge of compromise between them? A mash-up of sorts, in terms of reconciling the need to keep the cash register ringing without losing sight of the bigger picture. I call this long-term sales. Whereas the short-term initiative is akin to a traditional campaign, the long-term sales effort is a form of commitment.

3. *Short-term wins:* Don't think I'm letting you off the hook that easily. Accountability is not an optional extra anymore, as it's still important to have something to show for your efforts off the bat. It's a modern-day marketing equivalent of the bird in the hand versus the two in the bush. Only this time, consider the large "W" (big win), the small "w" (small win), or in some cases even the small "l" (small loss), which represents failing fast or failing smart, insights, lessons, learnings, or pleasing initial results.

Now imagine a long-term sales effort infused with medium-term metrics and unified by short-term wins thanks to data residue. Sound alien? I hope not. We come in peace.

Maarten's Response: In Chapter 14, I talked about measurement and the need for a real dashboard, as well as analysts who can make sense of the data. I also recommend you pair the brilliant analyst with an equally brilliant "insights person" —someone who understands the difference between what happened and what it means. Too many times I see the following items listed as insights when they are really merely facts:

- The population is aging.
- Sales in the West have gone down.
- The promotion did not work.

A true insights person will bring you reasons, hypotheses, and, well, insights into the why and what it means. These in turn will spark ideas as to what to do next.

Equally important is the need to address your organizational structure so that these insights are shared between all key stakeholders within the organization.

From Campaigns to Commitments to Ecosystems

L et me start right off the bat[1] with a mea culpa as it relates to the four buzzwords or clichés that are anywhere on the continuum of painful to putrid: *big data, native advertising, transmedia,* and *ecosystem.*

Now that I've got that out there, let me concede in the spirit of "If you can't beat 'em, join 'em" that I've reconciled myself internally to say *big data* and *ecosystem* without using air quotes or wincing. I'm even coming around to the term *native advertising,* although I still think that this is nothing more than classic branded content integration—even advertorial, if you think about it.

As far as *transmedia* is concerned, you can forget about it. I'm just not going there, although I'm all for gender equality among vampires. According to Wikipedia, this is the definition of an ecosystem:

*An **ecosystem** is a community of living organisms (plants, animals and microbes) in conjunction with the nonliving components of their environment (things like air, water and mineral soil), interacting as a system. . . . As ecosystems are defined by the network of interactions among organisms, and between organisms and their environment, they can come in any size but usually encompass specific, limited spaces (although some scientists say that the entire planet is an ecosystem).*

Interestingly enough, the entry begins with a small caveat: For the business metaphor, see "Business ecosystem." This entry cites James Moore as having first introduced the strategic planning term in his book *The Death of Competition: Leadership and Strategy in the Age of Business Ecosystems*[2] (1990) and later in a *Harvard Business Review* article titled "Predators and Prey: A New Ecology of Competition" (1993). Moore defines *business ecosystem* as:

> *An economic community supported by a foundation of interacting organizations and individuals—the organisms of the business world. The economic community produces goods and services of value to customers, who are themselves members of the ecosystem. The member organisms also include suppliers, lead producers, competitors, and other stakeholders. . . .*

Personally, I prefer the original definition, which encompasses several key themes worth expounding on:

- *community*—a strong recurring theme from *The Cluetrain Manifesto* describing a central component of social media.
- *living organisms*—human beings: employees, partners, customers, stakeholders.
- *in conjunction with the nonliving organisms*—technology.
- *interacting as a system/linked together*—connecting the dots so that employees can connect with other employees; employees, with customers; and customers, with customers.
- *they can come in any size*—ecosystems within ecosystems; size doesn't matter; the ultimate leveling of the playing fields.

The basic concept of an ecosystem implies evolution, codependence, interconnectedness, health and wellness, balance, and ultimately survival. Take one critical piece of the puzzle out of the equation (let's say bees pollinating flowers), and the ecosystem itself can wither (plant life dying and food chain collapsing).

Thank you, Barry B. Benson.[3]

In my book, *Join the Conversation*, I introduced the concept that marketing is not a campaign; it's a commitment. That statement is still true, except it's now time to upgrade or evolve this idea into a vision of an interconnected organism that is dynamic, fluid, flexible, agile, growing, and *alive*.

On one level, an ecosystem is a hybrid collection or amalgamation of complementary, ongoing, and symbiotic commitments. On another level, it is simply a better way of doing business—a more progressive, more productive, and more profitable model.

Google Is an Ecosystem

Apple's cloud-based App store is an ecosystem. Hell, the entire company is an ecosystem, albeit one that is closed to the outside world but is a bustling ant colony within.

Nike's FuelBand is an ecosystem.

Red Bull's Human Traffic Content Factory is an ecosystem.

Innovation at 128,000 Feet[4]

When I mention the name Baumgartner, you may immediately think of San Francisco Giants pitcher Madison Bumgarner, but I'm referring to Felix Baumgartner, an Austrian skydiver, daredevil, and BASE jumper who, in October 2012, set a world record for free-fall skydiving

That previous statement is a gross understatement. This is what he did: He jumped at a distance of 24 miles, or 39 kilometers, above the Earth. (A plane flying at 35,000 feet is only 6.6 miles above the Earth. Baumgartner was in a space-suit in a space capsule, and could see the curvature of the Earth!)

He became the first person in history to break the sound barrier, putting him in the same category as the *Concorde*. He reached an estimated speed of 834 miles per hour, or 1,342 kilometers per hour, traveling faster than a Boeing 777.

During the fall, Baumgartner went into a spin, where he was seen hurtling through space like a tumbleweed on amphetamines. Remarkably, he stabilized—and said this spinning was anticipated and under control—and landed on his feet.

The mission itself was five years in the making and has delivered several key insights that will help scientists and aviation experts on the development of equipment, clothing, safety, tourism, and space ship evacuation procedures of space travel.

Most remarkably, this jump was essentially a giant ad for Red Bull. Ordinarily, I would be on my *Life after the 30-Second Spot* or *Join the Conversation* soapbox, lambasting brands for elongated, protracted, and procrastinated planning cycles in favor of a real-time, dynamic shortened time to market. But not this time.

Red Bull, yet again, hasn't just raised the bar; it pretty much obliterated the bar by demonstrating the relevance, role, purpose, and utility associated with a brand that has truly invested and vested itself in extreme sports and lifestyle. Calling Red Bull a content marketer is an insult to Red Bull. Red Bull is so much more.

Not only did it almost literally bring its core positioning, "Red Bull gives you wings," to life but it also showed an acute understanding and mastery of pure and unadulterated innovation in the form of a unique and original idea that had zero precedent and, quite frankly (and again quite literally), no safety net.

I cannot even begin to fathom the 1,000 ways this could have gone wrong and the huge risks that were at stake. The experiment itself was already aborted once because of weather conditions, but the blunt risk here was the very real possibility and scenario of witnessing a live death. (All brought to you by Red Bull.)

Ironically (and it is a monstrous—pun intended—irony), a competitor in the form of Monster Energy drink is currently being sued and subsequently investigated by the U.S. Food and Drug Administration for a number of alleged consumption-related deaths.

Conversely, Red Bull brought a symphony to life, with more than 8 million people worldwide watching YouTube's live stream of the free fall. Within four days, and across 1,700 related clips, it was the second-fastest video to reach 50 million views in history. (The first was KONY 2012.)

I look at the average NASCAR driver, tattooed, or should I say littered, with a cacophony of conflicting brand logos and juxtapose this with the clean and clinical branding 24 miles up in the air. I raise a can in congratulations to this marketer.

I speak to marketers worldwide, representing every major corporation. They all envy and want to be like two brands: Nike and Apple. Well, make that three brands: Red Bull joins the hall of fame trinity.

The combined jealousy and respect are palpable, and so is my advice to every Red Bull wannabe: "Just do It," or to quote Baumgartner's mentor, retired U.S. Air Force Colonel Joseph Kittinger: "Start the cameras, and our guardian angel will take care of you."

Red Bull is the quintessential Z.E.R.O. marketer, with a truly connected ecosystem that is fueled by passion, innovation, a sense of purpose and identity, and its own asset-driven machine that authentically leverages the humans that power the brand, and are in turn powered by it.

Find Your (Brand) Greatness[5]

In August 2012, Nike launched its "Find Your Greatness" activation platform for the Nike FuelBand. Featuring "reality" stars like morbidly obese 12-year-old Nathan Sorrell from London, Ohio, it was a bizarre twist on Dove's Campaign for Real Beauty, which used real, flawed, plus- or minus-sized humans as spokespeople, versus the celebrity-laden, retouched incumbent approach.

So what happens when you put one (technology) and one (creativity) together? You get 12, August 12, 2012, to be specific: #findyourgreatness Day. On August 12, all FuelBand users had an opportunity to set a world record of Fuel earned in a single day, a global challenge uniting every single customer. In addition, individuals had the opportunity to set or break their own personal best records.

I started my day with an eight-mile run, followed it up with baseball and soccer in the backyard with my son, and went for a two-mile stroll with my daughter. Clearly, I wasn't backing down. This is what I had to do to eclipse my long four-and-a-half-hour walk spoiled by playing golf a month before. I broke my record. I tweeted it, Facebooked it, checked in, checked out, rested, iced, compressed, and elevated. At the end of the day, I proudly stroked my two "collectors" badges to prove to my adoring fan base of tens that I had found my individual greatness and played my part in this virtual activity-fest.

Looking back, I see yet another way that Nike has been able to connect the dots and live large in a world where technology-led innovation is a blessing and a not-so-secret weapon in terms of walking the talk of consumer engagement, communal activity, advocacy, and passion-led conversation, all while earning plenty of consumer credits in the form of Fuel in the process.

Figure 19.1　The Nike+ API developer community

Nike hasn't stopped there. In 2013, they launched a developer initiative (see Figure 19.1), designed around hacking their own API (what's your heresy?) and ultimately innovating around their own innovation. Reprise.

Q: What's the best way to keep innovating?
A: Keep innovating!

So what's *your* equivalent of FuelBand?
Where's *your* (brand) greatness?

Does it exist? If so, how are you bringing it to life? If it doesn't exist, isn't it time to explore your own intersection of Madison Avenue and Mountain View? I'll even give you a complimentary hashtag to get you motivated.

Everything Is Connected to Everything, and Everyone Is Connected to Everyone

The idea of an ecosystem is the ability to connect the dots—every single dot, or node, or interaction, or transaction. Ten years ago, we might have referred to early signs of a holistic operating framework as integration, but truly—at least in the world of paid media—this was nothing more than duplication or imitation— things that looked and felt the same instead of the real prize: differentiation and ultimately transformation.

Of course, 10 years ago, we had no clue as to what extent the innovation continuum would obliterate all forms of convention and status quo as we knew it then or know it now. Jim Bush's words of wisdom are already outdated. This is not about generic people; it's about specific customers. The customers that will make or break your very existence, the same ones that—if successfully leveraged, recognized, rewarded, empowered, and activated—can help you flip the funnel. These are the same people who are bursting with ideas, suggestions, and recommendations to crowdsource your way to marketing nirvana. It's also not as much a generic business as it is an ecosystem: a living, breathing, thriving, fluid, and unpredictable collection of human beings, peers, partners, lovers, and haters who all play their own unique role in a fascinating reality show known as your life.

Thanks, Jim, I'll Take It from Here

The ant is a marvelous creature. Technically it's an insect, but it's really a freak of nature (the good kind). The ant can carry 10 to 50 times its body weight. Some ants are actually capable of carrying up to 100 times their body weight. Ants aren't exactly loners. They work well in groups (colonies), but it is more than that. They form a completely collaborative band of brothers (or ants) operating in unison, a perfect ecosystem of like-minded individuals (or ants) acting as a slick, well-oiled community. There are even reports in Texas, Florida, and other southern states of a subspecies called "crazy ants," because of their unpredictable movements and swarming populations. Said crazy ants are actually changing their own ecosystem—and by definition the ecosystem around them—based on their actions.

I'm not saying we should behave like ants. They also have tiny brains and their womenfolk kill the men; I am, however, suggesting that we could learn a lot from operating as a cohesive group or collective.

This Is a Customer-Centric Ecosystem Powered by Technology

This is not about random or generic people; it's about specific people. First and foremost, it is about your customers, but equally so, it is about your employees, business and channel partners, and various constituencies and communities that house and fuel the ecosystem itself.

How Do You Scale Humanity?

Ultimately, the vision of a customer-centric ecosystem powered by technology is about balance and equilibrium. It's one that currently does not exist; it's out of whack. We either exist in a technophobic world of inefficient humans (we are flawed and imperfect at our core) or an abundant world of ubiquitous technology that has similar inefficiencies in the form of stripping out every last bit of common sense left in us.

At what point will airlines dispense of the dot matrix printers they use for passenger manifests (I mean we have 3D printers now!) and pay attention to their most loyal and valuable customers sitting in the cabins, wondering if someone will remember them. *Do you know who I am?* Service without technology is too haphazard, random, and serendipitous. Consistency is table stakes.

Corporations see technology and immediately think of cost, cost efficiencies to be exact. They look to streamline, automate, simplify. They look to scale through science instead of customizing and personalizing through art.

Think of the current state of the supermarket. Every day, another checkout counter manned by a cashier and bagger gets replaced with a self-service checkout kiosk that is about as user-friendly and easy to operate as a YouTube video on how to perform open-heart surgery, fill out a government form, or program your universal remote. The goodwill of supermarkets giving jobs to people with handicaps is nothing but the faded fumes of a time when we still possessed a thread of humanity.

The real challenge and prize is to find the perfect mix between humans and machines. When we do it well, the effects are sublime. The key is technology that is like the old-fashioned child: seen, but not heard. Technology should be invisible and transparent, yet indispensable like oxygen. Technology should remind us to wish a customer happy birthday or provide salespeople with an orchestra of apps that help them do their jobs and serve their customers better.

If technology is the oxygen that powers the ecosystem, then data represents the DNA that bonds it to itself and hydrogen and the concept of "universal currency" (Fuel, Rewards, Points, Miles) is the water that keeps everything alive. Sure you can put a pretty bow around it, or actually a bowtie, to help you flip a funnel, create an ambassador program, and activate advocacy. And while you're doing it, consider drizzling in a startup cocktail or two.

Now is not the time to take your foot off the throttle. Now is the time to press, to push the limits and boundaries of what is possible and what might be possible. The innovation imperative is teaming with unlimited possibilities, especially when it too becomes its own ecosystem of entrepreneurs, intrapreneurs, advisors, mentors, and thought leaders.

One Step Back to Take One Step Forward

Hold on a moment. This chapter is incomplete. Let's ask the question again (it's not rhetorical): *How do you scale humanity?* One step at time. One human step at a time. Technology can help, but it is not the be all and end all.

Technology is like sound at a rock concert. You never come home and say, *"Man, that reverb was off the hizzle!"* (Hopefully you never use the word, *hizzle*. Ever) In fact, the only time you ever talk about the sound at a rock concert is when it sucks! Technology should be exactly the same. Transparent. Seamless. Functional. Supportive.

And going back to the Web banner vs. McDonald's tray table comparison: sometimes technology is not the answer at all.

Take Dulux and their Let's Colour Project (www.letscolourproject .com) that hit the proverbial Z.E.R.O. jackpot by elevating themselves beyond product (cans or tins of paint) and brand ("Dulux. We know the colours that go" or "Worth doing, worth Dulux") to the coveted echelons of experience and community (using P.B.E.C., as introduced in Chapter 16).

The goal of Let's Colour was *to uplift people's lives by adding color to communities globally.* To date, Dulux has donated 570,612 liters of paint across every major continent to empower and inspire local communities to better their neighborhoods. They've helped restore pride among locals in their surrounding environments such as in the Favelas of Rio, and in doing so created a growing community of brand ambassadors (Z of Z.E.R.O.) using the ultimate owned assets (O of Z.E.R.O.) in the form of brick buildings, employees, community, and, of course, cans of paint!

When a Honda owner named Joe was about to see his car pass the million-mile mark, Honda threw him a parade. When another Honda lover mowed Honda's "H-Mark" into his lawn, Honda mowed the Honda owner's name—Chris—into the lawn of campus in Torrance, California.

And then came the love Honda gave toward the band "Monsters Calling Home," an unsigned act that recorded a music video in a member's Honda.

Honda loved them back, and how—by booking them on *Jimmy Kimmel Live!*

It's almost impossible to campare this to the dreadful television commercials from *the same brand* that quote tweets. Corporate schizophrenia rules!

Maarten's Response: Customer-centric ecosystems are incredibly important, because they form the backbone of your Z.E.R.O. approach. Investing time and money into listening, understanding, and empowering this lifeline will pay big dividends.

Personally, I believe one of the best investments you can make is in creating a listening infrastructure.

The second—or perhaps other first—investment you should make is to ensure you can connect with your consumers directly. As we have said before, social media is rented space. Getting people to share their contact details with you is the ultimate relationship commitment. It is like marrying: Brand and consumer are now directly linked a hopefully long and happy relationship that you need to work on to keep it working.

CHAPTER
20

That's Great ... Now What the Hell Do I Do Next?

What's next? The short answer: anything. Something. The longer answer is to make a genuine and earnest commitment to change. Make a pledge or take the pledge to Z.E.R.O. Embrace your heresy. Define your legacy. Challenge your internal team, your constituents, and your external partners to bring new ideas to the table, to fire themselves before you fire them, to reboot as Mitch Joel would have you do.

The opportunity cost of doing nothing is armageddon. The stakes are ultimately survival, but death by a thousand paper cuts—or, in this case, a thousand thousandths of a percentage point of market share translates into millions of dollars of revenue lost.

Hey, Chubby, Get into That Gym

This book begins by discussing the obesity epidemic, and here we are at the tail end of the book talking about your seat once again—the seat of your *derriere*, the seat at the strategic and decision-making table, and the seat at your consumer's consideration set table.

Paid media's waste has become nuclear, and it's time to figure out ways to address the problem and concoct a series of triangulated solutions, be

241

they defensive (*"What if we're wrong?"* aka protecting the cash cow) or offensive (*"What if we're right?"* aka sacred cow burgers).

We chose to go straight for the jugular instead of pussyfooting around the elephant in the room. We aren't doing you any favors by telling you what a great job you're currently doing. (By the way, have you lost weight?) We're not yes men, and if you hire us to help you at some point, whether it's for a keynote speech, communications planning audit, or innovation assessment, we're still not going to stroke your ego. What we will do, however, is guide you toward what we think is a safe haven amid a turbulent sea of violent change, clutter, and competitive pressure.

Work Out Workshop

It begins with a workshop, not dissimilar to any workshop you've done before in the past, in that you invite key stakeholders and external partners to attend. We'd recommend dividing the day into three parts that mirror this book's approach:

1. *The problem:* This is where you assess threats and determine from a probability standpoint what will happen, what won't happen, and what may happen. This is where you contingency plan and discuss your heresy and legacy.

2. *The solution:* Z.E.R.O., aka ground zero. It's time to lay the table with the four pillars of advocacy, innovation, customer centricity, and real estate. This is where you discuss in great detail exactly how you intend to activate and invest accordingly. To be clear, you're not building a three-legged table; that's called a tripod. You're also not building a table with different-sized legs; that's called a mess.

3. *The action plan:* Now it's time to be actionable, practical, and even tactical. Our feeling is that you have a choice across the spectrum to (1) evaluate, (2) prioritize, and (3) deploy accordingly. Our recommendation is to come up with both a laundry list of to-dos and a resulting project plan for each selected action item. Once this is in place, we recommend doing just one at a time—no point in boiling the ocean. Rank and rate the 10 action items, as well as the plan to roll them out. Perhaps you'll give priority to what is actually possible, as opposed to theoretically achievable but realistically impossible.

Forrester recently conducted a Global Marketing Innovation Study (May 2013) and segmented companies into four categories, based on their marketing innovation cultures. Eight percent were classified as "Risk-averse," 61 percent as "Pragmatists," 27 percent as "Experimenters," and only 3 percent "Customer-obsessed." The description for Pragmatists was essentially reactive, slow-moving and conservative, and when combined with the Risk-averse, represents a whopping 7 out of every 10 companies.

So which one are you? Don't answer that!

There are two clear takeaways here:

1. Roughly one-third of companies have an inside shot at pulling away from the pack.

2. Experimentation is the bridge or conduit toward this differentiation.

It's time to become a lean (brand), mean experimenter.

Jaffe and Albarda's Law of Z.E.R.O. Motion

With apologies to Newton's "for each action, there is an equal and opposite reaction," we believe that every action you take needs short-term wins, medium-term metrics, and long-term sales baked into the ecosystem and infrastructure.

When it comes to zealots, for example, start at the beginning:

1. Do you know who your raving fans are?

2. What are you doing to grow this base of promoters?

3. How are you activating the advocates?

With respect to innovation, start with an internal mandate to conduct four experiments over the course of the next calendar year. That's one per quarter. Or, if you need a little more breathing room, go with three over four-month intervals. It probably helps to benchmark your digital progress to date. At Evol8tion, we do this through our signature Innovation Assessment score. Feel free to use your own if you like; this is not a bait and switch.

On the customer service side, it's time to implement the new rules of customer service against a segmented customer base. Do the exercises. Calculate:

1. The revenue split by the number of returning customers (retention) versus the number of first-time buyers (acquisition) bucket respectively

2. The investment against these two segments and, with it, the opportunities for optimization

3. The breakout within the retention bucket (the 80/20 rule), which isolates and highlights the power customers

The final exercise is to map this against the influencer evaluation, namely, those who buy a lot, talk a lot, and do both. How can you scale this?

Finally, it's time to take your real estate test if you truly want to get into the landlord business. It begins with a full audit of all your assets: owned, leased, and rented. Where are the gaps to migrate or upgrade from leased to owned? To what extent are you fully integrating and optimizing the potential of your suite of assets: your people, packaging, stores, website, and apps? Where are the opportunities to move from indirect to direct engagement? What are the possibilities of transitioning from tenant to landlord?

You Have a Long Way to Go

A Forrester and Heidrick & Struggles report suggests that there is still too much lethargy built into the model. Put differently, you have a long way to go. As Figure 20.1 suggests, you're still obsessed with acquisition above

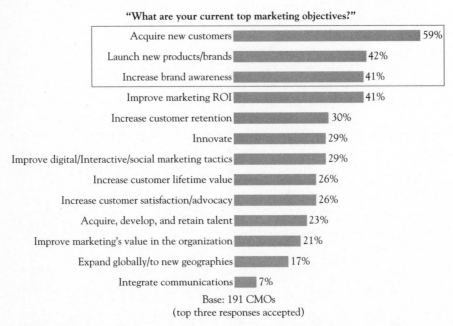

"What are your current top marketing objectives?"

Acquire new customers	59%
Launch new products/brands	42%
Increase brand awareness	41%
Improve marketing ROI	41%
Increase customer retention	30%
Innovate	29%
Improve digital/Interactive/social marketing tactics	29%
Increase customer lifetime value	26%
Increase customer satisfaction/advocacy	26%
Acquire, develop, and retain talent	23%
Improve marketing's value in the organization	21%
Expand globally/to new geographies	17%
Integrate communications	7%

Base: 191 CMOs
(top three responses accepted)

Source: Q3 2011 Forrester/Heidrick & Struggles Global Evolved CMO Online Survey
Source: Forrester Research, Inc.

Figure 20.1   Obsessing on acquiring customers

all else (what's the point in fishing when your net is full of holes?). You're still too focused on your reflection, you're not customer-centric, and innovation is too low on your priority lists.

When You Come to a Fork in the Road, Take It

In the second quarter of 2013, we were treated[1] to two very intriguing—and yet seemingly contradictory—pieces of research concerning the state of marketing and the relative health and wellness of its fearless leader, the chief marketing officer (CMO).

As mentioned earlier in this book, a Spencer Stuart study reported that the average tenure of the CMO has doubled, from 23 months in 2006 to 45 months in 2013.

Contrast that with an Accenture study that reflects a whopping 40 percent of marketers feel they are ill-prepared to meet their objectives. The study listed key impediments to marketing performance being inefficient business practices (19 percent) and lack of funding (17 percent).

Cut to Spencer Stuart crowing about how chief executive officers (CEOs) are finally coming round to giving credit to the tough job of CMOs (after giving them such a tough time previously!) in these current recessionary times, combined with credence on the responsibility associated with a CMO's burgeoning portfolio to include so many more technology-enabled components perhaps previously associated with information technology—along with an expanded role including the mission-critical specialties of customer service, social media, and the like.

And back to Accenture, indicating that 48 percent of marketers will spend more on managing customer data; 40 percent will increase spending on Web analytics; and 39 percent will boost spending on marketing analytics—with their limited, insufficient funding, of course. Furthermore, half of the respondents indicated they would begin an internal reorganization to become more digitally savvy, and 52 percent said they would be hiring more digital talent.

So let me see if I've got this correct: CMOs are living large and enjoying unprecedented job security and tenure in a time of unprecedented economic pressure, organizational upheaval, business volatility, and technology-enabled change, despite the fact that they don't have enough processes, budget, and/or talent to do their jobs effectively.

And then there was the Fournaise study from Chapter 3 that concluded that CMOs have lost certain decision-making powers (pricing, distribution, cost of goods) to other department heads. Perhaps the real reason they are lasting longer: they are making less business mission critical decisions.

Is it just me, or is something a little off here?

I've tried to reconcile these insights in an effort to come out with a warm, fuzzy, glass-half-full outcome. My feeling is that this is a classic case of lesser evils. On one hand, we have CEOs giving CMOs a little more respect and autonomy to do their jobs. This is a good thing, a *very* good thing, in fact. It's imperative that CMOs have enough time to execute on a longer-term vision and mission.

On the other hand, this may just be a signal to essentially throw in the towel, with CEOs conceding that scapegoating CMOs is not necessarily a sustainable practice while at the same time not exactly shaking up the status quo to empower CMOs to do their jobs and achieve their goals with appropriate budgets, talent, and/or resources.

Arguably, the one common thread that connects, unifies, and even explains these two disparate findings is the acceleration and proliferation of disruptive technology-based innovation in the marketing world. The goalposts continue to shift and become elusively more challenging to reach from month to month.

Put metaphorically: We're still chasing our own tails; the only thing that has changed is the frantic and frenzied (read: manic) pace at which we're doing it.

Firing the CMO does nothing more than place the organization even further into an arguably insurmountable back foot posture and laggard position. That said, without implementing dramatic changes associated with the egregious gaps in investment and talent, the company is no closer to exponentially adapting and powering forward. Restructuring may help, but only if it's painfully cathartic, profound, and sustained.

The solution? I'm afraid I don't have a silver bullet, but giving CMOs more room to breathe is a definite start, if—and only if—CMOs take this as a golden opportunity to effect meaningful change within their business unit, company, and even industry.

Perhaps CMO should stand for chief muddled officer or chief morphed officer. Which one are you? The latter is a new brand of officer for a new world of brands, a new age marketer incorporating equal parts chief listening or conversation officer, chief customer or experience officer, chief innovation officer, chief data officer, and pretty much anything else a consultant or author can throw at you. The chief morphed officer is both a generalist (jack-of-all-trades) and a specialist at one: marketing.

Marketing is everything.

Embrace Your Inner Masochist[2]

I had the opportunity to deliver the keynote speech at Compete's Annual Digital CMO Conference in 2013. After the sessions, a small group of senior marketing executives had an intimate lunch and discussion about organizational change and cultural transformation.

One of the paradigms and frameworks we discussed came from Stephen DiMarco, Compete's CMO, who referenced a very simple matrix of pain and pleasure as motivational forces and catalysts of change. The continuum looks something like this (in order from most important to least important):

Pain now

Pain later

Pleasure now

Pleasure later

What struck me with this very simple and yet effective breakdown is how pain trumps pleasure—both in the present and future.

Intuitively, this makes sense if you think about disrupting norms and the status quo: Fear of failure (losing one's job, being lambasted by the trades and blogosphere, market share loss) is the known devil versus the unknown devil of wild success (new revenue streams, competitive advantage, viral mania, and best-in-show creative).

And yet, it makes no sense at all. The downside is always known and somewhat finite. Our goal here is to minimize or mitigate the cost of failure. On the flipside, the upside is limitless and infinite. And yet, we resist or choose to stick with the tried and tested instead of framing inaction as an opportunity cost—the cost of doing nothing.

The second surprise from this breakout is how pain later trumps pleasure now. One would think the pecking order would place pleasure now just above pain later. The result is the quintessential rock and a hard place—a purgatory or limbo of sorts between the pain of clutter, confusion, and lack of metrics with the looming noose of missed goals. I guess this is where the phrase *paralyzed with fear* comes into play.

Completing the matrix in Table 20.1 is definitely a helpful exercise, but I think it's time we also flip the matrix by redefining pain and pleasure and rethinking time frames, thereby separating fear from failure.

It is widely held that change happens (action) when the cost of not changing is greater than the cost of changing. Put differently, when the pain associated with inactivity outweighs the pain (risk, fear, uncertainty, etc.) associated with venturing out of one's comfort zone.

The problem is that we typically either misinterpret these signs or don't always act in a smart, strategic, and holistic way. Cases in point: A bad Twitter experience results in closing down an account or joining Twitter in the first place, respectively.

Today, we are surrounded by forces of change that jolt us into action. Often, these are sadly knee-jerk reactions that are forced rather than voluntary and mired in short-term thinking and instant gratification.

If it is true (and it is) that the incumbent paid media world continues to erode—both in terms of efficacy and efficiency—and if it is true (and it is) that the emerging digital landscape continues to expand and evolve, then

Table 20.1   The Pain-Pleasure Matrix

	Now	Later
Pain	Analysis paralysis, confusion and clutter, talent shortage, etc.	Missing goals, earnings, sales quotas
Pleasure	Better optimized and allocated budgets, better investment	Transformational change

Table 20.2   Z.E.R.O. Pain and Pleasure

	Now	Later
Pain (Push)	Failing fast and failing smart	Pivoting and course correction
Pleasure (Pull)	Patents, proprietary IP, barriers to entry and exit	Competitive advantage and transformational change

surely now would be the time to rework the matrix to essentially blend together both pain and pleasure as positive stimuli, working in tandem under the unified banner of innovation.

The takeaway here is to embrace pain now in order to avoid it later but equally to embrace future pleasure in order to avoid the soft, artificial, and increasingly temporary appearance of pleasure now (status quo).

Slay the Sacred Cow

We challenge you and your partners to justify every single line item and colored rectangle on your flowchart with real and meaningful data and metrics. We don't mind if they are short-term wins, medium-term metrics, or long-term sales validation. Everything that cannot earn its place should be on the chopping block.

By the way, calm down—we're not telling you to hemorrhage the system. Prioritize and plan accordingly. Start small, but get bigger quickly. Start slow, but speed up quickly. Start safe, but take on more calculated risk quickly.

Robin Hood Marketing

We agree, *Robin Hood Marketing is* a great-sounding name for our next book, but for now, it speaks to the fact that all four pillars of Z.E.R.O. have optimization implications, and we're being very clear that the money you *need* to properly and sufficiently invest in these four areas must come from paid media.

We recommend looking (you won't need to look too hard) for these entry points—from obvious and glaring wasteful line items to less obvious inefficiencies.

Vertical or Horizontal Routes

Of course, you can take the Chuck Fruit approach as well. Chuck, in his tenure at both Anheuser-Busch and then Coca-Cola (just like coauthor Maarten, only Maarten did it the other way around), mandated 5 percent of all television network budgets go toward cable. It soon became the kind of stake in the ground that was the norm in the industry. If you are creating innovation budgets, improvised budgets, or speculative or opportunistic budgets, remember that although imitation is the sincerest form of flattery, in the world of marketing it becomes white noise. Rather, consider putting that same stake through the heart of your competitor. Business transformation is not as effusive as you think.

Today, when you look at the failing networks losing ground by the day to basic and premium cable networks, Fruit looks like the greatest genius in somewhat-modern-day media. And Bud TV doesn't seem as silly nowadays as it did then, although I suspect it still stings as bad.

First mover advantage counts more than ever before. Bonon Buugh is doing a Chuck Fruit by mandating 10 percent of media budgets should go toward mobile.

Press. Press. Press.

You'll never win at blackjack if you don't have a betting strategy. The house will always win if you don't press your advantage, especially when the perceptual wind is in your sails. Doubling down and splitting in less obvious circumstances, placing additional chips on the hand to capitalize on momentum, or even unpredictable betting can help pull one over the dealer without being thrown out the casino. What would have happened if Budweiser had doubled its commitment when everyone else dabbled around the 5 percent ceiling?

The best way to keep innovating—is to keep innovating.

Setting an innovation budget is one thing; keeping it is another. By properly managing expectations throughout the process and getting the buy-in from the very top down, as well as middle out (beware the middle manager) and outside in (those pesky agencies and media companies can be quite persuasive), Z.E.R.O. budget setting and investment becomes a cultural imperative and strategic mandate for the business and brand.

Translation: When Budgets Are Cut, It Is Not the First to Go, but the Last

The very same justification for setting budgets up in the first place (the waste) should be the same reason why they are protected and insulated against short-term and reactive thinking.

One More Thing: Z.E.R.O. Is Not *Free*

With thanks to Jeff Rohrs, a fellow thought leader and newly minted author of *Audience*, who, in a conversation on the twentieth floor of the Hyatt Hotel in Sao Paulo, Brazil, scratched his head and said something to the effect of, "The genius is that Z.E.R.O. does not necessarily mean free, right?" I pretended to be completely on the same page and then exhaled a sigh of relief knowing that I almost omitted one of the most important takeaways from this entire book!

Z.E.R.O. is most certainly not free. That's part of the problem in the industry, which is to justify wasteful paid media with the crutch and three-card Monte of earned media, aka free media. Z.E.R.O. asserts that in a perfect world, brands would not need paid media because of the value derived from their existing customers and investments in technology, service, and/or owned assets. None of these investments are negligible, but they are almost always certainly more valuable, cost-efficient, and cost-effective than the incumbent alternatives. *All* can be considered investments, rather than expenditures. In some cases, they even become revenue generators, which flips the entire model on its head.

Keep It Simple, Stupid (KISS)

Just in case there is any ambiguity with your marching orders, here is a final summary: Media is a subset of marketing and is thus smaller than marketing. To make sense of the shifting media world, we gave you the acronym P.E.O.N. and four directives associated with rethinking how you plan, buy, and optimize dollars.

P.E.O.N. is a means to an end—and that end is Z.E.R.O.

Putting It All Together

There's a money slide in this book and it's coming up shortly. To set it up, let's go back to the Marketing Bowtie and consider who we're delivering against it.

Figure 20.2 shows where we are today, and the report card is not encouraging at all. Essentially, we are delivering predominantly against P.E.O. or paid-earned-owned.

An Incomplete Marketing Bowtie™

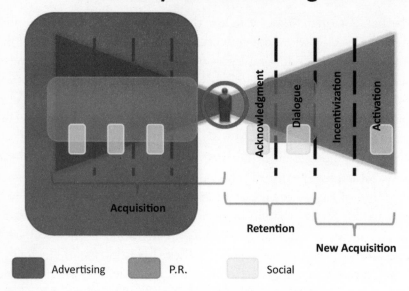

Figure 20.2   The Marketing Bowtie Scorecard

Four key takeaways from this analysis suggest a way forward:

1. We are completely absent at P.O.P. (Point of Purchase, Place of Purchase, Proof of Purchase).

2. We are completely underrepresented at the reward and recognize stage of the flipped funnel.

3. We are at absolute baby steps in terms of formalizing any sense of community.

4. Until steps 1 through 3 are met, the vision of a customer-centric ecosystem powered by technology cannot be reached.

We believe that Z.E.R.O. represents the final pieces of the puzzle (together with a profound investment and prioritization in nonmedia or human capital [aka talent]). See Figure 20.3.

Only one more step is required, and that is to synthesize and overlay both P.E.O.N. as it relates to media and the traditional funnel, and of course, Z.E.R.O., which not only gives us coverage across the flipped funnel but also provides support at the point in which the two funnels come together (P.O.P.). In addition, Z.E.R.O. reaches out across the aisle and,

Connecting the Dots with Z.E.R.O.

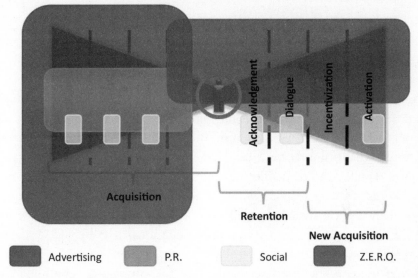

Figure 20.3   Z.E.R.O. fills the gaps across the Marketing Bowtie

The Marketing Bowtie™ with P.E.O.N. & Z.E.R.O. Overlays

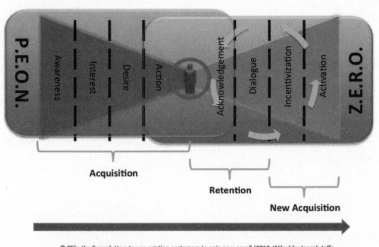

Figure 20.4   P.E.O.N. + Z.E.R.O. = Hero

in doing so, does not neglect the final mile in the acquisition cycle leading up to purchase (Figure 20.4).

This is the true connected ecosystem in action.

When All Else Fails, Don't Panic

Douglas Adams said it best in this line from *The Hitchhiker's Guide to the Galaxy*. He also said the magic number was 42, which is why we think you should move toward investing a minimum of 42 percent of your budget in direct versus indirect means. That number is completely arbitrary, of course. You'll need to determine your own benchmarks and milestones, but we do want to reassure you that things will be okay. Do not panic, especially if panic manifests itself in paralysis.

Z.E.R.O. represents, in our humble opinions, a bold and visionary approach to staying out in front of all the waves of innovation and change hitting us with increased regularity (see the innovation continuum in Chapter 17). It incorporates new budgets and significant shifts from acquisition to retention (a directional absolute 20 percent, or, put differently, a 25 percent reduction in acquisition in favor of retention), which would include the formalizing of advocacy and establishment of ambassador-type programs. This represents a firm stake in the innovation ground, including collaboration with entrepreneurs and their startups (up to 10 percent of your budget using the 60/30/10 rule), a rethink on content (assets versus media), and an evolution toward ecosystems powered by technology.

Shift Happens

Begin with whatever shift you prioritize as being the most important to the future of your business. Even if you follow Adams's lead and go with 42 percent, you won't lose. There's too much fat built into the model to allow you to fail by making these shifts. Give it a one-, three-, and five-year plan if you like, corresponding to short-, medium-, and long-term goals. Anything longer than that is just plain silly.

We're always just a tweet or text away if you want to bounce anything off us. We've seen Z.E.R.O. work before. It can work for you, too. In fact, it is already working for you. You have customers, right? Good. Stop wasting your time talking to us and get cracking.

EPILOGUE

Still stewing on the Z.E.R.O. value proposition? Well, what if we told you that you're proving Z.E.R.O. right now by reading this book? In May 2013, we launched a Kickstarter campaign to essentially self-fund our publishing effort. The idea was to use new marketing to prove new marketing (UNM2PNM) by turning this book into its own case study.

UNM2PNM was coined by Joseph when he launched his first book. Instead of sending out review copies to influencers in the hopes that they would write something, Joseph turned the convention on its head by making a review a condition of getting the book in the first place. Potential reviewers had to explicitly promise to review the book in order to receive a copy. Anyone from anywhere could participate. In taking this strategy, Joseph created a substantial set of reviews and "link love" through a combination of communal marketing (a concept that later became known as social media) and consumer-generated content.

With *Join the Conversation*, Joseph attempted to "bum rush the charts," a flash mob tactic that was originally used by independent artists Black Lab, as well as Scott Sigler in his book *Ancestor*. By encouraging their community to simultaneously purchase the MP3 and book, respectively, Black Lab was able to get their single, "Mine Again" (a very good track, I might add) to number 2 in the charts. Black Lab was the only unsigned band to feature on the charts that day. Scott Sigler hit number 4 on Amazon, with only Harry Potter, Oprah, and *The Secret* in front of him.

Joseph hit twenty-sixth overall and second in the business book charts, with only Alan Greenspan's *The Age of Turbulence* pipping him to the posts (see the figure on page 256).

The most popular items in **Business & Investing**. Updated hou

1.
    ### The Age of Turbulence: Adver
    by Alan Greenspan (Author)
    Average Customer Review: ★★★★☆
    In Stock

    List Price: $~~35.00~~
    Price: $20.99
    You Save: $14.01 (40%)
    120 used & new from $15.15

2.
    ### Join the Conversation: How to
    ### Community, Dialogue, and Pa
    by Joseph Jaffe (Author)
    Average Customer Review: ★★★★☆
    In Stock

    List Price: $~~29.95~~
    Price: $19.77
    You Save: $10.18 (34%)
    3 used & new from $18.75

Bum rush the charts: Alan, meet Joseph. Joseph, meet Alan

Kickstarter launched in 2009 as a resource to raise funds for creative projects. This process has since become known as crowdfunding (raising funds via the crowd).

It seemed opportune to prove the Z.E.R.O. theorem by self-liquidating the self-publishing investment (Z.E.R.O. is not *free*). By tapping into fans (Z) of Joseph's previous books and the authors' combined thought leadership portfolio, using an innovative new technology platform (E), offering experiential rewards to those who essentially preordered the book (R), and leveraging both Maarten's and Joseph's networks of friends, family, fans, and followers (O), the Kickstarter campaign, if successful, would become the book's own case study.

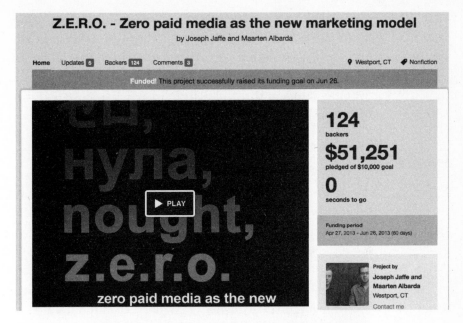

The final numbers for Z.E.R.O. on Kickstarter

The funding goal was set at $10,000, which conveniently approximated to the initial investment. The goal was reached within a week of going live, and in doing so, both Maarten and Joseph could say, "How much did it cost us to publish our book? Zero!"

The Twist

When the Kickstarter campaign was complete, 124 backers had pledged a collective $51,251, making this the second-most funded business or marketing book in Kickstarter's history! Joseph was interviewed by About.com for their Entrepreneur column. Also, Say Media wrote a piece[1] called "10 Interesting Media Winners on Kickstarter," comparing Z.E.R.O. alongside heavyweights such as the Veronica Mars Movie Project and Zach Braff's Wish I Was Here campaign, which raised more than $3 million.

It also drew the attention of an old friend, John Wiley & Sons, the company that published Joseph's first three books and now this one as

well. The decision to put the self-publishing journey on hold was ultimately an easy one when faced with the pragmatic reality and belief that
this book needs to be sold in stores—good old brick-and-mortar stores as
the ultimate owned asset. But fear not, the authentic narrative was still
intact: What was the nature of the deal with John Wiley & Sons and the
advance negotiated and secured? Why it was zero, of course!

Logging Off

Earlier in the book, we introduced P.E.O.N. and introduced the idea that
there was an alternative to the default of starting with P. In fact, if you
take out the P, you're left with E.O.N., which stands for either a collective
problem-solving project or an indefinitely long period of time.

We believe Kickstarter represented the community-driven support
of this thesis, and if you contributed to this campaign with the Charles
Montgomery Burns level ($67) or higher (we named each reward after a
famous miser,) we thank you (A of acknowledgment in A.D.I.A.) here
with your 140-character plug.

Always happy to support the brightest of minds and these are they. Bill
Laidlaw, www.ninecloudsbeds.ca

Imagine a world with zero paid media.@jaffejuice predicts this is the
future—@katskrieger

@sprinklr #SocialAtScale and #ZeroPaidMedia go hand in hand www
.sprinklr.com

@holimage May the heroes of all zeroes bring infinite prosperity to all.

Brilliant innovative thinking to push brands to re-evaluate strategic
marketing decisions, proud to be a part of this project. @jessicapeltz

Love the concept. Love the work. Bring on the zero.—Michael Chase
@chasethisnow

Congrats Jaffe on your next big thing! @johnjwall

If you're waiting for the perfect time to change you might be waiting
for awhile. Thank you Brenna, Sam and Chloe for being my inspiration.
Mal Chia, malchia.com

If your customers are not happy how can you sleep at night? Melinda
Banks, Customer Experience Professional

@NEENZ Building communities with Z.E.R.O.#ponomedia

Content Marketing that Converts @emarketingcopy

Media strategy that hearts Joe and Maarten @markramseymedia http://markramseymedia.com

Why ZERO is a dangerous idea, especially in Marketing @ChrisBurggraeve

Michael Smallwood

TIM ISAAC

It's exciting to discover this new land together with you guys! Lot of success with the book! Ricardo dos Santos Miquelino, twitter @and_dos_Santos

Brands have all the means to turn the Paid-Owned-Earned model in their favour, but content remains King @HuHeHa.

Great work, Joe! @mitchjoel—www.twistimage.com/blog

Well done Joe and Maarten, great idea brought to life. @allenjaffe

Congrats on your new book! Not to mention, a fantastic demonstration of Z.E.R.O. through successfully crowdfunding it on Kickstarter! Bravo. (Vivian Gagliano, @vivve)

don't stop. give it all you've got. cheers from @eaonp in Melbourne

Mad props to our pal Adam Keats (@akeats) for his never-ending support of our creative and disruptive vision.

Congrats to Maarten & Joseph! The American Beverage Consortium is honored to be a part of the launch of such an important book! @BevConsortium

Inbound Marketing is the key to achieving your goal of ZERO paid media. Learn more at www.HubSpot.com

Brilliant Belgian copywriter/media strategist @sjanssens gets mentioned in Jaffe & Albarda book. With zero effort! Quite amazing indeed!

As technology continues to disrupt industries & empower customers, owned & earned media will become the most valuable assets for brands @wolfepereira

travel for Joseph Jaffe is provided by travelpro1975@twitter

@mediaphyter Raconteur. Comedienne. Hockey lover. Forbes tech contributor. Where cybersecurity meets marketing.

I am looking forward to receiving my copy SOON—Natalie Jaffe

Making the marketing world a better place—Jim Elms

Let's give them something to talk about . . . @GaryHagestad

@TCO we are evolving ideas for the always on world! www.theconscience.org @cliveburcham

@erwinpenland loves working with people using creativity for change. @jaffejuice has a history of it and continues that trend with Z.E.R.O.

To my beloved wife, Bia—@bobwollheim

Satmetrix is the defacto software solution for driving your customer experience and delivering results. Co-creators of NPS! www.satmerix.com

As marketers continue to evolve into mathematicians and mad scientists, we need the pressures of new thinking to drive great business results. @perkolo

Upenn sparked my entrepreneurial spirit; Joe lit it on fire! Privileged to be working with such brilliant minds—@evo18tion. #32red # Iexydp

Met Joseph on a thursday, quit my job on Monday, and haven't regretted a day since. Well done joe! #hereisacrazyidea . . . @gwaldhorn

Wishing you much success and prosperi-perity with Z.E.R.O.—Robbie Brozin and the rest of the Nandocas family

ZERO PAID MEDIA won't bring you free Super Bowl tickets . . . but that's exactly the point . . . winners can reinvent marketing based on true IMPACT—@sdimarco

The title might be Z.E.R.O., but the ideas in here are worth a fortune. Congrats on the new book @jaffejuice @malbarda—@jaybaer

Wishing Joseph and Maarten every success with this crowd-funded initiative. @jaffeblend—Digital Training & Consulting can't wait to read it!

Joseph and Maarten are marketing provocateurs grounded in business reality. We look forward to getting Z.E.R.O. from this book—and that's a good thing!—Team @ExactTarget

Now it's up to all of you to continue this momentum. Share the ideas in this book. Put the frameworks into your presentations (with attribution of course). Join the conversation on Twitter with the hashtag #zeropaid media. Live the change and the evolution from campaigns to commitments to ecosystems.

Be a hero. Commit to Z.E.R.O.

NOTES

Preface

1. Centers for Disease Control and Prevention (CDC), 2012.
2. Ogden CL, Carroll MD, Kit BK, and Flegal KM, "Prevalence of Obesity and Trends in Body Mass Index Among US Children and Adolescents, 1999–2010," *Journal of the American Medical Association* 307, no. 5 (2012): 483–490; and National Center for Health Statistics, *Health, United States, 2011: With Special Features on Socioeconomic Status and Health* (Hyattsville, MD: U.S. Department of Health and Human Services, 2012).

Chapter 1: Madison Avenue

1. http://www.businessinsider.com/martin-sorrell-up-to-25-of-our-clients-dollars-are-wasted-2013-5.
2. http://www.nielsen.com/us/en/newswire/2011/nielsens-tops-of-2011-television.html.
3. http://tvbythenumbers.zap2it.com/2008/04/04/we-look-back-at-the-top-tv-shows-of-1982/3203/.
4. http://www.dreamgrow.com/youtube-killed-tv-infographic/.
5. http://blogs-images.forbes.com/anthonykosner/files/2012/05/you-tube-uploads-72-hours-per-minute-2012.png.
6. http://techcrunch.com/2012/02/09/nielsen-cord-cutting-and-internet-tv-viewing-on-the-rise/.
7. http://www.ncta.com/who-we-are/our-story.
8. http://www.directsattv.com/directv/comparecable.html.

Chapter 2: A Perfect Storm Is Coming

1. Digital natives today are younger than 15 years of age according to Bob Johansen from www.iftf.org.
2. GE: http://focusforwardfilms.com/; Subway: http://www.youtube.com/user/The4to9ers.
3. http://www.poynter.org/latest-news/business-news/the-biz-blog/196031/newspapers-report-ad-revenue-loss-for-25th-quarter-in-a-row/.
4. http://www.huffingtonpost.com/2013/04/22/boston-bombings-media-mistakes_n_3135105.html.
5. http://en.wikipedia.org/wiki/Digital_Economy_Act_2010.

Chapter 3: The Economic Case

1. Bob Johansen, *Get There Early* (San Francisco, CA: Berrett-Koehler Publishers, 2007).
2. http://business.time.com/2013/05/16/airline-baggage-fees-on-the-rise-yet-more-passengers-deem-them-reasonable/#ixzz2TrHcAThq.
3. http://www.mediapost.com/publications/article/187276/survey-probes-the-ceo-marketer-divide.html?print#axzz2Zz8LcwFn.

Chapter 4: The Business Case

1. Carl F. Mela, Sunil Gupta, and Donald Lehmann, "The Long-Term Impact of Promotion and Advertising on Consumer Brand Choice," *Journal of Marketing Research 34*, no. 2 (May 1997): 248–261.

Chapter 5: The Media Case

1. NPD DisplaySearch Global TV Replacement Study, July 2012.
2. Nielsen Cross Platform Report, 2012.

Chapter 6: The Consumer Case

1. http://youtu.be/ruav0KvQOOg.

Chapter 8: Is It Time to Blow Up the Entire Model?

1. http://www.buzzfeed.com/mjs538/sao-paulo-the-city-with-no-outdoor-advertising.
2. http://business.ftc.gov/documents/alt129-qa-telemarketers-sellers-about-dnc-provisions-tsr.
3. http://www.washingtonpost.com/wp-dyn/content/article/2006/05/03/AR2006050302399.html.
4. http://www.nyc.gov/html/doh/downloads/pdf/cdp/calorie_compliance_guide.pdf.
5. http://www.bbc.co.uk/news/world-europe-18960770.
6. http://www.adexchanger.com/agencies/will-the-agency-business-survive-look-to-flying-cockroaches-as-the-model/.

Chapter 9: Introducing Z.E.R.O.

1. Urban Dictionary, http://www.urbandictionary.com/.
2. http://www.merriam-webster.com/dictionary/zealous
3. http://www.jaffejuice.com/2006/07/a_croc_of_sweet.html.
4. http://company.crocs.com/news-releases/crocs-inc-2012-third-quarter-financial-results/.
5. http://www.eturbonews.com/35008/airline-passenger-satisfaction-improves-its-highest-levels-2006.
6. Originally appeared in MediaPost: http://www.mediapost.com/publications/article/182190/survival-demands-innovation-and-creativity.html#ixzz2MIjl50Q5.
7. Credited to Leigh Reyes on an episode of "The BeanCast," a weekly marketing podcast.
8. Originally appeared in MediaPost: http://www.mediapost.com/publications/article/187065/revenge-of-the-brick.html#ixzz2MIjCHLMU.
9. http://www.nytimes.com/2012/02/03/business/media/some-super-bowl-ads-being-seen-long-before-the-game-advertising.html?_r=3&.
10. Calculated using most recent media costs and building in estimated production budgets and agency fees.
11. http://www.mediapost.com/publications/article/194539/twitter-is-the-new-youtube.html#ixzz2MIgCT7nm.

12. Article excerpted and originally published in MediaPost.
13. 360i, Oreo's Digital Agency.
14. Evolution of Beauty Case Study, InSites Consulting.
15. http://www.guardian.co.uk/media/2012/jul/27/olympic-brand-mcdonalds-twitter.
16. http://www.smh.com.au/travel/travel-news/qantas-stands-firm-despite-social-media-uproar-20130411–2hobo.html.
17. http://corp.visiblemeasures.com/news-and-events/blog/bid/13280/Old-Spice-s-Online-Video-Coup and http://wearesocial.net/blog/2010/07/social-media-buzz-advantage-spice/.

Section III: The Z.E.R.O. Action Plan

1. http://www.youtube.com/watch?v=IvDCk3pY4qo.

Chapter 10: Culture and Talent

1. http://www.youtube.com/watch?v=h7_UNu7zEVs.

Chapter 11: Z.E.R.O. Action Plan—Tenure

1. http://www.mckinsey.com/insights/organization/motivating_people_getting_beyond_money.

Chapter 12: Z.E.R.O. Action Plan—Compensation

1. http://adage.com/article/news/coke-pushes-based-agency-compensation-model/136266/.

Chapter 14: Measurement and Insights
1. Parts of the following section were published on Maarten's blog, "Connection Planning Perspectives."

Chapter 15: Use Existing Customers to Gain New Ones

1. http://www-01.ibm.com/software/marketing-solutions/benchmark-reports/black-friday-2012.html?cm_mmc=holiday2012-benchmark-reports-_-press-release-_-wire-_-text-link.

Chapter 16: Customer Experience Becomes the Key Strategic Differentiator

1. "The BeanCast" is an Evol8tion company and its host, Bob Knorpp, works for Evol8tion.
2. As introduced and laid out in *Flip the Funnel* (John Wiley & Sons, 2010).

Chapter 17: The Innovation Imperative

1. http://www.mediapost.com/publications/article/196789/absolute-and-relative-innovation.html#ixzz2QelbdmSg.
2. http://www.mediapost.com/publications/article/197835/why-was-penneys-ron-johnson-fired.html#ixzz2QelEpMeO.
3. Originally appeared as an Online Spin article on MediaPost: http://www.mediapost.com/publications/article/190269/failfail .html#ixzz2MIggJZnd.
4. Originally appeared as an Online Spin article in MediaPost: http://www.mediapost.com/publications/article/192385/fail-fast-or-fail-smart.html#ixzz2MIgSsbzA.

Chapter 18: Become a Data Junkie

1. *Ad Age*, September 2012.
2. With credit, in part, to the Upstream Group's Doug Weaver.

Chapter 19: From Campaigns to Commitments to Ecosystems

1. Originally appeared as a MediaPost Online Spin column: http://www.mediapost.com/publications/article/198919/from-campaigns-to-commitments-to-ecosystems.html#ixzz2RWYuNzwP.
2. http://en.wikipedia.org/wiki/The_Death_of_Competition:_Leadership_and_Strategy_in_the_Age_of_Business_Ecosystems.
3. http://www.imdb.com/character/ch0033133.
4. http://www.mediapost.com/publications/article/185877/innovation-at-128000-feet.html?edition=53177#ixzz2UR0EprUQ.
5. Originally appeared as a column in MediaPost: http://www.media-post.com/publications/article/182521/find-your-brand-greatness .html#ixzz2MIjXbJCq.

Chapter 20: That's Great . . . Now What the Hell Do I Do Next?

1. Originally appeared as a MediaPost Online Spin article: http://www
   .mediapost.com/publications/article/199984/cmo-the-chief-
   muddled-officer.html#reply#ixzz2THPyt79L.
2. http://www.mediapost.com/publications/article/201016/embrace-
   your-inner-masochist.html#ixzz2UAfXv85M.

Epilogue

1. http://saydaily.com/2013/05/10-interesting-media-winners-on-kick-
   starter.html.

INDEX

DATE DUE

			PRINTED IN U.S.A.